THE **BIG** BOOK OF
SAUCES

ANNE SHEASBY

THE **BIG** BOOK OF
SAUCES

365

QUICK AND EASY SAUCES, SALSAS, DRESSINGS, AND DIPS

DUNCAN BAIRD PUBLISHERS

LONDON

For Mum, Bunny, and Sjeord

THE BIG BOOK OF SAUCES
Anne Sheasby

Distributed in the USA and Canada by
Sterling Publishing Co., Inc.
387 Park Avenue South
New York, NY 10016-8810

This edition first published in the UK and USA in 2005 by
Duncan Baird Publishers Ltd
Sixth Floor, Castle House, 75–76 Wells Street, London W1T 3QH

Managing Editor: Julia Charles
Editor: Rachel Connolly
Managing Designer: Manisha Patel
Photographic Art Direction: Sailesh Patel
Studio Photography: William Lingwood
Photography Assistant: Estelle Cuthbert
Stylists: Lucy McKelvie (food) and Helen Trent

Library of Congress Cataloging-in-Publication Data Available

ISBN: 978-1-84483-186-9

10 9 8 7 6 5 4 3 2

Typeset in Trade Gothic Condensed
Color reproduction by Scanhouse, Malaysia
Printed in China by Imago

For information about custom editions, special sales, premium and corporate
purchases, please contact Sterling Special Sales Department at 800-805-5489 or
specialsales@sterlingpub.com.

Publisher's Note: While every care has been taken in compiling the recipes in this
book, Duncan Baird Publishers, or any other persons who have been involved in
working on this publication, cannot accept responsibility for any errors or omissions,
inadvertent or not, that may be found in the recipes or text, nor for any problems that
may arise as a result of preparing one of these recipes.

Contents

Introduction

A good sauce can provide the finishing touch to many dishes, complementing and enhancing the flavor of the most simple food without being overpowering. A broiled steak, chicken portion, or fish cutlet can be transformed into something really special with the addition of a good sauce. Sauces not only add flavor and color to dishes, they also add texture and moisture, and there is a whole variety of sauces to suit all tastes and palates – savory and sweet, rich and light, hot and cold.

This book is an inspirational collection of sauce recipes, suitable for all kinds of food and for all occasions, and it provides an essential guide to sauce-making.

A wide range of mouth-watering recipes is included in the book: many basic and classic sauces, tasty sauces for pasta, delicious sauces for fish, meat, and poultry, and a creative collection of salsas and relishes, together with a good selection of flavorful salad dressings and vinaigrettes. Also included is a chapter on lighter, healthier sauces for those who are watching their weight. Savory and sweet dips are also covered, followed by a tempting selection of delicious sweet sauces and coulis which you will find hard to resist!

Many of the recipes are quick and easy to make, combining just a few of a wide variety of different ingredients that are readily available. Useful information such as preparation and cooking times (where applicable) is included with each recipe, as well as a choice of serving suggestions. The number of servings and the quantity/volume of sauce that each recipe makes (where applicable) are also included, while ingredient variations and cook's tips appear at the end of many of the recipes.

So, your journey through the wonderful world of sauce-making begins here – enjoy adding that special finishing touch to your own dishes at home.

Sauce Basics

TYPES OF SAUCES

Sauces vary a great deal in texture and flavor – a sauce may be thick or thin, smooth or chunky, savory or sweet – but they should all form an essential part of every cook's repertoire of tried and trusted recipes.

There are several types of sauce, including roux-based, brown, or emulsified sauces, vegetable-based sauces and purées, gravies and flavored butters, as well as salsas, relishes, salad dressings and vinaigrettes, and savory and sweet dips. Last, but by no means least, are many people's favorite – sweet sauces, fruit pureés, and coulis, all of which are included in this definitive guide.

BASIC TECHNIQUES OF SAUCE-MAKING

THICKENING SAUCES

Sauces may be thickened in various ways at different stages of a recipe. Sometimes a sauce is thickened at the beginning of a recipe with a roux, or toward the end of a recipe using ingredients such as egg yolks, butter, and cream. Another thickener that is added toward the end of the preparation time is beurre manié, also known as 'kneaded butter' – equal quantities of softened butter and all-purpose flour are kneaded together to make a smooth paste, which is then gradually whisked into the hot cooked sauce or liquid until it thickens.

Sauces may also be thickened using cornstarch, arrowroot, or potato flour, which is blended with a little cold liquid such as milk or water, then added to the sauce and heated, while stirring, until the sauce comes to a boil and thickens. Sauces thickened with arrowroot or potato flour are served as soon as they have thickened – if they are allowed to simmer for more than 1 minute or so, they may lose their thickening power and become thin again. Sauces thickened with cornstarch need to be simmered gently for 2–3 minutes once they have thickened, to cook the cornstarch.

ROUX-BASED SAUCES

A roux is a blend of equal quantities of butter and all-purpose flour that are cooked together before liquid is gradually added to make the sauce. The butter is melted, the flour is stirred in and this is known as the 'roux'. The roux is then cooked for varying lengths of time, depending on the recipe.

With a classic White or Béchamel Sauce, the roux is cooked but not colored, whereas for brown sauces, such as Espagnole (Brown) Sauce, the roux is cooked until it becomes brown. The liquid, such as milk or stock, is then gradually stirred or whisked into the roux. The mixture is heated gently, stirring or whisking continuously, until the sauce comes to a boil and thickens. The thickened sauce is then simmered gently for 2–3 minutes to cook out the taste of the flour. For the same reason, all-in-one sauces (where the butter, flour, and liquid are put together in the pan, heated gently, whisking continuously, until the sauce boils and thickens) are also simmered gently for 3–4 minutes before serving.

EMULSIFIED SAUCES

Emulsified sauces are based on one of two emulsions – a butter emulsion (such as Hollandaise Sauce or Beurre Blanc) or a cold emulsion of oil and egg yolks, such as Mayonnaise. With a butter emulsion, the initial cooking liquid used for the sauce is reduced during cooking to give a more intense flavor to the sauce, which is then enriched and thickened with butter or eggs.

REDUCING SAUCES

An alternative method of thickening sauces or stocks is to boil the mixture rapidly until the sauce or liquid is reduced in volume, the reducing time varying with the quantity of liquid. Remember not to season the sauce until it is reduced, as reducing will intensify the flavors of the sauce.

As the stock or sauce is reduced, skim off any froth from the surface using a slotted or metal spoon. However, do not attempt to reduce a sauce containing ingredients such as eggs or yogurt by rapid boiling as the sauce is likely to curdle. Quick cream sauces can usually be reduced using this method, though crème fraîche may curdle when used in this way.

FRUIT PURÉES AND COULIS

Fruit purées and coulis are simple to make and create a delicious fruit sauce to accompany desserts such as fresh fruit, ice cream, sorbet, fruit tartlets, or meringues, as well as adding a lovely finishing touch to these desserts. Fruit coulis are made by firstly puréeing raw or lightly cooked fruit. The fruit purée is then sieved, sweetened and sometimes flavored with liqueur, resulting in a delicious and colorful pouring sauce.

Fruits such as raspberries, strawberries, mixed berries, mangoes, peaches, and apricots are ideal for making fruit coulis. Some fruit- or vegetable-based sauces can also be thickened by blending the ingredients together using a hand-held blender, or a small blender or food processor.

ENRICHING SAUCES

To enrich a sauce quickly and effectively, simply whisk a little chilled (diced), unsalted butter into the finished sauce to give it a richer, creamier flavor. This will also thicken the sauce slightly and give it an attractive, glossy finish.

HOME-MADE STOCKS

A good home-made stock will make all the difference to the overall flavor of a sauce, and it is well worth the small amount of effort it takes to make. Home-made stock also freezes well, so it is worth making a large batch, then cooling and freezing it in handy, small quantities ready for future use. Remember, it is important to use good-quality, fresh ingredients to make flavorful stock that will then form the basis of a wide range of delicious sauces.

There is also an improved range of stock products available on the market, including stock cubes, stock granules, bouillon powder, concentrated liquid stock, and chilled fresh stock. Home-made stocks are recommended for use in all the relevant recipes in this book, but if you are pushed for time and need a quick solution, choose bouillon powder, concentrated liquid stock, or chilled fresh stock rather than stock cubes and granules. Shop-bought stock cubes and granules tend to be stronger and quite salty in flavor, so use these sparingly. See the selection of simple, basic home-made stock recipes on pages 10–11, which are also referred to in some of the recipes.

EQUIPMENT FOR SAUCE-MAKING

You only need a few basic pieces of equipment to ensure successful sauce-making at home. A good-quality, small to medium-sized, heavy-based saucepan is vital to ensure slow, even cooking. Copper pans are ideal, but these are quite expensive, so a good-quality stainless steel pan is a good, practical choice for home cooks. A double saucepan or double boiler (or a bain marie) is also useful when making sauces that require gentle, even cooking, such as traditional Egg Custard Sauce (Crème Anglaise).

A stainless steel balloon or coiled whisk will help prevent lumps forming in the sauce and ensure a smooth, even result. A basic wooden spoon is another useful tool for sauce-making.

A non-reactive sieve is ideal for sieving fruit purées to make coulis, rather than using a metal sieve. Metal sieves may impart a little metallic flavor or even slight discoloration to the food being sieved, especially when sieving acidic fruits or foods, so always choose a non-reactive sieve for these sauces. Conical strainers are also useful for straining sauces or stocks.

A small blender or food processor is an invaluable piece of equipment when making some sauces, and pestles and mortars are useful for making pestos and other thick sauces. Electric sauce-makers are also available on the market.

SERVING SAUCES

Some sauces are best served hot, others are preferable served cold, while some sauces may be served either way – each recipe in this book indicates at what temperature each sauce should be served. If serving a thickened sauce, such as Egg Custard Sauce (Crème Anglaise), cold, cover the surface closely with damp non-stick baking paper after it is made, in order to prevent a skin forming as the sauce cools. This is also applicable to sauces that are made in advance to be reheated later when required.

TROUBLE-SHOOTING TIPS
HOW TO RESCUE LUMPY OR CURDLED SAUCES

• To rescue a lumpy sauce, whisk the sauce vigorously using a balloon whisk until the sauce is smooth. Alternatively, pour the lumpy sauce into a small blender or food processor and blend for about 1 minute, until it is smooth, or pour the sauce through a fine sieve into a clean pan to remove the lumps.
• When making emulsified sauces such as Mayonnaise or Hollandaise, using a small blender or food processor will help to prevent curdling or separation of the ingredients.
• If an emulsified sauce such as Hollandaise shows signs of curdling, add an ice cube to the sauce and whisk thoroughly until it is smooth – the sauce should re-combine.
• If an emulsified sauce such as Beurre Blanc turns greasy and splits during preparation, it has become too hot. Simply whisk in an ice cube and this should rescue it.
• When making emulsified sauces such as Mayonnaise, make sure all the ingredients are at room temperature. If eggs are used straight from the fridge, the Mayonnaise is liable to curdle.
• When making an Egg Custard Sauce such as Crème Anglaise, add 1 tsp cornstarch to the eggs and sugar to reduce the risk of curdling. Once the sauce has thickened, cook it gently for a little longer to ensure that the taste of the cornstarch disappears.
• If an Egg Custard Sauce shows signs of curdling or separating, strain it into a clean bowl, add one or two ice cubes and whisk briskly to reduce the temperature of the sauce – this should make it smooth once again.

A NOTE ABOUT THE RECIPES

• Please note that Imperial or cup measurements are given for the recipes. Follow either set of measures.
• All spoon measures are level unless otherwise stated. (1 tbsp = 1 tablespoon; 1 tsp = 1 teaspoon; 2 tbsp = 2 tablespoons; 2 tsp = 2 teaspoons, and so on.) Sets of measuring spoons are available in Imperial for accurate measurements.
• Medium eggs should be used in the recipes, except where otherwise specified.
• We have included cooking temperatures for electric and gas ovens on relevant recipes. If you have a fan-assisted oven you will need to reduce the oven temperature slightly (usually by around 20 degrees) and/or adjust the cooking times. Please refer to manufacturer's guidelines for more specific information on adjusting the temperature and time for your cooker, if applicable.
• Some of the recipes in this book may contain raw or lightly cooked eggs – these recipes are not recommended for babies and young children, pregnant moms, the elderly, and those convalescing.

Basic Home-made Stock Recipes

VEGETABLE STOCK

PREPARATION TIME *15 minutes* **COOKING TIME** *1 hour 15 minutes* **MAKES ABOUT** *5 cups*

1 large onion, chopped
2 leeks, washed & sliced
2 carrots, sliced
4 sticks of celery, chopped

1 cup rutabaga or turnip, diced
1 parsnip, thickly sliced
1 fresh bouquet garni or 2 bay leaves

8 black peppercorns
½ teaspoon salt
7½ cups water

1 Place all the prepared vegetables in a large saucepan with the bouquet garni or bay leaves, black peppercorns, and salt. Add the water and stir to mix.
2 Bring slowly to a boil, then reduce the heat and partially cover the pan. Simmer gently for about 1 hour, skimming off and discarding any scum that rises to the surface as the stock is simmering.
3 Remove the pan from the heat and cool slightly, then strain the stock through a fine sieve into a bowl and discard the contents of the sieve. Adjust the seasoning to taste, then set aside to cool.
4 Use the stock immediately, or cover and chill in the refrigerator for up to 3 days.

VARIATION *Use 6 shallots in place of onion.*
COOK'S TIP *This stock may be frozen in a covered container(s) for up to 3 months.*

FISH STOCK

PREPARATION TIME *10 minutes* **COOKING TIME** *45 minutes* **MAKES ABOUT** *3¾ cups*

2¼lb raw lean white fish bones & trimmings, washed
1 large onion, chopped
2 carrots, sliced

3 sticks of celery, chopped
1 bay leaf
A small bunch of fresh parsley

Sea salt & freshly ground white pepper
4 cups water

1 Place the fish bones and trimmings in a large saucepan with all the prepared vegetables. Add the bay leaf, parsley, and seasoning, then add the water and stir to mix.
2 Bring slowly to a boil, then reduce the heat and partially cover the pan. Simmer gently for about 30 minutes, skimming off and discarding any scum that rises to the surface as the stock is simmering.
3 Remove the pan from the heat and cool slightly, then strain the stock through a fine sieve into a bowl and discard the contents of the sieve. Adjust the seasoning to taste, then set aside to cool.
4 Use the stock immediately, or cover and chill in the refrigerator for up to 2 days.

VARIATIONS *Use 2 leeks or 6 shallots in place of onion. Use 2 parsnips, thickly sliced, in place of carrots.*
COOK'S TIP *This stock may be frozen in a covered container(s) for up to 1 month.*

MEAT (BEEF OR LAMB) STOCK

PREPARATION TIME *15 minutes* **COOKING TIME** *2 hours 45 minutes* **MAKES ABOUT** *3 cups*

1lb stewing beef or shoulder of
   lamb, diced
1lb raw beef or lamb bones
7½ cups water

6 shallots or 1 large onion,
   sliced
2 carrots, sliced
1 turnip, chopped
2 sticks of celery, sliced

1 fresh bouquet garni or
   2 bay leaves
Sea salt & freshly ground
   black pepper

1 Preheat the oven to 220°C/425°F/gas mark 7. Put the meat and bones in a roasting pan and
  bake in the oven for about 30 minutes, or until well browned, turning occasionally.
2 Transfer the meat, bones and juices to a large saucepan and add the water. Add all the prepared
  vegetables, the bouquet garni or bay leaves, and seasoning and stir to mix.
3 Bring slowly to a boil, then reduce the heat and partially cover the pan. Simmer gently for about
  2 hours, skimming off and discarding any scum and fat that rises to the surface as the stock is
  simmering.
4 Remove the pan from the heat and cool slightly, then strain the stock through a fine sieve into a
  bowl and discard the contents of the sieve. Adjust the seasoning to taste, then set aside to cool.
5 Use the stock immediately, or cover and chill in the refrigerator for up to 3 days. Remove and
  discard any fat from the surface of the stock before use, if necessary.

VARIATIONS *Use 2 leeks in place of shallots or onion. Use diced rutabaga in place of turnip.*
COOK'S TIP *This stock may be frozen in a covered container(s) for up to 3 months.*

CHICKEN STOCK

PREPARATION TIME *10 minutes* **COOKING TIME** *2 hours 15 minutes* **MAKES ABOUT** *3 cups*

1 large raw meaty chicken
   carcass
1 large onion, sliced

2 carrots, sliced
2 sticks of celery, chopped
2 bay leaves

Sea salt & freshly ground
   black pepper
7½ cups cold water

1 Break or chop the chicken carcass into pieces and place them in a large saucepan. Add all the
  prepared vegetables, the bay leaves, and seasoning, then add the water and stir to mix.
2 Bring slowly to a boil, then reduce the heat and partially cover the pan. Simmer gently for about
  2 hours, skimming off and discarding any scum and fat that rises to the surface as the stock is
  simmering.
3 Remove the pan from the heat and cool slightly, then strain the stock through a fine sieve into a
  bowl, and discard the contents of the sieve. Adjust the seasoning to taste, then set aside to cool.
4 Use the stock immediately, or cover and chill in the refrigerator for up to 3 days. Remove and
  discard any fat from the surface of the stock before use, if necessary.

VARIATIONS *Use 1 meaty turkey carcass in place of chicken. Use 6 shallots in place of onion.*
COOK'S TIP *This stock may be frozen in a covered container(s) for up to 3 months.*

CHAPTER 1

BASIC SAUCES

Basic sauces are an important element of everyday cooking and should be included in every home cook's repertoire of recipes. This chapter brings together a wide selection of good, basic sauces, which can be served simply, perhaps with meat, fish, or vegetables. Other essential sauces, such as Rich Tomato Sauce, which can be used as the basis for tempting recipes such as meat or vegetable lasagnes, are also covered.

Basic sauces are simple to make and ideal for those new to sauce-making. Choose from a wide selection, including Basic White Sauce, Cheese (Mornay) Sauce, Quick Tomato Sauce, Fruity Sweet and Sour Sauce, Bread Sauce, Mint Sauce, Traditional Gravy, Fresh Horseradish Cream, Nutty Satay Sauce, and Tomato Catsup. A recipe for Basic Gluten-Free White Sauce is also included, which is ideal for those with a sensitivity to gluten.

001 BASIC WHITE SAUCE (POURING SAUCE)

PREPARATION TIME *5 minutes* **COOKING TIME** *10 minutes* **SERVES 4** *Makes about 1¼ cups*

1 tbsp butter
2 tbsp all-purpose flour
1¼ cups milk

Sea salt & freshly ground
   black pepper

1 Melt the butter in a small saucepan, stir in the flour and cook, stirring, for 1 minute. Remove the pan from the heat and gradually stir or whisk in the milk.

2 Return to the heat and bring slowly to a boil, stirring or whisking until the sauce is thickened and smooth. Simmer gently for 2–3 minutes, stirring continuously. Season to taste with salt and pepper. Serve hot.

SERVING SUGGESTIONS *Serve with broiled ham steaks or chicken breasts. Alternatively, serve with broiled fillets of plaice or sole, or with cooked fava beans or green beans.*

002 CHEESE (MORNAY) SAUCE

PREPARATION TIME *5 minutes* **COOKING TIME** *10 minutes* **SERVES 4** *Makes about 1½ cups*

1 tbsp butter
2 tbsp all-purpose flour
1¼ cups milk

1 tsp Dijon mustard
½ cup mature cheddar or
   gruyère cheese, finely grated

Sea salt & freshly
   ground black pepper

1 Melt the butter in a small saucepan, stir in the flour and cook, stirring, for 1 minute. Remove the pan from the heat and gradually stir or whisk in the milk.

2 Return to the heat and bring slowly to a boil, stirring or whisking until the sauce is thickened and smooth. Simmer gently for 2–3 minutes, stirring continuously.

3 Remove the pan from the heat and stir in the mustard, then stir in the cheese until melted. Season to taste with salt and pepper. Serve hot

SERVING SUGGESTIONS *Serve with broiled or oven-baked fishcakes, or with cooked cauliflower or broccoli florets.*

003 BASIC GLUTEN-FREE WHITE SAUCE

PREPARATION TIME *5 minutes* **COOKING TIME** *10 minutes* **SERVES 4** *Makes about 1¼ cups*

2 tbsp gluten-free cornstarch
1¼ cups milk
1 tbsp butter

Sea salt & freshly
   ground black pepper

1 Place the cornstarch in a bowl and blend with 4 tbsp of the milk to make a smooth paste. Heat the remaining milk in a saucepan over a medium heat until boiling, then pour onto the blended mixture, whisking continuously to prevent lumps forming.

2 Return the mixture to the saucepan and bring slowly to a boil, stirring continuously, until the sauce thickens.

3 Lower the heat and simmer gently for 2–3 minutes, then stir in the butter until melted and blended. Season to taste with salt and pepper. Serve hot.

SERVING SUGGESTIONS *Serve with broiled halibut, or with cooked fava beans, or fresh minted peas.*

004 QUICK TOMATO SAUCE

PREPARATION TIME *5 minutes* **COOKING TIME** *40 minutes* **SERVES 4–6** *Makes about 3½ cups*

1 tbsp olive oil
1 onion, finely chopped
2 cloves garlic, crushed
2 x 14-oz cans chopped
  tomatoes

2 tbsp tomato paste
2 tbsp medium-dry sherry
  or red wine
½ tsp light soft brown sugar

Sea salt & freshly ground
  black pepper
1 tbsp chopped fresh mixed
  herbs (optional)

1 Heat the oil in a saucepan, add the onion and garlic and cook gently for 8–10 minutes, or until softened.

2 Add the tomatoes, tomato paste, sherry or wine, sugar, and salt and pepper to taste, and mix well.

3 Bring to a boil, then cook gently, uncovered, for about 25 minutes, or until the sauce is thick and pulpy, stirring occasionally.

4 Stir in the chopped herbs, if using, then adjust the seasoning to taste. Serve hot.

SERVING SUGGESTIONS *Serve with grilled lamb cutlets or chicken drumsticks.*

005 RICH TOMATO SAUCE

PREPARATION TIME *5 minutes* **COOKING TIME** *45 minutes* **SERVES 4–6** *Makes about 3¾ cups*

3 tbsp butter
1 red onion, finely chopped
2 cloves garlic, crushed

2 x 14-oz cans chopped
  tomatoes
⅔ cup red wine
2 tbsp tomato paste

½ tsp granulated sugar
1 bouquet garni
Sea salt & freshly
  ground black pepper

1 Melt the butter in a saucepan, add the onion and garlic and cook gently for about 10 minutes, or until softened.

2 Add the tomatoes, wine, tomato paste, sugar, and bouquet garni and mix well. Bring to a boil, then reduce the heat and cook gently, uncovered, for about 30 minutes, or until the sauce is thick and pulpy, stirring occasionally.

3 Discard the bouquet garni, and season to taste with salt and pepper. Serve hot.

SERVING SUGGESTIONS *Serve with hot pasta such as tagliatelle or fusilli, or use as the basis for a vegetable or meat lasagne. Alternatively, serve with meatballs or cooked vegetables.*

006 ANCHOVY SAUCE

PREPARATION TIME *5 minutes* **COOKING TIME** *10 minutes* **SERVES 4–6** *Makes about 1½ cups*

1 tbsp butter
2 tbsp all-purpose flour
1¼ cups milk

2-oz can anchovies in oil,
  drained & finely chopped
1 tbsp fresh lemon juice

Sea salt & freshly
  ground black pepper

1 Melt the butter in a small saucepan, stir in the flour and cook for 1 minute, stirring. Remove the pan from the heat, and gradually stir or whisk in the milk.

2 Return to the heat and bring slowly to a boil, stirring or whisking until the sauce is thickened and smooth. Simmer gently for 2–3 minutes, stirring continuously.

3 Stir in the anchovies and lemon juice, and reheat gently until hot. Season to taste with salt (if required) and pepper. Serve hot.

SERVING SUGGESTIONS *Serve with broiled or baked tuna steaks or shrimps.*

007 PARSLEY SAUCE

PREPARATION TIME *5 minutes* **COOKING TIME** *10 minutes* **SERVES 4** *Makes about 1¼ cups*

1 tbsp butter	1¼ cups milk	Sea salt & freshly
2 tbsp all-purpose flour	2–3 tbsp chopped	ground black pepper
	fresh parsley	

1 Melt the butter in a small saucepan, stir in the flour and cook, stirring, for 1 minute. Remove the pan from the heat and gradually stir or whisk in the milk.

2 Return to the heat and bring slowly to a boil, stirring or whisking until the sauce is thickened and smooth. Simmer gently for 2–3 minutes, stirring continuously.

3 Stir in the chopped parsley, and season to taste with salt and pepper. Serve hot.

SERVING SUGGESTIONS *Serve with broiled fillets of cod or haddock. Alternatively, serve with baked glazed ham, or with cooked fava beans, baby ears of corn, or fresh spinach.*

VARIATIONS *Use ⅔ cup vegetable stock or heavy cream in place of ⅔ cup of the milk. Use 1–2 chopped fresh mixed herbs in place of parsley.*

COOK'S TIP *For a thicker Parsley Sauce, simply follow the recipe above, increasing the butter to 2 tbsp and the flour to ¼ cup.*

008 TRADITIONAL GRAVY

PREPARATION TIME *5 minutes* **COOKING TIME** *30 minutes* **SERVES 2–4** *Makes about ¾ cup*

2 tbsp butter, softened
2 tbsp all-purpose flour
1 small onion, roughly
  chopped

Scant 1¼ cups meat or
  chicken stock *(see recipes
  on page 11)* or water from
  cooking vegetables, plus
  any juices from the roasted
  meat

¼ cup red or white wine (or
  50ml (2fl oz) extra stock)
1 tsp yeast extract
1 tsp dried mixed herbs
Sea salt & freshly ground
  black pepper

1 Put 1 tbsp butter and the flour in a small bowl and mix together until well blended to make beurre manié (*see Cook's Tip below*). Set aside.

2 Melt the remaining butter in a small saucepan, add the onion and cook gently for 8–10 minutes, or until softened.

3 Stir in the stock or vegetable water and meat juices, wine, yeast extract, and herbs and bring to a boil. Reduce the heat, cover, and simmer for 5 minutes.

4 Remove the onion using a slotted spoon and discard. Bring the liquid back to a boil, then add the beurre manié a little at a time, whisking continuously to blend in well with the liquid, until all the beurre manié has been added.

5 Continue to cook, whisking, until the gravy thickens. Simmer gently for 5 minutes, stirring continuously. Season to taste with salt (if required) and black pepper. Serve hot.

SERVING SUGGESTIONS *Serve with roast beef, lamb, pork, chicken, or turkey and all the trimmings. Alternatively, serve with pan-fried liver, kidneys, and bacon.*

VARIATIONS *Use 2 shallots in place of onion. A little gravy browning can be blended into gravy to intensify flavor and color, if desired.*

COOK'S TIP *Beurre manié, also known as kneaded butter, is added to a sauce toward the end of the preparation time as a thickener. Equal quantities of softened butter and all-purpose flour are kneaded together to make a smooth paste, which is then gradually whisked into the hot cooked sauce or liquid until it thickens.*

009 FRESH HORSERADISH CREAM

PREPARATION TIME *15 minutes* **COOKING TIME** *N/A* **SERVES 4–6** *Makes about 1¼ cups*

⅔ cup heavy cream
2–3 tbsp grated fresh
  horseradish, or to taste

2 tsp white wine vinegar
Sea salt & freshly
  ground black pepper

A little superfine sugar,
  to taste

1 Pour the cream into a bowl and whip until it forms thick, soft, peaks. Set aside.

2 Combine the horseradish and vinegar in a separate bowl, then gently fold the horseradish mixture into the whipped cream.

3 Add salt, pepper, and sugar, to taste. Cover and chill in the refrigerator until ready to serve.

SERVING SUGGESTIONS *Serve with hot or cold roast beef, or with broiled fresh or smoked mackerel, salmon, or trout.*

010 BREAD SAUCE

PREPARATION TIME *40 minutes* **COOKING TIME** *15 minutes* **SERVES 4–6** *Makes about 1½ cups*

4 whole cloves
1 small onion, peeled
6 black peppercorns
1 small bay leaf
1 fresh thyme sprig

1¼ cups milk
1½ cups fresh white bread
  crumbs
1 tbsp butter, diced

Sea salt & freshly
  ground black pepper
Freshly grated nutmeg
  (optional)
2 tbsp light cream

1 Press the cloves into the whole onion. Place the clove-studded onion in a saucepan with the peppercorns, bay leaf, fresh thyme, and milk. Bring gently to a boil, then remove the pan from the heat and set aside to infuse for 30 minutes.

2 Strain the milk into a clean pan, then discard the onion, spices, and herbs. Stir the bread crumbs into the milk, then bring gently to a boil and simmer for 5–10 minutes, or until thickened, stirring continuously.

3 Stir in the butter until melted, then season to taste with salt and pepper. Add a little grated nutmeg, if desired. Stir in the cream just before serving. Serve hot.

SERVING SUGGESTIONS *Serve with traditional roast turkey or partridge and all the trimmings.*

011 APPLE SAUCE

PREPARATION TIME *10 minutes* **COOKING TIME** *10–15 minutes* **SERVES 4**

1lb tart apples, peeled, cored
  & sliced
2 tbsp butter

½ tsp finely grated lemon zest
  (optional)

A little light soft brown sugar,
  to taste (optional)

1 Place the apples in a small saucepan with the butter and 2–3 tbsp water. Add the lemon zest, if using. Cover and cook gently for about 10 minutes, or until the apples are soft, thick, and pulpy, stirring occasionally.

2 Remove the pan from the heat, then mash or beat the apples with a wooden spoon to form a smooth purée.

3 Stir in a little sugar to taste, if desired. Set aside to cool, and serve warm or cold.

SERVING SUGGESTIONS *Serve with roast, broiled or pan-fried pork, turkey, duck, or goose.*

012 MINT SAUCE

PREPARATION TIME *10 minutes, plus standing* **COOKING TIME** *N/A* **SERVES 4** *Makes about 3 tbsp*

A small bunch of fresh mint,
  stalks removed

2 tsp superfine sugar
1 tbsp boiling water

1 tbsp white wine vinegar

1 Wash the mint leaves and shake them dry. Finely chop the mint leaves, then place them in a small bowl with the sugar.

2 Pour the boiling water over the mint leaves and sugar and stir to mix, then set aside for 5 minutes, or until the sugar has dissolved.

3 Add the vinegar and stir to mix. Set aside and leave to stand for 1–2 hours before serving. Serve at room temperature.

SERVING SUGGESTIONS *Serve with broiled or pan-fried lamb steaks, chops, or sausages.*

013 CRANBERRY AND ORANGE SAUCE

PREPARATION TIME *5 minutes* **COOKING TIME** *30 minutes* **SERVES 6–8** *Makes about 1¼ cups*

1 small orange
2 cups fresh cranberries

½ cup superfine sugar
⅔ cup water

1–2 tbsp ruby port wine
(optional)

1 Finely grate the zest from the orange and squeeze the juice. Place the cranberries in a saucepan with the orange juice, sugar, and water.

2 Bring gently to a boil, then cook, uncovered, for 20–30 minutes, or until the cranberries are soft, stirring occasionally.

3 Remove the pan from the heat and cool slightly. Using a slotted spoon, remove half the cranberries and place in a bowl. Purée the remaining cranberries and juices in a blender or food processor.

4 Add the cranberry purée to the reserved cranberries in the bowl, then stir in the orange zest, and port wine, if using, mixing well. Let cool, then serve warm or cold.

SERVING SUGGESTIONS *Serve with hot or cold roast turkey, chicken, pork, or duck.*
COOK'S TIP *Fresh cranberries are in season and at their peak between October and December, but they usually remain available some time into January. You can also purchase them frozen all year round.*

014 GREEN PEPPERCORN SAUCE

PREPARATION TIME *5 minutes* **COOKING TIME** *25 minutes* **SERVES 2–4** *Makes about 1 cup*

⅔ cup dry white wine
2 tbsp brandy
Scant 1 cup crème fraîche
 or heavy cream

1 tsp Dijon or wholegrain
 mustard
1 tbsp green peppercorns in
 brine, rinsed, & drained

2 tbsp chopped fresh parsley
 or snipped fresh chives
Sea salt & freshly ground
 black pepper

1 Put the wine and brandy in a small saucepan and bring to a boil. Simmer, uncovered, for
 about 10 minutes, or until the liquid has reduced by about half.
2 Whisk the crème fraîche or heavy cream into the sauce, bring slowly to a boil, then
 bubble for about 10 minutes, or until the sauce has thickened slightly.
3 Whisk the mustard into the sauce, then stir in the green peppercorns and chopped
 parsley or chives. Season to taste with salt and pepper. Serve hot.

SERVING SUGGESTIONS *Serve with pan-fried duck breasts, or with grilled salmon steaks.*

015 GREEN SAUCE

PREPARATION TIME *10 minutes* **COOKING TIME** *10 minutes* **SERVES 4** *Makes about 1½ cups*

1 tbsp butter
2 tbsp all-purpose flour
1¼ cups milk

2 bunches of watercress,
 trimmed, washed
 & finely chopped

Sea salt & freshly ground
 black pepper

1 Melt the butter in a small saucepan, stir in the flour and cook, stirring, for 1 minute.
 Remove the pan from the heat and gradually stir or whisk in the milk.
2 Return to the heat and bring slowly to a boil, stirring or whisking until the sauce is
 thickened and smooth. Simmer gently for 2–3 minutes, stirring continuously.
3 Stir in the watercress and cook for 1–2 minutes. Season to taste with salt and pepper.
4 Remove the pan from the heat and cool slightly, then purée the sauce in a blender or
 food processor until smooth.
5 Return the sauce to the pan and reheat gently before serving. Adjust the seasoning and
 serve hot.

SERVING SUGGESTIONS *Serve with roast lamb, chicken, or turkey, or with broiled tuna steaks.*

016 PIQUANT PAPRIKA SAUCE

PREPARATION TIME *5 minutes* **COOKING TIME** *15 minutes* **SERVES 4–6** *Makes about 1¼ cups*

2 tbsp butter
1 small onion, finely chopped
¼ cup all-purpose flour

1 tsp paprika
1 cup milk
4–5 tbsp dry sherry

Sea salt & freshly ground
 black pepper

1 Melt the butter in a saucepan, add the onion and sauté for about 5 minutes, or until
 softened. Stir in the flour and paprika and cook gently for 1 minute, stirring.
2 Remove the pan from the heat and gradually stir in the milk, followed by the sherry.
3 Return to the heat and bring slowly to a boil, stirring, until the sauce thickens. Simmer
 gently for 2–3 minutes, stirring. Season to taste with salt and pepper. Serve hot.

SERVING SUGGESTIONS *Serve with oven-baked chicken thighs or turkey breast steaks.*

017 RED BELL PEPPER SAUCE

PREPARATION TIME *20 minutes* **COOKING TIME** *35 minutes* **SERVES 2–4** *Makes about ¾ cup*

1 tbsp sunflower oil
1 red onion, chopped
1 clove garlic, crushed
1 large red bell pepper,
  skinned, seeded, & chopped

3 ripe plum or vine-ripened
  tomatoes, skinned, seeded,
  & chopped
½ cup vegetable stock *(see
  recipe on page 10)*

1 fresh bouquet garni
Sea salt & freshly ground
  black pepper

1 Heat the oil in a saucepan, add the onion, garlic, and red bell pepper and cook gently for about 10 minutes, or until softened.

2 Stir in the tomatoes, stock, bouquet garni, and seasoning. Bring to a boil, then reduce the heat and simmer, uncovered, for 20 minutes. Remove and discard the bouquet garni.

3 Remove the pan from the heat and cool slightly, then purée the mixture in a blender or food processor until smooth. Push the purée through a sieve and discard the contents of the sieve.

4 Return the sauce to the pan and reheat gently. Adjust the seasoning to taste, and serve hot. Alternatively, once sieved, the sauce may be left to cool, and served chilled.

SERVING SUGGESTIONS *Serve with stir-fried zucchini or steamed green beans or asparagus. Alternatively, serve with broiled fillets of plaice or lemon sole.*

COOK'S TIPS *To skin tomatoes, cut a small cross in the base of each tomato. Place the tomatoes in a bowl and cover them with boiling water. Leave for about 30 seconds, then, using a slotted spoon, transfer the tomatoes to a bowl of cold water. Remove the tomatoes from the water and peel off and discard the skins. To remove the seeds, cut each tomato in half and scoop out and discard the seeds.*

To skin bell peppers, cut each bell pepper in half and place them, cut-side down, on the rack in a broiler pan. Place under a preheated hot broiler for about 10–15 minutes, or until the skin is blackened and charred. Remove from the heat, cover the bell peppers with a clean, damp dish towel and let cool. Once cool, remove and discard the skin, cores, and seeds from the bell peppers.

018 FRUITY SWEET AND SOUR SAUCE

PREPARATION TIME *5 minutes* **COOKING TIME** *15–20 minutes* **SERVES 4** *Makes about 1¼ cups*

1 tbsp cornstarch
½ cup unsweetened
  pineapple juice
2 tbsp light soy sauce

2 tbsp light soft brown sugar
2 tbsp tomato paste
2 tbsp dry sherry
2 tbsp cider vinegar

1–2 tbsp chopped fresh
  parsley or cilantro
  (optional)
Sea salt & freshly
  ground black pepper

1 Blend the cornstarch with the pineapple juice in a small saucepan, then add the soy sauce, sugar, tomato paste, sherry, and vinegar and stir to mix.

2 Heat gently, stirring continuously, until the sauce comes to a boil and thickens slightly. Simmer gently for 10 minutes, stirring occasionally.

3 Stir in the chopped parsley or cilantro, if using, and season to taste with salt and pepper. Serve hot.

SERVING SUGGESTIONS *Serve with cooked mixed beans. Alternatively, serve with grilled pork or chicken kebabs, or with stir-fried strips of beef or chicken.*

019 NUTTY SATAY SAUCE

PREPARATION TIME *10 minutes* **COOKING TIME** *30 minutes* **SERVES 6–8** *Makes about 2¼ cups*

¾ cup dry roasted peanuts or
   unsalted (toasted) peanuts
1 tbsp olive oil
3 shallots, finely chopped
2 cloves garlic, crushed

1 fresh red or green chili,
   seeded, & finely chopped
1-inch piece of fresh root
   ginger, peeled & finely
   chopped

14-oz can coconut milk
Juice of 1 lime
1 tbsp light soft brown sugar
Sea salt, to taste

1 Place the peanuts in a blender or food processor and process until they are finely chopped. Set aside.

2 Heat the oil in a saucepan, add the shallots and sauté for about 5 minutes, or until softened. Add the garlic, chili, and ginger and sauté for 2 minutes.

3 Remove the pan from the heat, then add the shallot mixture to the peanuts in the processor and process briefly to mix.

4 Return the mixture to the saucepan, then stir in the coconut milk, lime juice, and sugar.

5 Bring slowly to a boil, stirring, then reduce the heat and simmer, uncovered, for 10–15 minutes, or until the sauce is thickened, stirring occasionally. Season to taste with salt, if required. Serve hot.

SERVING SUGGESTIONS *Serve as a dipping sauce with marinated broiled or grilled beef or lamb kebabs. Alternatively, serve with a selection of cooked or raw vegetable crudités.*

020 WILD MUSHROOM AND WINE SAUCE

PREPARATION TIME *15 minutes* **COOKING TIME** *25 minutes* **SERVES 4–6** *Makes about 2¼ cups*

2 tbsp butter
4 shallots, finely chopped
3 cups chestnut or brown
   cap mushrooms, sliced
3 cups fresh mixed wild
   mushrooms, sliced

1 clove garlic, crushed
½ cup dry white wine
½ cup vegetable stock *(see
   recipe on page 10)*
⅔ cup crème fraîche

1 tsp dried Italian herb
   seasoning
Sea salt & freshly ground
   black pepper

1 Melt the butter in a saucepan, add the shallots and sauté for about 5 minutes, or until softened.

2 Add all the mushrooms and garlic, and sauté over a fairly high heat for 5 minutes, or until softened.

3 Add the wine and bring to a boil, then bubble until the wine has reduced by about half.

4 Stir in the stock, crème fraîche, dried herbs, and seasoning, then bring to a boil and simmer for about 7 minutes, or until the sauce is thickened, stirring occasionally. Serve hot.

SERVING SUGGESTIONS *Serve with roast or broiled lamb steaks or chicken breasts. Alternatively, serve with broiled or pan-fried polenta slices.*
VARIATIONS *Use heavy cream in place of crème fraîche.*

021 CREAMY MUSHROOM SAUCE

PREPARATION TIME *10 minutes* **COOKING TIME** *15 minutes* **SERVES 4–6** *Makes about 2½ cups*

⅔ cup vegetable stock *(see recipe on page 10)*
1¼ cups heavy cream
3 tbsp butter

3 cups chestnut or brown cap mushrooms, sliced
2 cups button mushrooms, sliced

1–2 tbsp chopped fresh mixed herbs such as parsley, chives, & marjoram or oregano
Sea salt & freshly ground black pepper

1 Pour the stock and cream into a saucepan. Bring slowly to a boil, then simmer gently until the sauce thickens slightly to a coating consistency, stirring frequently.

2 Meanwhile, melt the butter in a skillet, add all the mushrooms and sauté for about 5 minutes, or until softened. Increase the heat slightly and cook, stirring frequently, until all the liquid has evaporated.

3 Add the mushrooms and chopped herbs to the cream sauce and reheat gently until hot, stirring continuously. Season to taste with salt and pepper. Serve hot.

SERVING SUGGESTIONS *Serve with broiled chicken breasts or grilled beef steaks. Alternatively, serve with baked cod or haddock fillets, or tuna steaks.*

VARIATIONS *Use crème fraîche in place of heavy cream. Use fresh mixed wild mushrooms in place of chestnut or button mushrooms.*

022 BARBECUE SAUCE

PREPARATION TIME *10 minutes* **COOKING TIME** *20 minutes* **SERVES 4–6** *Makes about 2¼ cups*

2 tbsp butter
1 red onion, finely chopped
14-oz can chopped tomatoes

4 tbsp light beer or lager
  (such as Budweiser)
1 tbsp red wine vinegar
1 tbsp Worcestershire sauce

1 tbsp tomato paste
1 tbsp light soft brown sugar
2 tsp Dijon mustard
Sea salt & freshly ground
  black pepper

1 Melt the butter in a saucepan, add the onion and sauté for about 5 minutes, or until softened.

2 Add the tomatoes, beer, vinegar, Worcestershire sauce, tomato paste, sugar, and mustard, and stir to mix well.

3 Bring gently to a boil, stirring, then simmer, uncovered, for 10–15 minutes, or until the sauce thickens slightly, stirring occasionally. Season to taste. Serve hot.

SERVING SUGGESTIONS *Serve with grilled vegetable or chicken kebabs, or chicken drumsticks.*

023 TOMATO CATSUP

PREPARATION TIME *5 minutes* **COOKING TIME** *40 minutes* **SERVES 4–6** *Makes about 2¼ cups*

2 tbsp olive oil
1 small red onion, finely
  chopped
2 cloves garlic, crushed
14-oz can chopped tomatoes

1 tbsp tomato paste
2 tbsp red wine
⅓ cup light soft brown sugar
2 tbsp red wine vinegar
2 tsp Dijon mustard

Sea salt & freshly ground
  black pepper

1 Heat the oil in a saucepan, add the onion and garlic and sauté for 5 minutes. Stir in the
  tomatoes, tomato paste, and red wine.
2 Bring to the boil, then reduce the heat and simmer, uncovered, for about 25 minutes, or
  until most of the liquid has evaporated and the sauce has reduced to a very thick pulp,
  stirring occasionally.
3 Remove the pan from the heat and cool slightly, then purée the mixture in a blender or
  food processor until smooth.
4 Return the mixture to the rinsed-out pan, stir in the sugar, vinegar, mustard, and
  seasoning, then bring to a boil, reduce the heat and simmer gently for 5 minutes.
5 Remove the pan from the heat and let the sauce cool a little, then taste and adjust the
  seasoning, and serve warm. Alternatively, let the sauce cool completely, and serve cold.

SERVING SUGGESTIONS *Serve with broiled or grilled beef burgers, sausages, spare ribs, lamb chops, or
chicken drumsticks.*

024 QUICK CHILI SAUCE

PREPARATION TIME *10 minutes* **COOKING TIME** *20 minutes* **SERVES 6** *Makes about 2 cups*

1 tbsp olive oil or chili-
  flavored olive oil
5 scallions, finely chopped
1 fresh red chili, seeded &
  finely chopped

1 clove garlic, crushed
14-oz can chopped tomatoes
A squeeze of fresh lemon
  juice
1 tbsp light soft brown sugar

Sea salt & freshly ground
  black pepper
2 tsp cornstarch
Medium chili sauce, to taste
  (optional)

1 Heat the oil in a small saucepan, add the scallions, chili, and garlic and sauté for about
  5 minutes, or until softened.
2 Add the tomatoes, lemon juice, sugar, and salt and pepper to taste, and mix well. Bring
  slowly to a boil, then cover and simmer gently for 10 minutes, stirring occasionally.
3 In a small bowl, blend the cornstarch with 1 tbsp cold water, then stir the cornstarch
  mixture into the sauce. Bring the sauce to a boil, stirring continuously, then reduce the
  heat and simmer gently for 3 minutes, stirring.
4 Adjust the seasoning and add a dash or two of chili sauce to taste, if desired. Serve hot.

SERVING SUGGESTIONS *Serve with broiled or pan-fried monkfish, halibut, or tiger prawns. Alternatively,
serve with stuffed baked zucchini, marrows, or bell peppers.*

CHAPTER 2

CLASSIC SAUCES

This book would not be complete without a chapter dedicated to classic sauce recipes. Many of these, such as Mayonnaise, Aïoli, and Hollandaise, will be familiar to you, but perhaps you have not tried to make recipes such as these before now. Once you have mastered a few easy basic techniques, you can enjoy creating a whole range of classic sauces at home.

In the following pages, you will find a tempting selection of recipes, with easy-to-follow instructions. It is well worth that extra bit of effort to make your own delicious sauces. Once you have tried making many of these home-made classics, you will never want to go back to ready-made products again!

Other classic sauce recipes included are Béchamel Sauce, Soubise (Onion) Sauce, Velouté Sauce, Espagnole (Brown) Sauce, Chasseur Sauce, Tartare Sauce, Remoulade, Beurre Blanc, Classic Pesto, Saffron Sauce, and Cumberland Sauce.

025 BÉCHAMEL SAUCE

PREPARATION TIME *35 minutes* **COOKING TIME** *10 minutes* **SERVES 4** *Makes about 1¼ cups*

1¼ cups milk
1 small onion or shallot,
  cut in half
1 small carrot, thickly sliced
1 bay leaf

6 black peppercorns
A few fresh parsley stalks
1 tbsp butter
2 tbsp all-purpose flour

Sea salt & freshly ground
  black pepper
Freshly grated nutmeg,
  to taste (optional)

1 Pour the milk into a small saucepan and add the onion or shallot, carrot, bay leaf, black
peppercorns, and parsley stalks. Bring almost to a boil, then remove the pan from the
heat and set aside to infuse for 30 minutes.

2 Strain the mixture into a jug, reserving the flavored milk and discarding the contents of
the sieve. Melt the butter in a separate small saucepan, stir in the flour and cook,
stirring, for 1 minute. Remove the pan from the heat and gradually stir or whisk in the
flavored milk.

3 Return to the heat and bring slowly to a boil, stirring or whisking until the sauce is
thickened and smooth. Simmer gently for 2–3 minutes, stirring continuously. Season to
taste with salt and pepper, and a little nutmeg, if using. Serve hot.

SERVING SUGGESTIONS *Serve with broiled or pan-fried fillets of plaice or sole, broiled chicken breasts,
or with cooked petit pois or small carrots.*
COOK'S TIP *For a thicker sauce, follow the recipe above, increasing the butter to 2 tbsp and the flour
to ¼ cup.*

026 SOUBISE (ONION) SAUCE

PREPARATION TIME *10 minutes* **COOKING TIME** *20 minutes* **SERVES 4** *Makes about 1½ cups*

3 tbsp butter
1 large onion, finely chopped

3 tbsp all-purpose flour
1¼ cups milk

Sea salt & freshly ground
  black pepper

1 Melt 4 tsp butter in a pan, add the onion and cook gently for 10–15 minutes, or until
softened. Remove the pan from the heat and set aside.

2 Melt the remaining butter in a separate saucepan, stir in the flour and cook, stirring, for
1 minute. Remove the pan from the heat and gradually stir or whisk in the milk.

3 Return the sauce to the heat and bring slowly to a boil, stirring or whisking until it is
thickened and smooth. Simmer gently for 2–3 minutes, stirring continuously.

4 Stir in the cooked onion and reheat gently until hot, stirring continuously. Season to
taste with salt and pepper. Serve hot.

SERVING SUGGESTIONS *Serve with baked ham, roast chicken, or with broiled haddock or monkfish.*
VARIATION *Use 1 large red onion in place of regular onion.*
COOK'S TIP *Leave the root end intact when slicing or chopping an onion. This will prevent the release
of the strong juices and fumes that cause eyes to water.*

027 CHASSEUR SAUCE

PREPARATION TIME *15 minutes* **COOKING TIME** *35 minutes* **SERVES 4–6** *Makes about 2¼ cups*

½ cup butter
1 small onion, finely chopped
4 cups button mushrooms, sliced
¼ cup all-purpose flour
¾ cup dry white wine

1¼ cups chicken or beef stock
  (see recipes on page 11)
1 tbsp tomato paste
1 tbsp chopped fresh mixed herbs such as parsley, basil, & oregano

1 tbsp brandy
Sea salt & freshly ground black pepper

1 Melt the butter in a saucepan, add the onion and mushrooms and sauté for about 5 minutes, or until softened. Remove the vegetables from the pan using a slotted spoon, set aside and keep hot.
2 Stir the flour into the juices in the pan, then cook for about 2 minutes, stirring continuously, until the mixture is brown. Remove the pan from the heat and gradually whisk in the wine, stock, and tomato paste.
3 Return to the heat and bring slowly to a boil, stirring or whisking until the sauce is thickened slightly. Simmer gently for about 15 minutes, or until the sauce is smooth and glossy, stirring occasionally.
4 Stir in the sautéed onion and mushrooms, the chopped herbs, and brandy, and season to taste with salt and pepper. Serve hot.

SERVING SUGGESTIONS *Serve with oven-baked chicken breasts, or with pan-fried strips of beef.*

028 VELOUTÉ SAUCE

PREPARATION TIME *5 minutes* **COOKING TIME** *10 minutes* **SERVES 4** *Makes about 1½ cups*

4 tsp butter
3 tbsp all-purpose flour
1¼ cups chicken, fish, vegetable or meat stock
  (see recipes on pages 10–11)

2 tbsp heavy cream
½ tsp fresh lemon juice
Sea salt & freshly ground black pepper

1 Melt the butter in a small saucepan, stir in the flour and cook, stirring, for about 2 minutes, or until light golden in color. Remove the pan from the heat and gradually stir or whisk in the stock.
2 Return the pan to the heat and bring slowly to a boil, stirring or whisking until the sauce is thickened and smooth. Simmer gently for 2–3 minutes, stirring continuously.
3 Stir in the cream, then stir in the lemon juice. Season to taste with salt and pepper. Serve hot.

SERVING SUGGESTIONS *Serve with broiled or baked chicken breasts, or fillets of cod or plaice. Alternatively, serve with broiled lamb or pork chops.*

029 RICH CHEESE SAUCE

PREPARATION TIME *10 minutes* **COOKING TIME** *10 minutes* **SERVES 4** *Makes about 1½ cups*

1 tbsp butter
2 tbsp all-purpose flour
1¼ cups full-fat milk
¾ cup mature cheddar
 cheese, grated

¼ cup fresh Parmesan
 cheese, finely grated
1 tsp Dijon mustard
Sea salt & freshly ground
 black pepper

Freshly grated nutmeg,
 to taste (optional)

1 Melt the butter in a small saucepan, stir in the flour and cook, stirring, for 1 minute.
Remove the pan from the heat and gradually stir or whisk in the milk.
2 Return to the heat and bring slowly to a boil, stirring or whisking until the sauce is
thickened and smooth.
3 Stir in the cheeses and mustard and cook over a gentle heat for about 5 minutes, or
until the cheeses have melted and the sauce is smooth and glossy, stirring continuously.
Season to taste with salt and pepper, and a little nutmeg, if using. Serve hot.

SERVING SUGGESTIONS *Serve with oven-baked ham, or with broiled cod or halibut. Alternatively, serve
with cooked cauliflower or broccoli florets, or with hot gnocchi or macaroni.*
VARIATIONS *Use red Leicester or double Gloucester cheese in place of cheddar and Parmesan cheeses.
Use English mustard in place of Dijon mustard.*

030 BORDELAISE SAUCE

PREPARATION TIME *10 minutes* **COOKING TIME** *1 hour 15 minutes* **SERVES 4–6** *Makes about 1¾ cups*

2 tbsp butter
1 slice of rindless unsmoked
  bacon, finely chopped
2 shallots, finely chopped
1 carrot, finely chopped

1 cup mushrooms, finely
  chopped
3 tbsp all-purpose flour
1¼ cups beef stock *(see
  recipe on page 11)*

1¼ cups red wine
1 bouquet garni
Sea salt & freshly ground
  black pepper

1 Melt the butter in a saucepan. Add the bacon and cook for 2 minutes, stirring. Add the
shallots, carrot and mushrooms and sauté for about 8 minutes, or until softened and
lightly browned.

2 Stir in the flour and cook, stirring, until the flour is lightly browned. Remove the pan
from the heat and gradually stir in the stock and wine.

3 Bring slowly to a boil, stirring continuously, and continue to cook until the mixture thickens. Add the bouquet garni and seasoning. Cover and simmer gently for 1 hour, stirring
occasionally.

4 Remove the pan from the heat, cool slightly, then strain the sauce through a sieve.
Discard the contents of the sieve. Return the strained sauce to the rinsed-out saucepan
and reheat gently before serving. Adjust the seasoning to taste. Serve hot.

SERVING SUGGESTIONS *Serve with pan-fried beef medallions, or with roast lamb, pheasant, or rabbit.*
VARIATION *Use smoked bacon in place of unsmoked bacon.*

031 ESPAGNOLE (BROWN) SAUCE

PREPARATION TIME *10 minutes* **COOKING TIME** *1 hour 15 minutes* **SERVES 4** *Makes about 1¼ cups*

2 tbsp butter
1 slice of rindless streaky
   bacon, chopped
1 small onion, finely chopped
1 small carrot, finely chopped
1 stick of celery, finely chopped

1 cup button mushrooms,
   finely chopped
¼ cup all-purpose flour
2 cups beef or meat
   stock *(see recipe on page
   11)*

2 tbsp tomato paste
1 fresh bouquet garni *(see
   Cook's Tip below)*
Sea salt & freshly ground
   black pepper

1 Melt the butter in a saucepan, add the bacon and cook for 2–3 minutes, stirring.
2 Add the onion, carrot, celery, and mushrooms and sauté gently for 6–8 minutes, or until softened. Stir in the flour and cook, stirring, until the mixture is brown.
3 Remove the pan from the heat and gradually whisk in the stock. Return to the heat and bring slowly to a boil, stirring or whisking until the sauce is thickened.
4 Add the tomato paste, bouquet garni, and seasoning. Partially cover the pan and simmer gently for about 1 hour, stirring occasionally.
5 Strain the sauce through a sieve into a clean pan and discard the contents of the sieve. Reheat the sauce gently until hot, stirring continuously, then adjust the seasoning to taste. Serve hot.

SERVING SUGGESTIONS *Serve with broiled or pan-fried beef or venison steaks, or with fried lamb's liver or kidneys.*
COOK'S TIP *A fresh bouquet garni usually consists of 3 sprigs of fresh parsley, 2 sprigs of fresh thyme and a bay leaf, tied up in a celery stick or a section of leek.*

032 DEMI-GLACE SAUCE

PREPARATION TIME *5 minutes* **COOKING TIME** *20 minutes* **SERVES 4–6** *Makes about 1¼ cups*

1 quantity Espagnole (Brown)
   Sauce *(see recipe above)*
1¼ cups beef stock
   (see recipe on page 11)

Sea salt & freshly ground
   black pepper
A knob of butter (optional)

1 Combine the Espagnole Sauce and beef stock in a saucepan. Bring the mixture to a boil, then boil until reduced to half the original quantity, skimming off any impurities as they rise to the surface.
2 Remove the pan from the heat, then pass the sauce through a fine sieve and return the sauce to the pan, adjust the seasoning to taste, and reheat gently until hot, stirring continuously.
3 For added gloss and flavor, whisk in the knob of butter, if desired. Serve hot.

SERVING SUGGESTIONS *Serve with roast beef or pheasant. Alternatively, serve with pan-fried lamb cutlets or venison steaks.*
COOK'S TIP *For the best results, be sure to use a well-flavored home-made beef stock for this recipe (for more details on making and storing home-made stocks, see pages 10–11).*

033 SAUCE ROBERT

PREPARATION TIME *10 minutes* **COOKING TIME** *25 minutes* **SERVES 4–6** *Makes about 1½ cups*

1 tbsp butter
2 shallots, finely chopped
½ cup dry white wine
3 tbsp white wine vinegar
1¼ cups Demi-Glace
   Sauce *(see recipe on page
   32)*

2 tsp Dijon mustard
½ cup gherkins (drained
   weight), finely chopped
   (optional)
2 tsp chopped fresh parsley
Sea salt & freshly ground
   black pepper

1 Melt the butter in a saucepan, add the shallots and sauté for about 5 minutes, or until softened.
2 Stir in the wine and vinegar, then increase the heat, bring the mixture to a boil and boil rapidly until the liquid has reduced to about 3 tbsp.
3 Stir in the Demi-Glace Sauce, bring the mixture to a boil, then reduce the heat and simmer, uncovered, for 10 minutes, stirring occasionally.
4 Remove the pan from the heat and whisk in the mustard until smooth. Stir in the gherkins, if using, and the chopped parsley, then season to taste with salt and pepper. Serve hot.

SERVING SUGGESTIONS *Serve with broiled or oven-baked pork or lamb chops, pan-fried beef olives or broiled herby sausages.*
COOK'S TIP *The cooking process completed in Step 2 of this recipe is known as 'reduction' – where the flavor of the sauce is concentrated by rapid boiling.*

034 MOUSSELINE SAUCE

PREPARATION TIME *5 minutes* **COOKING TIME** *10 minutes* **SERVES 4–6** *Makes about 1¼ cups*

2 egg yolks
1 tbsp fresh lemon juice
½ cup butter, at room
   temperature, diced

6 tbsp heavy cream, lightly
   whipped
Sea salt & freshly ground
   black pepper

1 Put the egg yolks in a heatproof bowl with the lemon juice, and whisk together to mix. Place the bowl over a pan of barely simmering water and whisk the egg mixture for about 4 minutes, or until pale and thick.
2 Gradually whisk in the butter, one piece at a time, until the mixture begins to thicken and emulsify. Make sure each piece of butter is incorporated into the sauce before adding the next piece.
3 Once all the butter has been added and the sauce has become smooth and glossy, remove the bowl from the heat. Whisk for 1 minute.
4 Fold the whipped cream into the sauce, then add salt and pepper to taste. Stir in a little extra lemon juice to taste, if desired. Serve cold.

SERVING SUGGESTIONS *Serve with broiled chicken breasts, or with cooked artichoke hearts or asparagus.*

035 RÉMOULADE

PREPARATION TIME *10 minutes* **COOKING TIME** *N/A* **SERVES 4–6** *Makes about 1 cup*

2 tsp capers, drained & finely chopped

3 cocktail gherkins, drained & finely chopped

1 canned anchovy fillet, drained & finely chopped

⅔ cup Mayonnaise *(see recipe on page 37)*

1 tsp Dijon mustard

2 tsp finely chopped fresh tarragon

2 tsp chopped fresh parsley

Sea salt & freshly ground black pepper

1 Place the chopped capers, gherkins, and anchovy in a small bowl and stir to mix.

2 Add the mayonnaise, mustard, and chopped herbs and mix well. Season to taste with salt and pepper. Serve cold.

SERVING SUGGESTIONS *Serve with slices of cold beef, pork or chicken, or with whole shrimp or hard-cooked eggs.*

036 HOLLANDAISE

PREPARATION TIME *20 minutes* **COOKING TIME** *2–3 minutes* **SERVES 4–6** *Makes about ¾ cup*

3 tbsp white wine vinegar

6 black peppercorns

1 slice of onion or ½ a shallot

1 bay leaf

1 blade of mace

2 egg yolks

½ cup butter, at room temperature, diced

Sea salt & freshly ground black pepper

Freshly squeezed lemon or lime juice, to taste

1 Place the vinegar in a heavy-based saucepan with the peppercorns, onion or shallot, bay leaf, and mace. Bring to a boil, then reduce the heat and simmer until the mixture has reduced to about 1 tbsp of liquid. Remove the pan from the heat and set aside.

2 Place the egg yolks in a heatproof bowl with 1 tbsp butter and a pinch of salt, and beat together using a balloon whisk. Strain the reduced vinegar into the egg mixture and stir to mix.

3 Place the bowl over a pan of barely simmering water and whisk the egg mixture for 3–4 minutes, or until it is pale and beginning to thicken.

4 Gradually whisk in the remaining butter, one piece at a time, until the mixture begins to thicken and emulsify. Make sure each piece of butter is incorporated into the sauce before adding the next piece.

5 Once all the butter has been added and the sauce has become light and thick, remove the bowl from the heat. Whisk for 1 minute. Adjust the seasoning and add a little lemon or lime juice to taste. Serve immediately.

SERVING SUGGESTIONS *Serve with broiled or pan-fried salmon fillets or king prawns, or with steamed asparagus or globe artichokes.*

COOK'S TIPS *Hollandaise will curdle if allowed to overheat, and it will set too firmly if allowed to get cold. If Hollandaise begins to curdle, add an ice cube and whisk well; the sauce should re-combine.*

Hollandaise can also be made in a small food processor. Melt the butter and cool until tepid. Put the strained reduced vinegar in a small food processor with the egg yolks and a pinch of salt and process lightly to mix. With the motor running and blades turning, gradually add the melted butter in a thin, steady stream through the feeder tube, and process until light, thick, and emulsified. Adjust the seasoning and add fresh lemon or lime juice to taste.

037 HERBY LEMON HOLLANDAISE

PREPARATION TIME *20 minutes* **COOKING TIME** *2–3 minutes* **SERVES 4–6** *Makes about ¾ cup*

3 tbsp white wine vinegar
6 black peppercorns
1 slice of onion or ½ a shallot
1 bay leaf
1 blade of mace

2 egg yolks
½ cup butter, at room
   temperature, diced
Sea salt & freshly ground
   black pepper

1 tbsp chopped fresh
   mixed herbs
Freshly squeezed lemon
   juice, to taste

1 Place the vinegar in a heavy-based saucepan with the peppercorns, onion or shallot, bay leaf, and mace. Bring to a boil, then reduce the heat and simmer until the mixture has reduced to about 1 tbsp of liquid. Remove the pan from the heat and set aside.

2 Place the egg yolks in a heatproof bowl with 1 tbsp butter and a pinch of salt and beat together using a balloon whisk. Strain the reduced vinegar into the egg mixture and stir to mix.

3 Place the bowl over a pan of barely simmering water and whisk the egg mixture for 3–4 minutes, or until it is pale and beginning to thicken.

4 Gradually whisk in the remaining butter, one piece at a time, until the mixture begins to thicken and emulsify. Make sure each piece of butter is incorporated into the sauce before adding the next piece.

5 Once all the butter has been added and the sauce has become light and thick, remove the bowl from the heat. Whisk for 1 minute. Stir in the chopped herbs, then adjust the seasoning and add a little lemon juice to taste. Serve immediately.

SERVING SUGGESTIONS *Serve with broiled or pan-fried salmon fillets or whole rainbow trout.*

038 TARTARE SAUCE

PREPARATION TIME *10 minutes, plus standing* **COOKING TIME** *N/A* **SERVES 8–10** *Makes about 1¼ cups*

4 tbsp gherkins, drained & finely chopped

2 tbsp capers, drained & finely chopped

scant 1¼ cups Mayonnaise *(see recipe on page 37)*

4 tbsp extra-thick heavy cream

1 tbsp tarragon vinegar

1 tbsp chopped fresh flat-leaf parsley

1 tbsp snipped fresh chives

2 tsp chopped fresh tarragon

Sea salt & freshly ground black pepper

1 Combine the gherkins and capers in a bowl. Add the mayonnaise and mix well, then fold in the cream.

2 Fold in the vinegar and chopped herbs and mix well. Season to taste.

3 Cover and leave in a cool place for about 30 minutes before serving, so the flavors develop. Serve cold.

SERVING SUGGESTIONS *Serve with broiled or baked fishcakes or fish goujons. Alternatively, serve with fried breadcrumbed or battered cod, plaice, or haddock.*

VARIATIONS *Use plain fromage frais or crème fraîche in place of cream. Use white wine vinegar or freshly squeezed lemon juice in place of tarragon vinegar.*

COOK'S TIP *Capers are the small, unopened buds of a thorny, wild Mediterranean plant, which are picked and then pickled in salty vinegar, or preserved in salt. Capers should be rinsed (if preserved in salt) and drained before use. They can be used whole or finely chopped, depending on the recipe.*

039 MAYONNAISE

PREPARATION TIME *10 minutes* **COOKING TIME** *N/A* **SERVES 6–8** *Makes about 1½ cups*

2 egg yolks
1 tsp Dijon mustard
1 tbsp fresh lemon juice or
  white wine vinegar

A pinch of superfine sugar
Sea salt & freshly ground
  black pepper

1¼ cups light olive oil
  or sunflower oil

1 Place the egg yolks, mustard, lemon juice or vinegar, sugar, a little salt and pepper, and
  1 tbsp oil in a small blender or food processor. Blend for about 20 seconds, or until
  smooth, pale and creamy.
2 With the motor running and blades turning, gradually add the remaining oil to the
  blender or food processor, pouring it through the feeder tube in a slow, continuous
  stream until the mayonnaise is thick, creamy and smooth.
3 Adjust the seasoning to taste, then use immediately or cover and chill until required.
  Store in a covered container in the refrigerator for up to 3 days. Remove the mayonnaise
  from the refrigerator 30 minutes before serving. Serve cold.

SERVING SUGGESTIONS *Serve with salads, sliced cold cuts or smoked fish, or use as the basis for
sauces such as Tartare Sauce or flavored mayonnaises.*
VARIATION *Use fresh lime juice in place of lemon juice or white wine vinegar.*
COOK'S TIPS *The ingredients for mayonnaise should all be at room temperature. If eggs are used
straight from the refrigerator, the mayonnaise may curdle.*

040 AÏOLI

PREPARATION TIME *10 minutes* **COOKING TIME** *N/A* **SERVES 6–8** *Makes about 1½ cups*

2 egg yolks
1 tbsp fresh lemon juice
4 cloves garlic, crushed

½ tsp sea salt
Freshly ground black pepper,
  to taste

1¼ cups light olive oil
  or sunflower oil

1 Place the egg yolks, lemon juice, garlic, salt, a little black pepper, and 1 tbsp oil in a
  small blender or food processor. Blend for about 20 seconds, or until pale and creamy.
2 With the motor running and blades turning, gradually add the remaining oil to the
  blender or food processor, pouring it through the feeder tube in a slow, continuous
  stream until the aïoli is thick, creamy, and smooth.
3 Adjust the seasoning to taste, then use immediately, or cover and chill until required.
  Store in a covered container in the refrigerator for up to 2 days. Serve cold.

SERVING SUGGESTIONS *Serve with sliced cold roast chicken or salmon fillets, tiger prawns, or with
Mediterranean fish soups. Alternatively, serve with hard-cooked eggs or as a dip for potato wedges,
crisps, or vegetable crudités.*
VARIATIONS *Use fresh lime juice in place of lemon juice. Use smoked garlic in place of regular garlic.*
COOK'S TIPS *When buying garlic, choose plump garlic bulbs with tightly packed cloves and dry skin.
Avoid bulbs with soft, shrivelled cloves, or green shoots.*
  *When using a garlic press, leave the peel on the garlic clove. The soft garlic flesh will be pressed
through the mesh, and the peel/skin will be left behind in the garlic press, making it easy to clean
out after use.*

041 BÉARNAISE SAUCE

PREPARATION TIME *5 minutes* **COOKING TIME** *15 minutes* **SERVES 4–6** *Makes about ⅔ cup*

3 tbsp tarragon or white wine
  vinegar
½ tsp black peppercorns
2 shallots, finely chopped
A few fresh tarragon sprigs
1 bay leaf

2 egg yolks
½ cup butter, at room
  temperature, diced
Sea salt & freshly ground
  black pepper

1–2 tbsp chopped fresh
  mixed herbs such as
  tarragon, parsley & chervil
Fresh lemon juice, to taste
  (optional)

1 Place the vinegar in a small saucepan with the peppercorns, shallots, tarragon sprigs, bay leaf, and 1 tbsp water. Bring to a boil, then simmer until the mixture has reduced to about 1 tbsp of liquid. Remove the pan from the heat and set aside.

2 Place the egg yolks in a heatproof bowl with 1 tbsp butter and a pinch of salt and beat together using a balloon whisk. Strain the reduced vinegar into the egg mixture and stir to mix.

3 Place the bowl over a pan of barely simmering water and whisk the egg mixture for about 4 minutes, or until pale and beginning to thicken.

4 Gradually whisk in the remaining butter, one piece at a time, until the mixture begins to thicken and emulsify. Make sure each piece of butter is incorporated into the sauce before adding the next piece.

5 Once all the butter has been added and the sauce has become light and thick, remove the bowl from the heat. Whisk for 1 minute. Stir in the chopped herbs and adjust the seasoning to taste. Add a little lemon juice to taste, if desired. Serve immediately.

SERVING SUGGESTIONS *Serve with broiled cod or salmon steaks. Alternatively, serve with broiled or pan-fried beef or lamb steaks, or with steamed asparagus, green beans, or small zucchini.*

042 BEURRE BLANC

PREPARATION TIME *20 minutes* **COOKING TIME** *2–3 minutes* **SERVES 4–6** *Makes about 1 cup*

3 tbsp white wine
3 tbsp white wine vinegar
2 small shallots, finely
  chopped

1 cup butter, chilled &
  diced
Sea salt & freshly ground
  black pepper

Freshly squeezed lemon
  juice, to taste
1 tbsp chopped fresh parsley
  or finely snipped fresh
  chives (optional)

1 Put the wine, vinegar, and shallots in a small saucepan, bring to a boil and boil until the liquid has reduced to about 2 tbsp.

2 Reduce the heat to very low, then gradually whisk in the butter, piece by piece. The sauce should become pale, thick, and creamy as the butter melts.

3 Remove the pan from the heat, and season to taste with salt and pepper and a squeeze of lemon juice. Stir in the chopped parsley or chives, if desired. If you prefer a smooth sauce, simply pass the cooked sauce through a sieve before serving. Serve hot.

SERVING SUGGESTIONS *Serve with steamed or poached salmon steaks, whole plaice, or scallops.*
VARIATIONS *Use chopped fresh tarragon or chervil in place of parsley or chives. For a Beurre Rouge sauce, use red wine and red wine vinegar in place of white wine and white wine vinegar.*

043 REDCURRANT AND CRANBERRY SAUCE

PREPARATION TIME *5 minutes* **COOKING TIME** *25 minutes* **SERVES 4** *Makes about ⅔ cup*

⅓ cup redcurrant jelly
1 cup fresh cranberries
Finely grated zest & juice
   of 1 orange

1 cinnamon stick
2 tbsp ruby port wine

1 Place the redcurrant jelly in a saucepan, add the cranberries, orange zest, and juice, cinnamon stick, and port and stir to mix.
2 Bring gently to a boil, stirring, then simmer, uncovered, for about 20 minutes, or until the cranberries are soft and the sauce thickens slightly, stirring frequently.
3 Serve warm or cold. If serving cold, remove the pan from the heat and set aside until cold. Remove and discard the cinnamon stick before serving.

SERVING SUGGESTIONS *Serve with broiled or pan-fried lamb cutlets or beef steaks, or with roast venison, pheasant, or turkey.*
VARIATION *Use fresh blueberries in place of cranberries.*
COOK'S TIP *Frozen cranberries can also be used for this recipe. If using frozen cranberries, they may be used frozen (preferable) or defrosted — you may also need to reduce the overall cooking time a little.*

044 SORREL SAUCE

PREPARATION TIME *10 minutes* **COOKING TIME** *10 minutes* **SERVES 4** *Makes about 1½ cups*

1 tbsp butter
2 small shallots, finely
  chopped
1 bunch young sorrel leaves
  (stalks removed), shredded

1 quantity of Béchamel
  Sauce *(see recipe on page
  28)*, made using 4 tsp of
  butter & 3 tbsp flour
2 tbsp heavy cream

Sea salt and freshly ground
  black pepper
Pinch of freshly grated
  nutmeg, or to taste

1 Melt the butter in a small saucepan, add the shallots and sauté for about 5 minutes, or
   until softened. Add the sorrel and sauté for a further 2 minutes, or until wilted.
2 Stir the mixture into the warm Béchamel Sauce in a separate pan, along with the cream.
3 Heat gently, stirring continuously, until the sauce comes to a gentle simmer, then
   simmer for 2 minutes. Adjust the seasoning and add nutmeg to taste. Serve hot.

SERVING SUGGESTIONS *Serve with broiled or oven-baked chicken goujons or halibut fillets.*

045 SAFFRON SAUCE

PREPARATION TIME *20 minutes* **COOKING TIME** *20 minutes* **SERVES 4** *Makes about 1¼ cups*

½ tsp saffron strands
3 tbsp butter, chilled
  & diced
2 shallots, finely chopped

4 tbsp dry white wine
1¼ cups Velouté Sauce *(see
  recipe on page 29)*

Sea salt & freshly ground
  black pepper

1 Crumble the saffron strands into a small bowl, add 2 tbsp hot water and let to soak for
   15 minutes.
2 Melt 1 tbsp butter in a saucepan, add the shallots and sauté for 5 minutes, or until
   softened. Add the wine and bubble gently until the liquid has reduced to about 1 tbsp.
3 Add the saffron and liquid to the pan, and whisk in the Velouté Sauce. Heat gently until
   boiling, stirring, then simmer gently for 10 minutes, stirring occasionally.
4 Remove the pan from the heat, and season to taste with salt and pepper. Gradually
   whisk in the remaining butter until well blended. Serve hot.

SERVING SUGGESTIONS *Serve with broiled or poached haddock fillets or monkfish tail.*

046 CREAMY WHITE WINE SAUCE

PREPARATION TIME *10 minutes* **COOKING TIME** *20 minutes* **SERVES 4–6** *Makes about 1¼ cups*

¾ cup dry white wine
1 cup heavy cream
½ cup fish or vegetable
  stock *(see recipes on
  page 10)*

1 tbsp chopped fresh dill or
  chervil (optional)
1 tbsp chopped fresh parsley
Sea salt & freshly ground
  black pepper

1 Pour the wine into a saucepan, bring to a boil and boil rapidly until reduced by half.
2 Stir in the cream and stock and bring to a boil, then reduce the heat and simmer,
   uncovered, for 10–15 minutes, or until the sauce thickens slightly, stirring occasionally.
3 Remove the pan from the heat and stir in the chopped dill or chervil, if using, and
   chopped parsley. Season to taste with salt and pepper. Serve hot.

SERVING SUGGESTIONS *Serve with broiled, baked, or pan-fried whole plaice or lemon sole.*

047 CLASSIC PESTO

PREPARATION TIME *10 minutes* **COOKING TIME** *N/A* **SERVES 4–6** *Makes about 1¼ cups*

2½ cups fresh basil leaves,
  roughly torn into pieces
½ cup pine nuts
1 clove garlic, crushed
½ cup extra-virgin olive oil

½ cup fresh Parmesan
  cheese, finely grated
Sea salt & freshly ground
  black pepper

1 Place the basil in a mortar with the pine nuts, garlic, and a little of the oil. Pound or grind with a pestle to make a paste.

2 Gradually work in the remaining oil, then stir in the Parmesan cheese, and season to taste with salt and pepper.

3 Alternatively, put the basil, pine nuts, garlic, and olive oil in a small blender or food processor and blend to form a fairly smooth paste. Add the Parmesan cheese and seasoning, and process briefly to mix.

4 Store the pesto in a screw-topped jar, covered with a thin layer of oil, in the refrigerator for up to 1 week. Serve cold.

SERVING SUGGESTIONS *Serve with hot gnocchi or linguine. Alternatively, serve with broiled or roast chicken portions or haddock cutlets.*

VARIATION *Use 1¼ cups fresh parsley in place of 1¼ cups basil.*

048 RED WINE SAUCE

PREPARATION TIME *10 minutes* **COOKING TIME** *15 minutes* **SERVES 4–6** *Makes about 1¼ cups*

2 tbsp butter
2–3 shallots, finely chopped
1 small clove garlic, crushed
2 tbsp all-purpose flour
2 tsp light soft brown sugar

1¼ cups burgundy or red
 wine
1 tbsp medium-dry sherry
1 tsp chopped fresh thyme or
 rosemary

Sea salt & freshly ground
 black pepper

1 Melt the butter in a small saucepan, add the shallots and garlic and cook gently for about 8–10 minutes, or until softened.
2 Stir in the flour and sugar and cook for 1 minute, stirring. Remove the pan from the heat and gradually stir or whisk in the wine and sherry.
3 Return the pan to the heat and bring slowly to a boil, stirring or whisking continuously, until the sauce is thickened. Simmer gently for 2–3 minutes, stirring.
4 Stir in the chopped thyme or rosemary, and season to taste. Serve hot.

SERVING SUGGESTIONS *Serve with roast beef, or with broiled lamb or pork chops.*
COOK'S TIPS *Once the sauce has been cooked, cool slightly, then purée in a blender or food processor until smooth, if desired. Reheat gently before serving.*

Choose a red wine with a fairly robust flavor, but one that is not too expensive for this sauce. When wine is used in cooking, the alcohol evaporates as the wine is heated, but the flavor intensifies, so you need to choose an enjoyable wine.

049 CUMBERLAND SAUCE

PREPARATION TIME *10 minutes* **COOKING TIME** *10 minutes* **SERVES 4–6**

Finely grated zest & juice
of 1 orange
Finely grated zest & juice
of 1 lemon

4 tbsp redcurrant jelly
2 tbsp red wine vinegar
1 tsp Dijon mustard
Sea salt & freshly ground
black pepper

1 tbsp cornstarch
4 tbsp ruby port wine

1 Place the orange zest and juice, lemon zest and juice, redcurrant jelly, vinegar, mustard, a good pinch of salt and pepper, and 4 tbsp water in a saucepan and mix well. Bring slowly to a boil, stirring occasionally.

2 In a small bowl, blend the cornstarch with 1 tbsp water and the port wine. Stir the cornstarch mixture into the sauce, mixing well.

3 Bring slowly to the boil, stirring continuously, until the sauce thickens, then simmer gently for 2–3 minutes, stirring.

4 Remove the pan from the heat and set aside to cool. Adjust the seasoning to taste and serve warm or cold.

SERVING SUGGESTIONS *Serve with grilled gammon or pork steaks, or with roast pheasant or venison.*
COOK'S TIP *The zest is the outermost part of the rind of fruit such as oranges, lemons, limes, and grapefruit, which contains the highly flavored, volatile oil used to give an intense flavor to many savory and sweet dishes.*

050 GOOSEBERRY SAUCE

PREPARATION TIME *10 minutes* **COOKING TIME** *10 minutes* **SERVES 6** *Makes about 2¼ cups*

1 lb gooseberries
Finely grated zest & juice
of 1 orange
⅔ cup water

2 tbsp butter, diced
2 tbsp light soft brown
sugar

¼ tsp freshly grated nutmeg,
or to taste

1 Place the gooseberries in a saucepan with the orange zest and juice, and water and stir to mix. Bring the mixture slowly to a boil, then cover and simmer gently for 5–10 minutes, or until the gooseberries are cooked and soft, stirring occasionally.

2 Remove the pan from the heat and set aside to cool slightly, then purée the gooseberry mixture in a blender or food processor until smooth.

3 Return the mixture to the rinsed-out saucepan and stir in the butter, sugar, and nutmeg. Bring slowly to a boil, stirring continuously, then simmer gently for 1 minute. Serve hot.

SERVING SUGGESTIONS *Serve with broiled, grilled, or oven-baked oily fish such as mackerel or trout. Alternatively, serve with roast pork or goose, or with deep-fried camembert.*
VARIATION *Use superfine sugar in place of soft brown sugar.*
COOK'S TIPS *Gooseberry Sauce is a traditional English accompaniment to savory fatty foods such as mackerel, pork, and goose, or deep-fried creamy cheeses. It is a refreshing, pale green sauce made from ripe gooseberries, which creates a pleasantly sharp contrast to the fatty foods.*
Retaining the gooseberry skins and pulp adds texture and color to this sauce, but if you prefer a smooth sauce, the cooked purée can be pressed through a sieve then reheated gently before serving.

CHAPTER 3

SAUCES FOR PASTA

Pasta comes in a vast array of shapes and sizes and it cries out for the addition of a delicious, home-made sauce. Pasta sauces should be served with freshly cooked hot pasta, either on top of the pasta or tossed lightly together with the pasta.

With each recipe in this chapter, a couple of serving suggestions are included, specifying which type of pasta is recommended, but there are no hard and fast rules as to which pasta to serve with a particular sauce, so use these as a guide only.

A wide selection of tempting pasta sauces are included. Choose from Garlic and Chili, Spicy Tomato, Hazelnut Pesto, Chorizo and Plum Tomato, Frazzled Prosciutto and Zucchini, Bacon and Blue Cheese, Pancetta and Tomato, or Creamy Smoked Salmon, as well as old favorites such as Fresh Tomato and Basil, Bolognese, Primavera, or Classic Spaghetti Carbonara.

051 MUSHROOM AND ZUCCHINI

PREPARATION TIME *15 minutes* **COOKING TIME** *20 minutes* **SERVES 4**

¼ cup butter
1 onion, finely chopped
1 clove garlic, crushed
3 cups closed cup
  mushrooms, sliced

3 small zucchini,
  thinly sliced
¼ cup all-purpose flour
2 cups milk
1 cup cheddar or red
  leicester cheese, grated

1–2 tbsp chopped fresh
  mixed herbs
Sea salt & freshly ground
  black pepper

1 Melt 2 tbsp butter in a saucepan, add the onion, garlic, mushrooms, and zucchini and cook gently for 8–10 minutes, or until softened. Transfer the vegetables to a plate using a slotted spoon, set aside, and keep hot. Discard any left-over juices from the pan.

2 Melt the remaining butter in the pan, add the flour and cook for 1 minute, stirring. Remove the pan from the heat and gradually stir or whisk in the milk.

3 Return to the heat and heat gently, stirring or whisking continuously, until the sauce comes to a boil and thickens. Simmer gently for 2–3 minutes, stirring.

4 Add the cooked vegetables, the cheese, and chopped herbs to the sauce and stir to mix. Reheat gently until the cheese has melted and the sauce is hot, then season to taste with salt and pepper. Serve hot.

SERVING SUGGESTIONS *Serve with hot pasta such as tagliatelle, spaghetti, or penne.*

052 PRIMAVERA

PREPARATION TIME *15 minutes* **COOKING TIME** *25 minutes* **SERVES 4**

2 carrots, finely diced
2 zucchini, sliced
2 cups small broccoli
  florets
1 cup fresh asparagus,
  cut into 1-inch lengths
1 cup frozen peas

1 bunch of scallions,
  chopped
1 clove garlic, crushed
14-oz can chopped
  tomatoes
⅔ cups vegetable stock
  (see recipe on page 10)

Sea salt & freshly ground
  black pepper
1 tbsp chopped fresh parsley
1 tbsp chopped fresh basil

1 Place the carrots, zucchini, broccoli, asparagus, peas, scallions, garlic, tomatoes, stock, and salt and pepper to taste, in a saucepan and bring slowly to a boil, stirring occasionally. Reduce the heat, cover and simmer for 10 minutes, stirring occasionally.

2 Uncover the pan, increase the heat slightly and cook for a further 5–10 minutes, or until the vegetables are cooked and tender, stirring occasionally.

3 Stir the chopped herbs into the vegetable mixture, and adjust the seasoning to taste. Serve hot.

SERVING SUGGESTIONS *Serve with hot pasta such as fusilli, spirali, or riccioli. Sprinkle with freshly grated Parmesan cheese just before serving, if desired.*
VARIATION *Use sugar-snap peas or frozen baby fava beans in place of peas.*

053 GREEN PESTO

PREPARATION TIME *10 minutes* **COOKING TIME** *N/A* **SERVES 4**

2 cups fresh basil leaves
¾ cup fresh parsley
½ cup pine nuts
½ cup extra-virgin olive oil
2 small cloves garlic, crushed

½ cup fresh Parmesan
  cheese, finely grated
Sea salt & freshly ground
  black pepper

1 Place the basil leaves, parsley, pine nuts, olive oil, and garlic in a blender or small food processor and blend until fairly smooth and thoroughly mixed.

2 Add the Parmesan cheese and seasoning, and process briefly to mix.

3 Store the pesto in a screw-topped jar, covered with a thin layer of olive oil, in the refrigerator for up to 1 week. Serve cold.

SERVING SUGGESTIONS *Serve with hot pasta such as tagliatelle or fettucine. Alternatively, serve with hot gnocchi, or broiled or pan-fried slices of polenta.*

VARIATIONS *Use extra fresh basil in place of parsley. Omit 1 clove garlic, if preferred.*

COOK'S TIP *You could also make the pesto using a pestle and mortar, as follows. Place the basil and parsley in a mortar with the pine nuts, a little of the oil, and the garlic. Pound or grind with a pestle to make a paste. Gradually work in the remaining oil, then stir in the Parmesan cheese, and season to taste with salt and pepper.*

054 GARLIC AND CHILI

PREPARATION TIME *10 minutes* **COOKING TIME** *10 minutes* **SERVES 4**

5 tbsp olive oil
1 small onion, finely chopped
3–4 cloves garlic, finely
  chopped or crushed
2 small fresh red chilies,
  finely chopped (for a
  milder flavor, remove &
  discard the seeds)

4 sun-dried tomatoes in oil,
  drained, patted dry &
  finely chopped
2–3 tbsp chopped fresh
  parsley or basil
Sea salt & freshly ground
  black pepper

1 Heat 1 tbsp oil in a saucepan, add the onion, garlic, and chilies and sauté for about 5 minutes, or until softened.

2 Add the remaining oil to the pan together with the sun-dried tomatoes. Heat gently until hot, stirring continuously.

3 Stir in the chopped herbs, and season to taste with salt and pepper. Serve hot.

SERVING SUGGESTIONS *Serve with hot pasta such as spaghetti, spaghettini, or tagliatelle. Sprinkle the tossed pasta with a generous amount of finely grated fresh Parmesan cheese, just before serving.*

VARIATIONS *Use fresh green chilies in place of red chilies. Use ¼ –⅓ cup chopped or sliced pitted black olives in place of sun-dried tomatoes.*

055 FRESH TOMATO AND BASIL

PREPARATION TIME *15 minutes* **COOKING TIME** *30–35 minutes* **SERVES 4**

1 tbsp olive oil
6 shallots, finely chopped
2 cloves garlic, finely chopped
2 sticks of celery, finely chopped

1½ lb tomatoes, skinned, seeded, & chopped
4 sun-dried tomatoes in oil, drained, patted dry, & finely chopped
2 tbsp medium sherry

1 tbsp tomato paste
½ tsp light soft brown sugar
Sea salt & freshly ground black pepper
2–3 tbsp chopped fresh basil

1 Heat the oil in a saucepan, add the shallots, garlic, and celery and sauté for about 5 minutes, or until softened.

2 Add the tomatoes, sun-dried tomatoes, sherry, tomato paste, sugar, and salt and pepper to taste, and mix well. Bring to a boil, then reduce the heat, cover and simmer for 15 minutes, stirring occasionally.

3 Uncover the pan, increase the heat slightly and cook for a further 10–15 minutes, or until the sauce is cooked and thickened, stirring occasionally. Stir in the chopped basil. Serve hot.

SERVING SUGGESTIONS *Serve with hot pasta such as penne or fusilli. Sprinkle with grated fresh Parmesan cheese and garnish with fresh basil sprigs. This sauce is also delicious served with hot filled pasta such as tortelloni or ravioli.*

VARIATIONS *Use 1–2 leeks in place of shallots. Use 2 small carrots in place of celery. Use chopped fresh mixed herbs in place of basil.*

056 SPICY TOMATO

PREPARATION TIME *20 minutes* **COOKING TIME** *30 minutes* **SERVES 4**

1½ lb tomatoes
3 tbsp butter
1 leek, washed & finely chopped
1 small red bell pepper, seeded & finely chopped

1 clove garlic, crushed
1 tsp *each* of ground cumin, ground coriander, & hot chili powder
3 cups mushrooms, finely chopped

⅔ cup dry white wine
1 tbsp tomato paste
Sea salt & freshly ground black pepper

1 Place the tomatoes in a large bowl and cover with boiling water. Leave for about 30 seconds, then remove the tomatoes using a slotted spoon, and plunge them into cold water. Drain the tomatoes and remove the skins, then deseed them and chop the flesh. Set aside.
2 Melt the butter in a saucepan, add the leek, red bell pepper, and garlic and sauté for about 5 minutes, or until softened. Add the ground spices and cook gently for 1 minute.
3 Add the tomatoes, mushrooms, wine, tomato paste, and seasoning and stir to mix. Bring to a boil, then reduce the heat, cover and simmer for 15 minutes, stirring occasionally.
4 Uncover the pan, increase the heat a little and cook for a further 10 minutes, or until the sauce has thickened slightly, stirring occasionally. Serve hot.

SERVING SUGGESTIONS *Serve with hot pasta such as fusilli, penne, or tortellini. Sprinkle with grated or shaved fresh Parmesan cheese just before serving, if desired.*
VARIATION *Use fresh plum or vine-ripened tomatoes in place of regular tomatoes.*

057 TASTY TOMATO

PREPARATION TIME *15 minutes* **COOKING TIME** *30–35 minutes* **SERVES 4–6**

2 tbsp olive oil
1 red onion, finely chopped
1 carrot, finely chopped
1 stick of celery, finely chopped
1 clove garlic, crushed

1½ lb ripe tomatoes, skinned, seeded, & chopped
⅔ cup dry white wine
⅔ cup vegetable stock (see recipe on page 10)
1 tbsp tomato paste

Sea salt & freshly ground black pepper
2 tbsp chopped fresh basil

1 Heat the oil in a saucepan, add the onion, carrot, celery, and garlic and sauté gently for about 10 minutes, or until softened.
2 Add the tomatoes, wine, stock, tomato paste, and salt and pepper to taste, and mix well.
3 Bring to a boil, then reduce the heat and simmer, uncovered, for 20–25 minutes, or until the sauce is slightly thickened and pulpy, stirring occasionally.
4 Stir in the chopped basil, and adjust the seasoning to taste. Serve hot.

SERVING SUGGESTIONS *Serve with hot pasta such as fusilli, penne, or riccioli.*
VARIATIONS *Use 1 regular onion in place of red onion. Use red wine in place of white wine.*

058 CHUNKY TOMATO, MUSHROOM, AND GARLIC

PREPARATION TIME *10 minutes* **COOKING TIME** *25 minutes* **SERVES 4**

3 tbsp butter
2 small leeks, washed &
   finely chopped
2 cloves garlic, crushed

1½ lb tomatoes, skinned,
   seeded, & roughly chopped
4 cups chestnut or brown
   cap mushrooms, sliced
⅔ cup red wine

1 tbsp tomato paste
Sea salt & freshly ground
   black pepper

1 Melt the butter in a saucepan, add the leeks and garlic and sauté for about 5 minutes, or until softened. Add the tomatoes, mushrooms, wine, tomato paste, and seasoning and stir to mix.

2 Bring to a boil, then reduce the heat, cover and simmer for 10 minutes, stirring.

3 Uncover the pan, increase the heat and cook for a further 10 minutes, or until the sauce has thickened slightly, stirring frequently. Serve hot.

SERVING SUGGESTIONS *Serve with hot pasta such as tagliatelle, fettucine, or linguine.*
VARIATIONS *Stir 1–2 tbsp chopped fresh basil into the sauce just before serving, if desired. Use closed cup or button mushrooms in place of chestnut mushrooms.*
COOK'S TIP *When preparing leeks, remove most of the green tops and make slits in the outer layers of the leeks to enable you to flush out any dirt and grit under cold running water. Alternatively, trim and slice or chop the leeks, then rinse them thoroughly under cold running water, or stand them in a bowl of cold water for 15–20 minutes to remove any dirt or grit. Drain well before use.*

059 FAVA BEAN AND PARSLEY

PREPARATION TIME *10 minutes* **COOKING TIME** *10 minutes* **SERVES 4**

2⅓ cups broad beans
   (shelled weight)
2 tbsp butter
¼ cup all-purpose flour
1¼ cups milk

⅔ cup vegetable stock
   (see recipe on page 10)
A large pinch of mustard
   powder
4 tbsp chopped fresh parsley

Sea salt & freshly ground
   black pepper

1 Cook the fava beans in a saucepan of boiling water for about 5–8 minutes, or until tender. Drain, set aside and keep hot.

2 Meanwhile, melt the butter in a saucepan, then add the flour and cook for 1 minute, stirring. Remove the pan from the heat and gradually stir or whisk in the milk and stock.

3 Return to the heat and heat gently, stirring or whisking continuously, until the sauce comes to a boil and thickens. Simmer gently for 2–3 minutes, stirring.

4 Stir in the fava beans, mustard powder, chopped parsley, and seasoning and reheat gently until hot, stirring continuously. Serve hot.

SERVING SUGGESTIONS *Serve with hot pasta such as fusilli, bucati, or radiatori.*
VARIATIONS *Use frozen fava beans if fresh ones are not available and follow cooking time on package. Stir ½ cup finely grated gruyère or cheddar cheese into the sauce just before serving, if desired.*

060 ZUCCHINI AND MIXED BELL PEPPER

PREPARATION TIME *10 minutes* **COOKING TIME** *25–30 minutes* **SERVES 4**

¼ cup butter
1 red onion, finely chopped
1 clove garlic, crushed
1 red bell pepper, seeded & diced
1 yellow bell pepper, seeded

& diced
4 zucchini, sliced
2 cups button mushrooms, sliced
14-oz can chopped tomatoes

⅔ cup red wine
1 tbsp tomato paste
Sea salt & freshly ground black pepper
2 tbsp chopped fresh basil

1 Melt the butter in a saucepan, add the onion, garlic, bell peppers, and zucchini and sauté for about 5 minutes, or until slightly softened.
2 Add the mushrooms, tomatoes, red wine, tomato paste, and salt and pepper to taste, and stir to mix. Bring to a boil, then reduce the heat, cover and simmer for 10 minutes, stirring occasionally.
3 Uncover the pan, increase the heat a little and cook for a further 10–15 minutes, or until the sauce has thickened slightly and the vegetables are tender and cooked to your liking, stirring occasionally. Stir in the basil, and adjust the seasoning to taste. Serve hot.

SERVING SUGGESTIONS *Serve with hot pasta such as spaghetti, fettucine, or tagliatelle.*
VARIATIONS *Use 1 regular onion or 4 shallots in place of red onion. Use dry white wine or vegetable stock in place of red wine.*

061 ROASTED CHERRY TOMATO AND BRIE

PREPARATION TIME *20 minutes* **COOKING TIME** *20 minutes* **SERVES 4–6**

1 lb cherry tomatoes, halved
3 tbsp olive oil
4 shallots, thinly sliced
2 cloves garlic, crushed
4 cups button mushrooms, sliced

1 cup mascarpone
½ lb brie (weight without rind), rind removed & cheese diced
4 tbsp chopped fresh basil

Sea salt & freshly ground black pepper

1 Preheat oven to 180°C/350°F/gas mark 4. Place the tomatoes, cut-side up, in a single layer in a large, shallow ovenproof dish and drizzle over 2 tbsp oil. Bake in the oven for 10–15 minutes, or until lightly cooked.

2 Meanwhile, heat the remaining oil in a saucepan, add the shallots, garlic, and mushrooms and sauté for about 5 minutes, or until softened. Add the mascarpone and heat gently until hot, stirring.

3 Add the brie and stir until just beginning to melt, then remove the pan from the heat and gently stir in the roasted tomatoes and their juices, and the chopped basil. Season to taste with salt and pepper. Serve hot.

SERVING SUGGESTIONS *Serve with hot pasta such as riccioli, radiatori, or spirali.*
VARIATIONS *Use 1 onion in place of shallots. Use camembert or Cambazola (blue brie) cheese (with rind removed) in place of brie.*

062 STILTON AND WALNUT

PREPARATION TIME *5 minutes* **COOKING TIME** *15 minutes* **SERVES 4**

1 tbsp olive oil
1 small onion, finely chopped
1 clove garlic, crushed
1 cup crème fraîche

½ cup Stilton cheese, crumbled
1 cup walnut halves, roughly chopped

2–3 tbsp snipped fresh chives or chopped fresh parsley
Sea salt & freshly ground black pepper

1 Heat the oil in a saucepan, add the onion and garlic and sauté gently for 8–10 minutes, or until softened.

2 Stir in the crème fraîche and heat gently until bubbling, then stir in the Stilton cheese and heat gently until melted, stirring continuously.

3 Remove the pan from the heat and stir in the walnuts and snipped chives or chopped parsley. Season to taste with salt and pepper. Serve hot.

SERVING SUGGESTIONS *Serve with hot pasta such as fusilli, farfalle, or penne.*
VARIATIONS *Use 2–3 shallots in place of onion. Use other blue cheeses such as gorgonzola or dolcelatte in place of Stilton. Use pecan nuts in place of walnuts.*
COOK'S TIP *Toast the walnut halves before chopping and adding them to the sauce, if desired.*

063 SPINACH AND BLUE CHEESE

PREPARATION TIME *15 minutes* **COOKING TIME** *15 minutes* **SERVES 4**

2 tbsp butter
4 shallots, finely chopped
1 clove garlic, crushed
¼ cup all-purpose flour

2 cups milk
¾ lb fresh spinach,
   cooked & drained
   thoroughly

1 cup Stilton cheese,
   crumbled
Sea salt & freshly ground
   black pepper

1 Melt the butter in a saucepan, add the shallots and garlic and sauté for about 5
minutes, or until softened. Add the flour and cook for 1 minute, stirring.

2 Remove the pan from the heat and gradually stir or whisk in the milk. Return to the heat
and heat gently, stirring or whisking continuously, until the sauce comes to a boil and
thickens. Simmer gently for 2–3 minutes, stirring.

3 Press any excess water out of the spinach using the back of a wooden spoon, then chop
the spinach. Add the spinach and Stilton to the sauce and mix well.

4 Reheat gently, stirring continuously, until the cheese has melted and the sauce is hot.
Season to taste with salt and pepper. Serve hot.

SERVING SUGGESTIONS *Serve with hot pasta such as tagliatelle, linguine or spaghetti.*
VARIATIONS *Use 1 onion in place of shallots. Use diced gorgonzola, diced Cambazola (blue brie), or
grated mature cheddar cheese in place of Stilton.*
COOK'S TIP *Another quick and easy way to squeeze excess water out of the spinach is to tip the
cooked spinach into a colander and press with a potato masher, or press between 2 plates.*

064 GRUYÈRE AND LEEK

PREPARATION TIME *15 minutes* **COOKING TIME** *15 minutes* **SERVES 4**

¼ cup butter
4 cups leeks (trimmed
   weight), washed & thinly
   sliced
4 shallots, finely chopped

1 clove garlic, crushed
¼ cup all-purpose flour
2 cups milk
1 cup gruyère cheese,
   grated

1 tbsp chopped fresh
   tarragon (optional)
Sea salt & freshly ground
   black pepper

1 Melt 2 tbsp butter in a saucepan, add the leeks, shallots, and garlic and cook gently for
8–10 minutes, or until softened. Transfer the vegetables to a plate using a slotted
spoon, set aside and keep hot. Discard any left-over juices from the pan.

2 Place the remaining butter in the pan with the flour and milk. Heat gently, whisking
continuously, until the sauce comes to the boil and thickens. Simmer gently for 3–4
minutes, stirring.

3 Add the cooked vegetables, cheese, and chopped tarragon, if using, to the sauce and stir
to mix. Reheat gently until the cheese has melted and the sauce is hot, then season to
taste with salt and pepper. Serve hot.

SERVING SUGGESTIONS *Serve with hot pasta such as linguine, fettucine, or tagliatelle.*

065 BOLOGNESE

PREPARATION TIME *10 minutes* **COOKING TIME** *1 hour 10 minutes* **SERVES 4–6**

1 tbsp olive oil
2 red onions, chopped
1 carrot, finely chopped
2 sticks of celery, finely
    chopped
1 clove garlic, crushed
2¼ cups lean ground beef
1 tbsp all-purpose flour

4 cups mushrooms,
    sliced
14-oz can chopped
    tomatoes
1 tbsp tomato paste
1¼ cups beef or
    vegetable stock *(see
    recipes on pages 10 and 11)*

1¼ cups dry red or white wine
2 tsp dried Italian herb
    seasoning
Sea salt & freshly ground
    black pepper

1 Heat the oil in a large saucepan, add the onions, carrot, celery, and garlic and sauté for about 5 minutes, or until softened.

2 Add the ground beef and cook until the meat is browned all over, stirring occasionally. Add the flour and cook for 1 minute, stirring.

3 Add the mushrooms, tomatoes, tomato paste, stock, wine, dried herbs, and seasoning and stir to mix.

4 Bring to a boil, then reduce the heat, cover and simmer for about 1 hour, stirring occasionally, until the meat is cooked and the sauce is well reduced. If desired, uncover the pan and increase the heat slightly 15–20 minutes before the end of the cooking time to thicken the sauce a little more. Serve hot.

SERVING SUGGESTIONS *Serve with hot pasta such as spaghetti or spaghettini. Serve sprinkled with finely grated fresh Parmesan cheese.*
VARIATIONS *Use lean ground lamb or pork in place of beef. Use extra stock in place of red wine.*

066 CLASSIC SPAGHETTI CARBONARA

PREPARATION TIME *10 minutes* **COOKING TIME** *15 minutes* **SERVES 4**

12 oz dried spaghetti
Sea salt & freshly ground
    black pepper
2 tbsp butter
1 tbsp olive oil
1 onion, finely chopped

1 cup smoked bacon slices,
    chopped
3 eggs, beaten
6 tbsp heavy cream
½ cup pecorino cheese,
    finely grated

¾ cup fresh Parmesan
    cheese, finely grated
2 tbsp chopped fresh parsley
    or snipped fresh chives

1 Cook the spaghetti in a large saucepan of lightly salted, boiling water for 10–12 minutes, or until just cooked or al dente.

2 Meanwhile, heat the butter and oil in a saucepan until the butter is melted. Add the onion and sauté for about 5 minutes, or until softened.

3 Add the bacon and cook for about 5 minutes, or until the bacon is cooked, stirring frequently. Remove the pan from the heat and set aside.

4 Mix the eggs, cream, pecorino cheese, ½ cup Parmesan, the chopped parsley or snipped chives, and seasoning together in a bowl.

5 Drain the pasta and return to a clean pan. Add the bacon mixture and toss to mix. Add the egg mixture and cook gently over a very low heat, tossing continuously, until the eggs are just lightly cooked. Sprinkle with the remaining Parmesan, and serve immediately.

SERVING SUGGESTIONS *Serve with hot pasta such as spaghetti, as directed above, or with tagliatelle in place of spaghetti.*
VARIATION *Use smoked pancetta, de-rinded, in place of bacon.*

067 HAZELNUT PESTO

PREPARATION TIME *10 minutes* **COOKING TIME** *N/A* **SERVES 4**

2½ cups fresh basil leaves, roughly torn into pieces
½ cup hazelnuts, lightly toasted

2 cloves garlic, crushed
½ cup olive oil
¾ cup fresh Parmesan cheese, finely grated

Sea salt & freshly ground black pepper

1 Place the basil, hazelnuts, garlic, and olive oil in a small blender or food processor and blend until fairly smooth and thoroughly mixed. Add the Parmesan cheese and seasoning, and process briefly to mix.
2 Alternatively, place the basil in a mortar with the hazelnuts, garlic, and a little of the oil. Pound or grind with a pestle to make a paste. Gradually work in the remaining oil, then stir in the Parmesan cheese, and season to taste with salt and pepper.
3 Transfer to a small bowl, cover and set aside in a cool place until ready to serve. Alternatively, store the pesto in a screw-topped jar, covered with a thin layer of oil, in the refrigerator for up to 1 week. Serve cold.

SERVING SUGGESTIONS *Serve with hot filled pasta such as ravioli. Alternatively, serve with hot pasta such as plain spaghetti, spinach tagliatelle, farfalle, or fusilli.*
VARIATION *Use lightly toasted pine nuts or almonds in place of hazelnuts.*
COOK'S TIP *Basil is a delicate-leaved herb which should be prepared carefully. To avoid losing valuable flavor and color too quickly from basil, simply tear the leaves with your fingers instead of chopping them with a knife. If you do chop basil with a knife or scissors, use the chopped leaves as quickly as possible.*

068 CHORIZO AND PLUM TOMATO

PREPARATION TIME *20 minutes* **COOKING TIME** *25–30 minutes* **SERVES 4**

¼ cup butter

1 red onion, finely chopped

1 small red bell pepper, seeded & finely chopped

2 sticks of celery, finely chopped

2 cloves garlic, crushed

6 oz cured (cooked) chorizo, thinly sliced

14-oz can chopped tomatoes

4 sun-dried tomatoes in oil, drained, patted dry, & finely chopped

6 tbsp dry white wine

1 tbsp sun-dried tomato paste

Sea salt & freshly ground black pepper

2–3 tbsp chopped fresh basil

1 Melt the butter in a saucepan, add the onion, red bell pepper, celery, and garlic and sauté for 5 minutes. Add the chorizo and sauté for 1 minute.

2 Add the canned tomatoes, sun-dried tomatoes, white wine, tomato paste, and salt and pepper to taste, and stir to mix. Bring to a boil, then reduce the heat, cover, and simmer for 15 minutes, stirring occasionally.

3 Uncover the pan, increase the heat slightly and cook for a further 5–10 minutes, or until the sauce is cooked and thickened slightly, stirring occasionally. Stir in the chopped basil. Serve hot.

SERVING SUGGESTIONS *Serve with hot pasta such as tagliatelle or fettucine.*

VARIATIONS *Use fresh tomatoes in place of canned tomatoes – skin and chop 1 lb 2 oz fresh ripe plum or vine-ripened tomatoes and use as directed. Use red wine in place of white wine.*

069 FRAZZLED PROSCIUTTO AND ZUCCHINI

PREPARATION TIME *10 minutes* **COOKING TIME** *20 minutes* **SERVES 4**

2 tbsp olive oil
6 oz thin slices of
   prosciutto
1 red onion, finely chopped
2 zucchini, finely chopped

1 tbsp chopped fresh
   flat-leaf parsley
1 tbsp chopped fresh basil
1 tbsp chopped fresh oregano
   or marjoram

1¼ cups crème fraîche
Sea salt & freshly ground
   black pepper

1 Heat 1 tbsp oil in a non-stick skillet, add the prosciutto, a few slices at a time, and cook over a fairly high heat, turning frequently, until crinkled and crisp. Transfer to a plate, set aside, and keep hot.

2 Add the remaining oil to the skillet and heat until hot, then add the onion and sauté for 3 minutes. Add the zucchini and sauté for a further 7 minutes, or until the vegetables are just cooked.

3 Stir in the chopped herbs and crème fraîche and heat gently until hot, stirring.

4 Snip the frazzled prosciutto into thin strips or pieces and stir into the herb sauce. Season to taste with salt and pepper. Serve hot.

SERVING SUGGESTIONS *Serve with hot pasta such as fusilli, rigatoni, amori, or spirali. Alternatively, serve with hot gnocchi.*

VARIATIONS *Use Parma ham in place of prosciutto. Use 4 shallots or 1 leek in place of red onion. Use heavy cream in place of crème fraîche.*

070 BACON AND BLUE CHEESE

PREPARATION TIME *10 minutes* **COOKING TIME** *20 minutes* **SERVES 4**

2 tbsp olive oil
2 small leeks, washed &
   sliced
4 cups button mushrooms,
   sliced
1 clove garlic, crushed

2 tbsp dry sherry
⅔ cup heavy cream or
   crème fraîche
Sea salt & freshly ground
   black pepper

⅔ cup cooked smoked bacon,
   diced
1 cup gorgonzola cheese,
   diced
2 tbsp chopped fresh parsley
   or snipped fresh chives

1 Heat the oil in a skillet, add the leeks, mushrooms, and garlic and cook gently for about 8–10 minutes, or until softened.

2 Add the sherry and cook over a fairly high heat, stirring frequently, until most of the liquid has evaporated.

3 Reduce the heat, stir in the cream or crème fraîche, and salt and pepper to taste, and cook gently for 1–2 minutes.

4 Stir in the bacon, cheese, and chopped parsley or snipped chives and heat gently until hot, stirring continuously. Serve hot.

SERVING SUGGESTIONS *Serve with hot pasta such as fettucine, tagliatelle, linguine, or spaghetti.*

VARIATIONS *Use Stilton or Cambozola (blue brie) in place of gorgonzola cheese. Use cooked lean smoked ham or chicken in place of bacon.*

071 PANCETTA AND TOMATO

PREPARATION TIME *15 minutes* **COOKING TIME** *20–25 minutes* **SERVES 4**

3 tbsp butter
1 large onion, chopped
2 cloves garlic, crushed
1 cup pancetta, diced

1½ lb tomatoes, skinned
& chopped
5 cups button
mushrooms, halved
1 tbsp tomato catsup

1 tbsp tomato paste
Sea salt & freshly ground
black pepper
2 tbsp chopped fresh
mixed herbs

1 Melt the butter in a saucepan, add the onion, garlic, and pancetta and sauté for about
5 minutes, or until the onion has softened.
2 Add the tomatoes, mushrooms, tomato catsup, tomato paste, and salt and pepper to
taste, and mix well.
3 Bring to a boil, then reduce the heat, cover and simmer for 20–25 minutes, or until
the vegetables are tender, stirring occasionally.
4 Stir in the chopped herbs and adjust the seasoning to taste. Serve hot.

SERVING SUGGESTIONS *Serve with hot pasta such as penne, fusilli, or riccioli.*
VARIATIONS *Use chorizo or bacon (smoked or unsmoked) in place of pancetta. Use 2 x 14-oz cans
chopped tomatoes in place of fresh tomatoes. Use chopped basil in place of mixed herbs.*
COOK'S TIP *Pancetta is an Italian bacon, available as smoked or unsmoked (green). It may be used in
recipes such as this one, or cured pancetta can be sliced and served as a cold cut.*

072 SMOKED HAM AND LEEK

PREPARATION TIME *10 minutes* **COOKING TIME** *15 minutes* **SERVES 4**

4 cups leeks (trimmed
weight), washed & sliced
2 tbsp butter
¼ cup all-purpose flour
1¼ cups milk

⅔ cup vegetable stock
*(see recipe on page
10)*, cooled
¾ cup cooked lean
smoked ham, diced
2–3 tbsp snipped fresh
chives

Sea salt & freshly ground
black pepper
½ cup mature cheddar
cheese, finely grated
(optional)

1 Steam the leeks over a saucepan of boiling water for about 10 minutes, or until cooked
and tender.
2 Meanwhile, place the butter, flour, milk, and stock in a saucepan and heat gently,
whisking continuously, until the sauce comes to a boil and thickens. Simmer gently
for 3–4 minutes, stirring.
3 Drain the leeks, squeezing out any excess water, then add the leeks to the white sauce
with the ham, snipped chives, and salt and pepper to taste, and mix well. Heat gently
until hot, stirring continuously. Stir in the cheese, if using, until melted. Serve hot.

SERVING SUGGESTIONS *Serve with hot pasta such as fettucine or linguine.*

073 FLAKED TUNA AND ZUCCHINI

PREPARATION TIME *10 minutes* **COOKING TIME** *20 minutes* **SERVES 4**

2 tbsp butter
3 cups leeks (trimmed
   weight), washed & thinly
   sliced
4 small zucchini, sliced
¼ cup all-purpose flour

2 cups vegetable stock *(see
   recipe on page 10)*
⅔ cup dry white wine
14-oz can tuna in spring
   water, brine or oil,
   drained & flaked

1–2 tbsp chopped fresh
   parsley or cilantro
A dash of Tabasco sauce
Sea salt & freshly ground
   black pepper
½ cup toasted flaked
   almonds

1 Melt the butter in a saucepan, add the leeks and zucchini, cover and cook gently for
about 10 minutes, or until softened, stirring occasionally. Add the flour and cook gently
for 1 minute, stirring.
2 Remove the pan from the heat and gradually stir or whisk in the stock and wine, then
bring slowly to a boil, stirring continuously, until the sauce thickens. Simmer gently for
2–3 minutes, stirring.
3 Stir the tuna, chopped parsley or cilantro, Tabasco sauce, and salt and pepper to taste,
into the sauce, then reheat gently until hot, stirring continuously. Stir in the flaked
almonds (or sprinkle the almonds over the top of the pasta and sauce) and serve hot.

SERVING SUGGESTIONS *Serve with hot pasta such as tagliatelle, fettucine, or linguine.*

074 TASTY TUNA

PREPARATION TIME *10 minutes* **COOKING TIME** *10–15 minutes* **SERVES 4**

¼ cup butter
3 cups leeks (trimmed
   weight), washed & sliced
4 cups closed cup
   mushrooms, sliced
¼ cup all-purpose flour

2 cups milk
14-oz can tuna in spring
   water, brine or oil,
   drained & flaked
2–3 tbsp chopped fresh
   parsley

A good pinch of cayenne
   pepper
Sea salt & freshly ground
   black pepper

1 Melt the butter in a saucepan, add the leeks and mushrooms and cook gently for about
10 minutes, or until softened. Add the flour and cook gently for 1 minute, stirring.
2 Remove the pan from the heat and gradually stir or whisk in the milk, then heat gently,
stirring or whisking continuously, until the sauce comes to a boil and thickens. Simmer
gently for 2–3 minutes, stirring.
3 Stir in the tuna, chopped parsley, cayenne pepper, and seasoning, then reheat gently
until hot, stirring. Serve hot.

SERVING SUGGESTIONS *Serve with hot pasta such as spaghetti, tagliatelle, linguine, or spaghettini.*
VARIATIONS *Use flaked canned salmon in place of tuna. Use sliced zucchini in place of mushrooms.
Use 1 tbsp chopped fresh tarragon or cilantro in place of parsley.*

075 CREAMY SMOKED SALMON

PREPARATION TIME *10 minutes* **COOKING TIME** *15 minutes* **SERVES 4**

2 tbsp butter
½ lb button mushrooms, halved
⅔ cup dry white wine
1¼ cups crème fraîche

10 oz smoked salmon, cut into thin strips or small pieces
1 tbsp chopped fresh dill

1 tbsp creamed horseradish sauce
Sea salt & freshly ground black pepper

1 Melt the butter in a saucepan, add the mushrooms and sauté for about 5 minutes, or until softened.
2 Add the wine, bring to a boil, then cook over a high heat until the liquid has reduced by half, stirring occasionally.
3 Reduce the heat, stir in the crème fraîche, and bring gently to a boil.
4 Stir in the smoked salmon, chopped dill, creamed horseradish sauce, and seasoning, and heat gently for 1–2 minutes. Serve hot.

SERVING SUGGESTIONS *Serve with hot pasta such as linguine, spaghetti, fettucine, or tagliatelle.*
VARIATIONS *Use sliced zucchini in place of mushrooms. Use heavy cream in place of crème fraîche. Use chopped fresh flat-leaf parsley or snipped fresh chives in place of dill.*
COOK'S TIP *You can buy smoked salmon trimmings which are ideal to use in this recipe, and these will be more economical too.*

076 SMOKED TROUT WITH ALMONDS

PREPARATION TIME *10 minutes* **COOKING TIME** *15 minutes* **SERVES 4–6**

2 tbsp sunflower oil

3½ cups leeks (trimmed weight), washed & thinly sliced

5 small zucchini (trimmed weight), sliced

2 tbsp butter

¼ cup all-purpose flour

2 cups fish or vegetable stock *(see recipes on page 10)*, cooled

⅔ cup dry white wine

1 cup skinless smoked trout fillets, flaked

2–3 tsp chopped fresh tarragon

½ cup toasted flaked almonds

Sea salt & freshly ground black pepper

1 Heat the oil in a skillet, add the leeks and zucchini and cook gently for about 8–10 minutes, or until softened.

2 Meanwhile, melt the butter in a saucepan, add the flour and cook gently for 1 minute, stirring. Gradually whisk in the stock and wine, then heat gently, whisking continuously, until the sauce comes to a boil and thickens. Simmer gently for 2–3 minutes, stirring.

3 Stir the leek mixture, smoked trout, and chopped tarragon into the sauce, then reheat gently until hot, stirring continuously.

4 Stir in the flaked almonds (or sprinkle the almonds over the top of the pasta and sauce), and season to taste with salt and pepper. Serve hot.

SERVING SUGGESTIONS *Serve with hot pasta such as tagliatelle, spaghetti, or fettucine.*

077 RED SALMON AND WATERCRESS

PREPARATION TIME *10 minutes* **COOKING TIME** *15 minutes* **SERVES 4**

4 tsp butter

3 shallots, finely chopped

1 clove garlic, crushed

2 bunches watercress, washed and patted dry

1¼ cups crème fraîche

1 tsp Dijon mustard

Sea salt & freshly ground black pepper

14-oz can red salmon in brine, drained

1 Melt the butter in a saucepan, add the shallots, garlic, and watercress and sauté for about 5 minutes, or until the shallots are softened.

2 Remove the pan from the heat and set aside to cool slightly, then place the watercress mixture in a blender or food processor. Add the crème fraîche, mustard, and salt and pepper to taste, and blend until smooth.

3 Transfer the mixture to a saucepan and heat gently until hot, stirring continuously.

4 Flake the salmon, removing any bones, then add the salmon to the sauce. Reheat gently until hot, stirring continuously. Adjust the seasoning to taste, and serve hot.

SERVING SUGGESTIONS *Serve with hot pasta such as farfalle, conchiglie, or penne.*

VARIATIONS *Use 1 small regular onion or red onion in place of shallots. Use flaked canned pink salmon or tuna in place of red salmon.*

078 FRESH MUSSEL AND TOMATO

PREPARATION TIME *20 minutes* **COOKING TIME** *30–35 minutes* **SERVES 4**

1 tbsp olive oil
1 onion, finely chopped
2 cloves garlic, finely chopped
2 sticks of celery, finely chopped
1 red bell pepper, seeded & finely chopped

2 cups button mushrooms, finely chopped
1½ lb ripe plum tomatoes, skinned, seeded, & roughly chopped
4 sun-dried tomatoes in oil, drained, patted dry, & finely chopped
6 tbsp red wine

1 tbsp tomato paste
Sea salt & freshly ground black pepper
½ lb cooked shelled fresh mussels (shelled weight)
2 tbsp chopped fresh basil

1 Heat the oil in a saucepan, add the onion, garlic, celery, red bell pepper, and mushrooms and sauté for about 5 minutes, or until softened.

2 Add the plum tomatoes, sun-dried tomatoes, wine, tomato paste, and salt and pepper to taste, and stir to mix. Bring to a boil, then reduce the heat, cover and simmer for 20–25 minutes, or until the vegetables are cooked and tender, stirring occasionally.

3 Stir the shelled mussels into the tomato sauce, increase the heat slightly and cook, uncovered, for about 5 minutes, or until the mussels are hot, stirring occasionally. Add the chopped basil and stir to mix. Serve hot.

SERVING SUGGESTIONS *Serve with hot pasta such as tagliatelle or linguine.*

079 CAJUN CHICKEN

PREPARATION TIME *15 minutes* **COOKING TIME** *15 minutes* **SERVES 4**

1 tbsp olive oil
1 onion, finely chopped
1 red bell pepper, seeded & sliced
2 small zucchini, cut into matchstick strips

4 cups button mushrooms, halved
1 lb skinless boneless chicken breasts, cut into thin strips
1 tbsp Cajun seasoning
1 tbsp cornstarch

2 tbsp dry sherry
1¼ cups chicken stock
  (see recipe on page 11)
2 tbsp tomato paste
Sea salt & freshly ground black pepper

1 Heat the oil in a wok or large skillet, add the onion, red bell pepper, zucchini, and mushrooms and stir-fry for 3 minutes.

2 Add the chicken and stir-fry for a further 3–4 minutes, or until the chicken is cooked, then add the Cajun seasoning and stir-fry for 1 minute.

3 Blend the cornstarch with the sherry until smooth, and add to the wok with the stock, tomato paste and seasoning. Stir-fry until hot and bubbling, then simmer gently for 2–3 minutes, stirring continuously. Serve hot.

SERVING SUGGESTIONS *Serve with hot pasta such as tagliatelle, fettucine, or spaghetti.*
VARIATIONS *Use 2 carrots in place of zucchini. Use turkey breast or lean pork in place of chicken. Use Chinese 5-spice or 7-spice seasoning in place of Cajun seasoning.*

080 CHICKEN, LEEK, AND MUSHROOM

PREPARATION TIME *15 minutes* **COOKING TIME** *20 minutes* **SERVES 4–6**

3 tbsp butter
2 leeks, washed & thinly
 sliced
4 cups mushrooms, sliced
⅓ cup all-purpose flour
1¼ pints milk

⅔ cup chicken stock
 (see recipe on page 11),
 cooled
¾ lb cooked skinless
 boneless chicken, cut into
 small pieces

1–2 tbsp chopped fresh
 parsley
Sea salt & freshly ground
 black pepper

1 Melt the butter in a saucepan, add the leeks and mushrooms and cook gently for about
 8–10 minutes, or until softened.
2 Add the flour and cook for 1 minute, stirring. Remove the pan from the heat and
 gradually stir or whisk in the milk and stock.
3 Return the pan to the heat and cook gently, stirring continuously, until the sauce comes
 to a boil and thickens. Simmer gently for 2–3 minutes, stirring.
4 Add the chicken to the sauce and bring back to a boil, stirring continuously, then
 simmer gently for 5 minutes, stirring occasionally.
5 Stir in the chopped parsley, and season to taste with salt and pepper. Serve hot.

SERVING SUGGESTIONS *Serve with hot pasta such as fusilli or riccioli.*
VARIATIONS *Use cooked turkey breast or cooked ham in place of chicken. Use 1 tbsp chopped fresh
tarragon, cilantro, or mixed herbs in place of parsley.*

CHAPTER 4

SAUCES FOR FISH AND SHELLFISH

Many types of fish and shellfish, including cod, haddock, monkfish, plaice, lemon sole, salmon, tuna, shrimp, and mussels, are often enhanced when served with a delicious sauce. Simply broiled, baked or pan-fried, and served with a flavorful sauce, they make an ideal and tempting meal to suit many occasions and palates.

This chapter covers an eclectic range of tasty sauces perfect for many types of fish and shellfish, including Marie Rose Sauce, Rich Parsley Sauce, Cheese and Chive Sauce, Dill and Mustard Sauce, Broiled Red Bell Pepper Sauce, Piquant Mushroom Sauce, Creamy Avocado Sauce, Fresh Lemon Sauce, Tomato Coulis, Rouille, Pistachio Butter, and Herb and Lime Butter.

081 MARIE ROSE SAUCE

PREPARATION TIME *15 minutes* **COOKING TIME** *N/A* **SERVES 4–6** *Makes about 1½ cups*

1 cup Mayonnaise *(see recipe on page 37)*
4 tbsp extra-thick heavy cream
2 tbsp tomato catsup

1 tsp Worcestershire sauce
1 tsp fresh lemon or lime juice
2 tsp creamed horseradish sauce (optional)

A few drops of Tabasco sauce
Sea salt & freshly ground black pepper

1 Place the mayonnaise and cream in a bowl and stir together until well mixed.

2 Add the tomato catsup, Worcestershire sauce, lemon or lime juice, creamed horseradish sauce, if using, and Tabasco sauce, and mix well.

3 Season to taste with salt and pepper. Serve immediately or cover and chill until ready to serve. Serve cold.

SERVING SUGGESTIONS *Serve with cooked cold king prawns, mixed seafood, or flaked crabmeat.*
COOK'S TIPS *Worcestershire sauce is a strongly flavored proprietary brown sauce/condiment, which can be served with roast or broiled meat and poultry, or added to recipes such as this one, or to salad dressings or other sauces to heighten the flavor.*
Fiery Tabasco sauce also adds heat and flavor to some sauces, marinades, and salad dressings.

082 RICH PARSLEY SAUCE

PREPARATION TIME *35 minutes* **COOKING TIME** *10 minutes* **SERVES 4** *Makes about 1¼ cups*

1¼ cups full-fat milk
1 shallot, cut in half
1 small carrot, thickly sliced
1 bay leaf

½ tsp black peppercorns
A few fresh parsley stalks
1 tbsp butter
2 tbsp all-purpose flour

2–3 tbsp chopped fresh parsley
Sea salt & freshly ground black pepper

1 Pour the milk into a small saucepan and add the shallot, carrot, bay leaf, black peppercorns, and parsley stalks. Bring almost to a boil, then remove the pan from the heat, cover and let infuse for 30 minutes.

2 Strain the mixture into a jug, reserving the flavored milk and discarding the contents of the sieve.

3 Melt the butter in a separate saucepan, stir in the flour and cook, stirring, for 1 minute. Remove the pan from the heat and gradually stir or whisk in the flavored milk.

4 Return the pan to the heat and bring slowly to a boil, stirring or whisking until the sauce is thickened and smooth. Simmer gently for 2–3 minutes, stirring continuously.

5 Stir in the chopped parsley, then season to taste with salt and pepper. Serve hot.

SERVING SUGGESTIONS *Serve with broiled cod, haddock, or turbot fillets. Alternatively, serve with oven-baked fishcakes or fish goujons.*
VARIATIONS *Use vegetable stock in place of half the milk. Use 1–2 tbsp chopped fresh mixed herbs, such as parsley, chives, oregano, and basil in place of parsley.*
COOK'S TIP *There are two types of parsley – curly and flat-leaf. Choose the more common curly parsley for this traditional British sauce.*

083 FRESH HERB SAUCE

PREPARATION TIME *5 minutes* **COOKING TIME** *10 minutes* **SERVES 4** *Makes about 1½ cups*

4 tsp butter
3 tbsp all-purpose flour
1¼ cups milk
½ cup cheddar cheese,
  grated

1 tsp Dijon mustard
3 tbsp chopped fresh mixed
  herbs, such as parsley,
  oregano, thyme, & chives

Sea salt & freshly ground
  black pepper

1 Place the butter, flour, and milk in a saucepan. Heat gently, whisking continuously, until the sauce comes to a boil and is thickened and smooth. Simmer gently for 3–4 minutes, stirring.
2 Remove the pan from the heat and stir in the cheese until melted, then stir in the mustard and chopped herbs. Season to taste with salt and pepper. Serve hot.

SERVING SUGGESTIONS *Serve with broiled or pan-fried whole plaice or lemon sole, or with pan-fried fish goujons or mixed seafood.*

084 WHOLEGRAIN MUSTARD SAUCE

PREPARATION TIME *5 minutes* **COOKING TIME** *10 minutes* **SERVES 4** *Makes about 1½ cups*

2 tbsp cornstarch
1¼ cups milk
1–2 tbsp wholegrain
  mustard, or to taste

1 tbsp butter
1–2 tbsp chopped fresh
  parsley

Sea salt & freshly ground
  black pepper

1 In a small saucepan, blend the cornstarch with a little of the milk until smooth, then stir in the remaining milk.
2 Heat gently, stirring continuously, until the sauce comes to a boil and thickens. Simmer gently for 3 minutes, stirring, to make a smooth, glossy white sauce.
3 Stir in the mustard, butter, and chopped parsley and heat gently until hot, stirring. Season to taste with salt and pepper. Serve hot.

SERVING SUGGESTIONS *Serve with broiled or grilled mackerel, trout, or salmon fillets.*

085 CELERY SAUCE

PREPARATION TIME *10 minutes* **COOKING TIME** *15–20 minutes* **SERVES 4–6**

2 tbsp butter
3 shallots, finely chopped
4 sticks of celery, finely
  chopped

2 tbsp cornstarch
1½ cups milk
2 tbsp chopped fresh parsley

Sea salt & freshly ground
  black pepper

1 Melt the butter in a saucepan, then stir in the shallots and celery. Cover and cook gently for 15–20 minutes, or until the vegetables are cooked and tender, stirring occasionally.
2 Meanwhile, in a separate saucepan, blend the cornstarch with a little of the milk until smooth, then stir in the remaining milk. Heat gently, stirring continuously, until the sauce comes to a boil and thickens. Simmer gently for 3 minutes, stirring.
3 Stir the hot cooked vegetables and chopped parsley into the white sauce, then season to taste with salt and pepper. Serve hot.

SERVING SUGGESTIONS *Serve with poached or broiled salmon, tuna, or haddock steaks.*

086 WILD MUSHROOM SAUCE

PREPARATION TIME *10 minutes* **COOKING TIME** *15 minutes* **SERVES 4**

2 tbsp butter
2 shallots, thinly sliced
1 clove garlic, crushed
¾ lb mixed fresh wild
   mushrooms, such
   as shiitake & oyster
   mushrooms, sliced

2 tbsp dry sherry
2–3 tsp chopped fresh
   thyme (optional)
2–3 tbsp crème fraîche
   or sour cream
Sea salt & freshly ground
   black pepper

1 Melt the butter in a large, non-stick skillet. Add the shallots and garlic and cook gently
for 3 minutes.
2 Add the mushrooms and sauté for about 5 minutes, or until tender.
3 Stir in the sherry and chopped thyme, if using. Increase the heat slightly and cook for
2–3 minutes, stirring continuously, until most of the liquid has evaporated.
4 Stir in the crème fraîche or sour cream, and season to taste with salt and pepper.
Serve hot.

SERVING SUGGESTIONS *Serve with broiled or pan-fried halibut or salmon steaks, or with broiled or
oven-baked whole trout or mackerel.*
VARIATIONS *Use button, chestnut, or closed cup mushrooms (or a mixture) in place of wild mushrooms.
Use brandy, ruby port wine or Madeira in place of sherry. Use chopped fresh sage or tarragon in place
of thyme. Use 1–2 tbsp chopped fresh parsley in place of thyme.*

087 TOMATO AND CILANTRO SAUCE

PREPARATION TIME *15 minutes* **COOKING TIME** *30–40 minutes* **SERVES 6**

1 tbsp olive or sunflower oil
2 cups leeks (trimmed weight), washed & thinly sliced
2 cloves garlic, crushed
2 sticks of celery, finely chopped

2 cups mushrooms, finely chopped *(see Cook's Tip below)*
1½ lb tomatoes, skinned, seeded, & finely chopped
1 tbsp tomato catsup

Sea salt & freshly ground black pepper
2–3 tbsp chopped fresh cilantro
4 tbsp light cream (optional)

1 Heat the oil in a saucepan, add the leeks, garlic and celery and sauté for about 5 minutes, or until softened.

2 Add the mushrooms and sauté for 1 minute. Add the tomatoes, tomato catsup, and salt and pepper to taste, and mix well.

3 Bring the mixture to a boil, stirring, then reduce the heat, cover, and simmer for 20–25 minutes, or until the vegetables are tender, stirring occasionally.

4 Uncover the pan and simmer for a further 5–10 minutes, or until the sauce has thickened slightly, stirring occasionally.

5 Stir in the chopped cilantro and light cream, if using. Adjust the seasoning to taste, and serve hot.

SERVING SUGGESTIONS *Serve with broiled or oven-baked cod or haddock steaks or monkfish tail.*
COOK'S TIP *Choose closed cup, button, or chestnut (brown cap) mushrooms for this recipe.*

088 CHUNKY FRESH TOMATO SAUCE

PREPARATION TIME *15 minutes* **COOKING TIME** *25–30 minutes* **SERVES 4–6**

1 lb ripe tomatoes, skinned & finely chopped
⅔ cup dry white wine
1 small onion, finely chopped

2 sticks of celery, finely chopped
1 clove garlic, crushed
1 tbsp tomato paste
1 tbsp tomato catsup

1 tbsp chopped fresh mixed herbs
Sea salt & freshly ground black pepper

1 Place the tomatoes, wine, onion, celery, garlic, tomato paste, tomato catsup, chopped herbs, and seasoning in a saucepan and stir to mix well.

2 Bring to a boil, then reduce the heat, cover, and simmer for 15 minutes, stirring occasionally.

3 Increase the heat slightly, uncover the pan and cook for a further 5–10 minutes to thicken the sauce, stirring frequently. Adjust the seasoning to taste, and serve hot.

SERVING SUGGESTIONS *Serve with broiled or barbecued fish kebabs or fish steaks such as cod, haddock or salmon.*
VARIATIONS *Use 14-oz can chopped tomatoes in place of fresh tomatoes. Use 1 tsp dried mixed herbs or dried Italian herb seasoning in place of fresh herbs.*

089 DILL AND MUSTARD SAUCE

PREPARATION TIME *5 minutes* **COOKING TIME** *20 minutes* **SERVES 6** *Makes about 1¼ cups*

1 cup dry white wine
¾ cup fish or vegetable
  stock *(see recipes on
  page 10)*

1 cup crème fraîche
  or heavy cream
2 tbsp wholegrain mustard
2 egg yolks, lightly beaten

2–3 tbsp chopped fresh dill
Sea salt & freshly ground
  black pepper

1 Place the wine and stock in a saucepan and bring to a boil, then boil rapidly until the liquid has reduced by about half.

2 Reduce the heat and stir in the crème fraîche or heavy cream, mustard, egg yolks, and chopped dill.

3 Cook gently, stirring continuously, for about 10 minutes, or until the sauce is thickened slightly. Do not allow the mixture to boil. Season to taste with salt and pepper. Serve hot.

SERVING SUGGESTIONS *Serve with pan-fried or broiled plaice, lemon sole, or halibut fillets, or with pan-fried or grilled tiger or king prawns.*

VARIATIONS *Use 1–2 tbsp Dijon mustard in place of wholegrain mustard. Use 1–2 tbsp chopped fresh tarragon or 2–3 tsp hot horseradish sauce (or to taste), in place of dill.*

COOK'S TIPS *Egg yolks are added to sauces such as this one toward the end of the cooking time. They will enrich and thicken a sauce, but remember, the eggs will curdle if the mixture is boiled.*

Once made, this sauce should be served immediately as it cannot be reheated.

090 CREAMY BROCCOLI SAUCE

PREPARATION TIME *10 minutes* **COOKING TIME** *20 minutes* **SERVES 4**

2 cups broccoli florets
3 shallots, chopped
1 tbsp butter
2 tbsp all-purpose flour

1¼ cups milk
½ cup cheddar cheese,
  finely grated

Sea salt & freshly ground
  black pepper

1 Cook the broccoli and shallots in a saucepan of boiling water for 5–7 minutes, or until tender. Drain, then place them in a blender or food processor with 2 tbsp of the cooking liquid, and blend to form a purée. Set aside.

2 Place the butter, flour, and milk in a saucepan. Heat gently, whisking continuously, until the sauce comes to a boil and thickens. Simmer gently for 3–4 minutes, stirring. Stir in the broccoli purée and reheat gently until hot, stirring.

3 Remove the pan from the heat and stir in the cheese until melted. Season to taste with salt and pepper. Serve hot.

SERVING SUGGESTIONS *Serve with broiled or oven-baked cod, haddock, or monkfish.*

VARIATIONS *Use red Leicester, double Gloucester, gruyère, or emmental cheese in place of cheddar. Use 1 small leek or 1 small onion in place of shallots. Use cauliflower florets in place of broccoli.*

COOK'S TIP *When buying broccoli, choose strong, firm stalks with bright green, compact florets. Avoid limp, yellow, or discolored heads.*

SAUCES FOR FISH AND SHELLFISH

091 CHEESE AND CHIVE SAUCE

PREPARATION TIME *5 minutes* **COOKING TIME** *10 minutes* **SERVES 4** *Makes about 1½ cups*

1 tbsp butter
2 tbsp all-purpose flour
⅔ cup milk
⅔ cup chicken stock
   (see recipe on page 11),
   cooled

½ cup mature cheddar
   cheese, grated
2–3 tbsp snipped fresh
   chives
Sea salt & freshly ground
   black pepper

1 Place the butter, flour, milk, and stock in a saucepan and heat gently, whisking continuously, until the sauce comes to a boil and thickens. Simmer gently for 3–4 minutes, stirring.
2 Remove the pan from the heat and stir in the cheese until melted. Stir in the snipped chives, and season to taste with salt and pepper. Serve hot.

SERVING SUGGESTIONS *Serve with poached smoked haddock fillets, or with pan-fried cod steaks.*
VARIATIONS *Use gruyère or emmental cheese in place of cheddar. Use chopped fresh parsley in place of chives.*

092 CHEESE AND CORN SAUCE

PREPARATION TIME *5 minutes* **COOKING TIME** *10 minutes* **SERVES 2–4**

1 tbsp butter
2 tbsp all-purpose flour
1¼ cups milk
⅔ cup canned corn kernels
 (drained weight), drained

½ cup cheddar cheese,
 grated
1–2 tbsp chopped fresh
 parsley
Sea salt & freshly ground
 black pepper

1 Place the butter, flour, and milk in a saucepan and heat gently, whisking continuously, until the sauce comes to a boil and thickens. Simmer gently for 3–4 minutes, stirring.
2 Add the corn kernels and heat gently until hot, stirring continuously. Remove the pan from the heat and stir in the cheese until melted.
3 Stir in the chopped parsley, and season to taste with salt and pepper. Serve hot.

SERVING SUGGESTIONS *Serve with broiled or pan-fried plaice fillets, or with broiled fishcakes.*
VARIATIONS *Use gruyère or emmental cheese in place of cheddar. Use 1–2 tbsp snipped fresh chives in place of parsley.*
COOK'S TIPS *For a stronger cheese flavor, choose a mature cheddar cheese for this sauce. For a milder cheese flavor, choose a medium or mild cheddar cheese.*
 Finely grated cheese will melt more quickly into the sauce than coarsely grated cheese, though the time difference is marginal.

093 ROASTED CHERRY TOMATO SAUCE

PREPARATION TIME *5 minutes* **COOKING TIME** *45 minutes* **SERVES 6** *Makes about 2½ cups*

2 lb cherry tomatoes or
 small plum tomatoes
1 tbsp olive oil

1 onion, finely chopped
2 cloves garlic, crushed
2 tbsp tomato paste

2–3 tbsp chopped fresh basil
Sea salt & freshly ground
 black pepper

1 Preheat the oven to 180°C/350°F/gas mark 4. Arrange the tomatoes in a single layer in a shallow baking dish. Roast the tomatoes for about 20 minutes, or until soft.
2 Remove from the oven and set aside to cool slightly, then purée the roasted tomatoes in a blender or food processor until smooth. Press the tomato purée through a sieve into a bowl, then discard the skins and seeds. Reserve the tomato sauce and set aside.
3 Heat the oil in a saucepan, add the onion and garlic and sauté for 5–7 minutes, or until softened. Add the reserved tomato sauce, tomato paste, chopped basil, and seasoning, and mix well.
4 Bring to a boil, then reduce the heat and simmer, uncovered, for 10 minutes, stirring occasionally. Adjust the seasoning to taste, and serve hot.

SERVING SUGGESTIONS *Serve with broiled or pan-fried cod steaks, mackerel fillets, or king prawns.*
VARIATIONS *Add 1 finely chopped, seeded red chili with the garlic, if desired.*

SAUCES FOR FISH AND SHELLFISH

094 PEPPERED TOMATO SAUCE

PREPARATION TIME *5 minutes* **COOKING TIME** *30 minutes* **SERVES 4**

3 tbsp butter
1 onion, finely chopped
1 tsp superfine sugar
14-oz can chopped
   tomatoes

1 tbsp tomato paste
1 tsp dried herbes de
   Provence
Sea salt & freshly ground
   black pepper

4 tbsp dry white wine

1 Melt the butter in a saucepan, add the onion and sauté for about 5 minutes, or until softened. Remove the pan from the heat and stir in the sugar.

2 Place the tomatoes, tomato paste, dried herbs, a pinch of salt and a good seasoning of pepper in a blender or food processor. Add the sautéed onions, and blend until well mixed.

3 Return the mixture to the saucepan. Bring the mixture almost to the boil, then stir in the wine. Bring gently to a boil, then reduce the heat and simmer, uncovered, for 15–20 minutes, or until the sauce is cooked and thickened, stirring occasionally. Serve hot.

SERVING SUGGESTIONS *Serve with broiled, oven-baked or grilled cod, tuna, or salmon steaks.*
VARIATIONS *Add 1 clove crushed garlic to the tomato sauce, if desired – sauté the garlic with the onion and continue as above. Use red wine in place of white wine.*
COOK'S TIP *Spices such as black peppercorns keep their flavor best when they are stored whole, so it is always best to grind them fresh, as and when you need them. Ground spices can be stored in small amounts, to be used within a short period of time.*

095 BROILED RED BELL PEPPER SAUCE

PREPARATION TIME *20 minutes, plus cooling* **COOKING TIME** *30–35 minutes* **SERVES 4–6**

1 tbsp olive oil
3 shallots, finely chopped
1 stick of celery, finely
   chopped

4 red bell peppers, skinned,
   seeded, and chopped (*see
   page 21*)
1 clove garlic, crushed
⅔ cup tomato juice
   or passata

½ cup vegetable stock
   (*see recipe on page 10*)
Sea salt & freshly ground
   black pepper

1 Heat the oil in a saucepan, add the shallots and celery and sauté gently for 8–10 minutes, or until softened. Add the bell pepper flesh and garlic and sauté for 1–2 minutes.

2 Add the tomato juice or passata, stock, and seasoning and mix well. Bring to a boil, then reduce the heat, cover, and cook gently for 15–20 minutes, stirring occasionally.

3 Remove the pan from the heat, cool slightly, then purée the mixture in a blender or food processor until smooth. Push the purée through a sieve, then discard the contents of the sieve. Reheat the red bell pepper sauce gently before serving and serve hot. Alternatively, cool and chill before serving and serve cold.

SERVING SUGGESTIONS *Serve with broiled or pan-fried whole plaice, sole, or dab.*

096 FRESH SPINACH AND NUTMEG SAUCE

PREPARATION TIME *10 minutes* **COOKING TIME** *25 minutes* **SERVES 6** *Makes about 2 cups*

½ lb fresh spinach leaves
4 tsp butter
1 small onion, finely chopped
1 clove garlic, crushed
⅓ cup vegetable stock
  (see recipe on page 10)

2 bay leaves
1 sprig of fresh thyme
5 tbsp crème fraîche or
  heavy cream
½ tsp freshly grated nutmeg,
  or to taste

Sea salt & freshly ground
  black pepper

1 Wash the spinach thoroughly, shake dry, then remove and discard any tough stalks. Chop the spinach roughly, then set aside.

2 Melt the butter in a saucepan, add the onion and sauté for 5 minutes. Add the garlic and sauté for 1 minute.

3 Add the spinach, stock, bay leaves, and sprig of thyme. Bring to a boil, then reduce the heat, cover and cook gently for 10 minutes, stirring occasionally.

4 Remove the pan from the heat and let cool slightly, then remove and discard the bay leaves and fresh thyme. Purée the spinach mixture in a blender or food processor until smooth.

5 Return the mixture to the rinsed-out pan and stir in the crème fraîche or heavy cream. Reheat gently until hot, stirring. Season to taste with nutmeg, salt, and pepper. Serve hot.

SERVING SUGGESTIONS *Serve with broiled or pan-fried haddock or halibut fillets, or monkfish tail.*
VARIATIONS *Use 3 shallots in place of onion. Use ground cumin or coriander in place of nutmeg.*
COOK'S TIP *Nutmeg is best bought whole and freshly grated when required. Special nutmeg graters and nutmeg mills are available for grating whole nutmegs; otherwise use a small, fine-holed grater.*

097 WHITE WINE AND MUSSEL SAUCE

PREPARATION TIME *10 minutes* **COOKING TIME** *10 minutes* **SERVES 4**

2 tbsp cornstarch
1½ cups dry or medium
  white wine
½ lb cooked shelled fresh
  mussels (shelled weight)
1 tbsp butter

3 tbsp crème fraîche
2 tbsp chopped fresh
  flat-leaf parsley
Sea salt & freshly ground
  black pepper

1 In a saucepan, blend the cornstarch with a little of the wine until smooth. Stir in the remaining wine, then heat gently, stirring continuously, until the sauce comes to a boil and thickens. Simmer gently for 3 minutes, stirring.

2 Stir in the mussels, butter, crème fraîche, chopped parsley, and seasoning, and heat gently until hot, stirring continuously. Serve hot.

SERVING SUGGESTIONS *Serve with broiled or grilled tuna or salmon steaks.*
COOK'S TIP *To clean fresh mussels, scrub the mussels in a sinkful of cold water, scraping off barnacles and pulling away the beards. Discard any mussels with broken shells or open mussels that don't close when tapped sharply.*

098 PIQUANT MUSHROOM SAUCE

PREPARATION TIME *10 minutes* **COOKING TIME** *10 minutes* **SERVES 4–6**

1 tbsp olive oil
1 small leek, washed &
  finely chopped
2 cloves garlic, crushed

4 cups fresh wild or large
  flat (field) mushrooms,
  sliced
4 cups chestnut or brown
  cap mushrooms, quartered

2 tbsp marsala or dry sherry
2–3 tbsp chopped fresh
  flat-leaf parsley
Sea salt & freshly ground
  black pepper

1 Heat the oil in a saucepan, add the leek and garlic and sauté for 3 minutes. Stir in all
the mushrooms and sauté for 3–4 minutes.
2 Add the marsala or sherry and cook over a high heat, stirring continuously, until some of
the liquid has evaporated.
3 Stir in the chopped parsley, and season to taste with salt and pepper. Serve hot.

SERVING SUGGESTIONS *Serve with broiled or oven-baked cod, salmon, or tuna steaks.*

099 CREAMY AVOCADO SAUCE

PREPARATION TIME *10 minutes* **COOKING TIME** *N/A* **SERVES 6–8** *Makes about 2½ cups*

2 ripe avocados
Finely grated zest & juice
  of 1 lime
1 cup natural yogurt

½ cup Mayonnaise (*see recipe
  on page 37*)
1 tbsp chopped fresh parsley
  or snipped fresh chives

Sea salt & freshly ground
  black pepper

1 Halve, pit and peel the avocados, then roughly chop the flesh. Place the avocado
flesh and lime zest and juice in a blender or food processor.
2 Add the yogurt and mayonnaise, and blend until smooth and well mixed.
3 Add the chopped parsley or snipped chives, and blend briefly to mix. Season to taste
with salt and pepper. Serve immediately.

SERVING SUGGESTIONS *Serve with broiled or grilled tuna or salmon steaks, or with broiled or cooked
(cold) tiger prawns.*
VARIATION *Use the finely grated zest and juice of 1 small lemon in place of lime.*

100 DILL AND CUCUMBER SAUCE

PREPARATION TIME *10 minutes, plus standing* **COOKING TIME** *N/A* **SERVES 4–6** *Makes about 2¼ cups*

½ cucumber, finely chopped
1 tbsp chopped fresh dill

1¼ cups natural yogurt
1 tsp Dijon mustard

Sea salt & freshly ground
  black pepper

1 Place the cucumber in a bowl, add the chopped dill, and mix well. Stir in the yogurt and
mustard, mixing well, then season to taste with salt and pepper.
2 Cover and let stand in a cool place for about 30 minutes before serving, so the flavors
develop. Serve cold.

SERVING SUGGESTIONS *Serve with broiled or grilled salmon steaks, whole mackerel, or king prawns.*
VARIATION *Replace ⅔ cup yogurt with natural Greek yogurt or plain fromage frais, if desired.*

101 SWEET BELL PEPPER AND LIME SAUCE

PREPARATION TIME *10 minutes, plus cooling* **COOKING TIME** *10–15 minutes* **SERVES 4**

2 tbsp olive oil
2 large red bell peppers,
 seeded & sliced
2 shallots, finely chopped

Finely grated zest & juice
 of 1 lime
6 tbsp tomato juice

2 tbsp chopped fresh
 flat-leaf parsley
Sea salt & freshly ground
 black pepper

1 Heat the oil in a saucepan, add the bell peppers and shallots, and sauté gently for 10–15 minutes, or until softened.

2 Remove the pan from the heat and cool slightly, then place the bell pepper mixture in a blender or food processor. Add the lime zest and juice, tomato juice, chopped parsley, and seasoning, and blend until smooth and well mixed.

3 Press the bell pepper purée through a sieve into a bowl and discard the contents of the sieve. Set the sauce aside to cool. Serve cold.

SERVING SUGGESTIONS *Serve with broiled or grilled whole sardines, pilchards, or mackerel.*

102 PIQUANT PEANUT SAUCE

PREPARATION TIME *5 minutes* **COOKING TIME** *10 minutes* **SERVES 4** *Makes about 1 cup*

2 tsp olive oil
2 scallions, finely chopped
½ cup fish stock
 (see recipe on page 10)
2 tbsp light soy sauce

2 tbsp smooth peanut butter
1 tbsp clear honey
1 tsp ground ginger
2 tsp cornstarch
3 tbsp dry sherry

Sea salt & freshly ground
 black pepper

1 Heat the oil in a small saucepan, add the scallions and sauté for about 5 minutes, or until softened. Stir in the stock, soy sauce, peanut butter, honey, and ginger.

2 In a small bowl, blend the cornstarch with the sherry until smooth, then add this mixture to the pan. Heat gently, stirring continuously, until the sauce comes to a boil and thickens. Simmer gently for 3 minutes, stirring. Season to taste with salt and pepper. Serve hot.

SERVING SUGGESTION *Serve with stir-fried mixed seafood tossed with cooked egg noodles.*

103 PIQUANT PIMENTO SAUCE

PREPARATION TIME *10 minutes* **COOKING TIME** *15 minutes* **SERVES 4** *Makes about 1¼ cups*

1 tbsp olive oil
1 red onion, finely chopped
6 oz pimentos in oil
(drained weight), drained,
 patted dry, & thinly sliced

2 tbsp tomato paste
¼ cup vegetable stock
 (see recipe on page 10)
A dash of Tabasco sauce or
 a pinch of cayenne pepper

Sea salt & freshly ground
 black pepper

1 Heat the oil in a saucepan, add the onion, and sauté for 8 minutes, or until softened.

2 Add the pimentos and sauté for 1 minute, then stir in the tomato paste, stock, and Tabasco sauce or cayenne pepper.

3 Bring gently to a boil, then simmer for 5 minutes, stirring occasionally. Season to taste with salt and pepper. Serve hot.

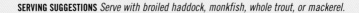

SERVING SUGGESTIONS *Serve with broiled haddock, monkfish, whole trout, or mackerel.*

104 CHILI SAUCE

PREPARATION TIME *10 minutes* **COOKING TIME** *20 minutes* **SERVES 4–6** *Makes about 2¼ cups*

14-oz can chopped tomatoes
2 shallots, finely chopped
2 sticks of celery, finely
  chopped

1 fresh red chili, seeded &
  finely chopped
1 clove garlic, crushed
⅔ cup dry white wine
1 tbsp tomato paste

Sea salt & freshly ground
  black pepper

1 Place the tomatoes, shallots, celery, chilli, garlic, wine, tomato paste, and seasoning in
a small saucepan and stir to mix.

2 Bring the mixture to a boil, then reduce the heat to medium/low and cook, uncovered, for
15–20 minutes, or until the sauce is cooked and thickened, stirring occasionally. Adjust
the seasoning to taste and serve hot.

SERVING SUGGESTIONS *Serve with stir-fried king prawns tossed with cooked rice noodles. Alternatively,
serve with broiled or oven-baked whole sardines or mackerel.*

VARIATIONS *Use red wine or unsweetened apple juice in place of white wine. Use 1–2 tsp hot chili
powder in place of the fresh chili. Use 1 lb fresh tomatoes, skinned and chopped, in place of
canned tomatoes.*

105 TOMATO COULIS

PREPARATION TIME *10 minutes* **COOKING TIME** *N/A* **SERVES 4** *Makes about 1 cup*

4 plum or vine-ripened
    tomatoes, skinned,
    seeded, & chopped
1 clove garlic, finely chopped

1 tbsp olive oil
1 tbsp tomato paste
2 tbsp chopped fresh oregano
1 tsp light soft brown sugar

Sea salt & freshly ground
    black pepper

1 Place the tomatoes, garlic, olive oil, tomato paste, chopped oregano, and sugar in a small blender or food processor, and blend until smooth.

2 Transfer the tomato coulis to a small bowl and season to taste with salt and pepper. Cover and set aside or chill until required. Serve cold.

3 Alternatively, the tomato coulis may be served hot — make the coulis as directed above, then place it in a saucepan and heat gently, until hot, stirring occasionally. Serve immediately.

SERVING SUGGESTIONS *Serve with marinated broiled monkfish tail, haddock, or salmon steaks.*

106 RED PESTO

PREPARATION TIME *10 minutes* **COOKING TIME** *N/A* **SERVES 4–6**

1¼ cups fresh basil leaves
1¼ cups fresh flat-leaf
    parsley
¼ cup pine nuts
1 clove garlic, crushed

6 sun-dried tomatoes in oil,
    drained & patted dry
1 tbsp tomato paste
6 tbsp extra-virgin olive oil

¼ cup fresh Parmesan
    cheese, finely grated
Sea salt & freshly ground
    black pepper

1 Place the basil, parsley, pine nuts, garlic, sun-dried tomatoes, tomato paste, and olive oil in a blender or food processor, and blend until well combined and relatively smooth.

2 Add the Parmesan cheese and seasoning and blend briefly to mix. Serve cold.

SERVING SUGGESTIONS *Serve with broiled or grilled monkfish or haddock, or with broiled mixed fish kebabs or king prawns.*

107 CILANTRO PESTO

PREPARATION TIME *10 minutes* **COOKING TIME** *N/A* **SERVES 4**

2½ cups fresh cilantro
    leaves
1 clove garlic, chopped

1 small fresh red or green
    chlli, seeded & chopped
    (optional)
¼ cup pine nuts

6 tbsp extra-virgin olive oil
Sea salt & freshly ground
    black pepper

1 Place the cilantro leaves in a mortar with the garlic, chili, if using, pine nuts and a little of the oil. Pound or grind with a pestle to make a paste. Gradually work in the remaining oil, then season to taste with salt and pepper.

2 Alternatively, put the cilantro leaves, garlic, chili, if using, pine nuts and oil in a small blender or food processor and blend to form a fairly smooth paste. Season to taste with salt and pepper.

3 Store the pesto in a screw-topped jar, covered with a thin layer of oil, in the refrigerator for up to 1 week. Serve cold.

SERVING SUGGESTIONS *Serve with broiled or pan-fried cod fillets, whole tiger prawns, or scallops.*

108 PEPPERED PARSLEY PESTO

PREPARATION TIME *10 minutes* **COOKING TIME** *N/A* **SERVES 4–6**

2½ cups fresh flat-leaf parsley
¼ cup pine nuts
1 clove garlic, crushed
6 tbsp extra-virgin olive oil

¼ cup fresh Parmesan cheese, finely grated
½ tsp cayenne pepper
½ tsp freshly ground black pepper

Sea salt, to taste
A squeeze of fresh lemon or lime juice (optional)

1 Place the parsley in a mortar with the pine nuts, garlic, and 1 tbsp oil. Pound or grind with a pestle to make a paste. Gradually work in the remaining oil, then stir in the Parmesan, cayenne, and black pepper. Season to taste with salt, and add a squeeze of lemon or lime juice, if desired. Add extra cayenne or black pepper, to taste, if desired.

2 Alternatively, put the parsley, pine nuts, garlic, 2 tbsp olive oil, the Parmesan, cayenne pepper, and black pepper in a small blender or food processor and blend to form a fairly smooth paste. With the motor running, gradually add the remaining oil through the feeder tube until it is well incorporated. Season to taste as above.

3 Store the pesto in a screw-topped jar, covered with a thin layer of oil, in the refrigerator for up to 1 week. Serve cold.

SERVING SUGGESTIONS *Serve with broiled or oven-baked cod fillets, monkfish tail, or tuna steaks.*

109 RHUBARB SAUCE

PREPARATION TIME *10 minutes* **COOKING TIME** *20–30 minutes* **SERVES 6–8**

1 lb fresh rhubarb, trimmed & cut into 1-inch slices

2 tart apples, peeled, cored & thinly sliced
⅔ cup water

½ cup superfine sugar
2 tbsp butter

1 Place the rhubarb and apples in a saucepan with the water. Bring slowly to a boil, then cover and simmer until the fruit is soft and pulpy, stirring occasionally.

2 Remove the pan from the heat and mash the fruit thoroughly with a fork or potato masher until smooth. Stir in the sugar and butter, mixing well.

3 Return the pan to the heat and bring slowly to a boil, stirring continuously, then simmer gently for 1–2 minutes, stirring. Serve hot or cold.

SERVING SUGGESTIONS *Serve with broiled whole mackerel, trout, sardines, or pilchards.*

110 CREAMY FRESH LEMON SAUCE

PREPARATION TIME *5 minutes* **COOKING TIME** *15 minutes* **SERVES 4**

1 tbsp sunflower oil
2 onions, thinly sliced
2 cloves garlic, crushed

1 fresh red or green chlli, seeded & finely chopped
Finely grated zest & juice of 2 lemons

⅔ cup crème fraîche
Sea salt & freshly ground black pepper

1 Heat the oil in a saucepan, add the onions, garlic, and chili and sauté for 5 minutes.

2 Add the lemon zest and juice, then cover and cook gently for about 10 minutes, or until the onions are soft, stirring occasionally.

3 Add the crème fraîche, and reheat gently until hot, stirring. Season to taste. Serve hot.

SERVING SUGGESTIONS *Serve with broiled haddock, cod, or halibut steaks.*

111 ROUILLE

PREPARATION TIME *10 minutes* **COOKING TIME** *N/A* **SERVES 6–8** *Makes about 1 cup*

2 cloves garlic, finely
chopped
1 fresh red chlli, seeded
& finely chopped

2 egg yolks
A pinch of salt
⅔ cup light olive oil
1 tbsp tomato paste

Cayenne pepper, to taste
(optional)

1 Place the garlic, chili, egg yolks, and salt in a small blender or food processor and blend
briefly to mix.

2 With the motor running and blades turning, gradually add the oil to the blender or food
processor, pouring it through the feeder tube in a slow, continuous stream until the
mixture is thick and creamy.

3 Add the tomato paste and a little cayenne pepper to taste, if desired, and blend briefly
to mix. Serve cold.

SERVING SUGGESTION *Serve with fish soups such as bouillabaisse.*

112 PISTACHIO BUTTER

PREPARATION TIME *10 minutes, plus chilling* **COOKING TIME** *N/A* **SERVES 4–6**

½ cup unsalted butter
(at room temperature)

1 tbsp pistachio nuts,
ground or very finely
chopped

Freshly ground black pepper,
to taste

1 Place the butter in a small bowl and beat until softened. Add the pistachio nuts, then
add black pepper to taste, and beat until well mixed.

2 Turn the flavored butter onto a piece of plastic wrap and shape into a log. Wrap the
flavored butter in the plastic wrap, then chill in the refrigerator for at least 1 hour before
serving. Cut into 4–6 even slices to serve. Serve chilled.

SERVING SUGGESTIONS *Serve a slice of flavored butter on top of broiled or pan-fried haddock fillets.*

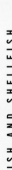

113 ANCHOVY BUTTER

PREPARATION TIME *10 minutes, plus chilling* **COOKING TIME** *N/A* **SERVES 4–6**

½ cup unsalted butter
(at room temperature)
2-oz can anchovy
fillets in oil, drained &
finely chopped

A squeeze of fresh lemon
juice
Freshly ground black pepper,
to taste

1 Place the butter in a small bowl and beat until softened. Mash the anchovies in a
separate bowl (or using a pestle and mortar) to form a paste.

2 Add the anchovy paste and lemon juice to the softened butter, then add black pepper to
taste, and beat until well mixed.

3 Turn the flavored butter onto a piece of plastic wrap and shape into a log. Wrap the
flavored butter in the plastic wrap, then chill in the refrigerator for at least 1 hour before
serving. Cut into 4–6 even slices to serve. Serve chilled.

SERVING SUGGESTIONS *Serve a slice of flavored butter on top of broiled or grilled cod, salmon, or
tuna steaks.*

SAUCES FOR FISH AND SHELLFISH

114 HERB AND LIME BUTTER

PREPARATION TIME *10 minutes, plus chilling* **COOKING TIME** *N/A* **SERVES 4–6**

½ cup unsalted butter
  (at room temperature)
Finely grated zest of 1 lime

2 tbsp chopped fresh parsley
1 tbsp chopped fresh
  cilantro

Freshly ground black pepper,
  to taste

1 Place the butter in a small bowl and beat until softened. Add the lime zest, chopped
  parsley, chopped cilantro, and black pepper to taste, and beat until well mixed.
2 Turn the flavored butter onto a piece of plastic wrap and shape into a log. Wrap the
  flavored butter in the plastic wrap, then chill in the refrigerator for at least 1 hour
  before serving. Cut into 4–6 even slices to serve. Serve chilled.

SERVING SUGGESTION *Serve a slice of flavored butter on top of
cooked hot, fresh mussels.*
VARIATIONS *Use finely grated zest of 1 lemon or 1 small
orange in place of lime zest. Use chopped fresh
tarragon, oregano, or basil in place of cilantro.*

CHAPTER 5

SAUCES FOR MEAT, POULTRY, AND GAME

Freshly broiled or pan-fried meat, poultry, or game served with a simple, tasty sauce is a hard combination to beat. In the following pages you'll find a wide variety of appetizing sauces, with something to suit every occasion.

Many of the sauces in this chapter are relatively quick and easy to make, and will add a delicious finishing touch to a meal. Some sauces are best served with a specific type of meat, whereas others are more flexible, giving you the chance to try various options, and typical serving suggestions are given with each recipe.

Choose from classics such as Creamy Caper Sauce, Black Bean Sauce, Barbecue Basting Sauce, Ruby Port and Cranberry Sauce, Madeira Sauce, Onion Gravy, Creamy Blue Cheese Sauce, and Creamy Tarragon Sauce. Or try something a little different such as Plum and Ginger Sauce, Spiced Green Lentil Sauce, Mustard and Horseradish Sauce, Aragula Pesto, or Cajun-Spiced Butter.

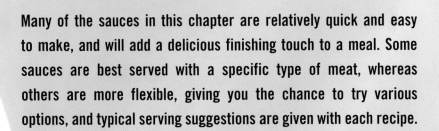

115 ONION GRAVY

PREPARATION TIME *10 minutes* **COOKING TIME** *40 minutes* **SERVES 6** *Makes about 2 cups*

2 tbsp butter
3½ cups onions, thinly
  sliced
1 small clove garlic, crushed
1 tsp chopped fresh thyme
¼ tsp superfine sugar

1 tbsp all-purpose flour
1¼ cups beef, chicken
  or vegetable stock *(see
  recipes on pages 10–11)*
½ cup red or white wine

Sea salt & freshly ground
  black pepper

1 Melt the butter in a saucepan, add the onions, garlic, chopped thyme, and sugar and
cook gently for about 30 minutes, or until golden and caramelized, stirring occasionally.
2 Stir in the flour and cook for 1–2 minutes, or until the flour is light brown in color,
stirring continuously.
3 Gradually stir in the stock and wine, then heat gently, stirring continuously, until the
sauce comes to a boil and thickens.
4 Simmer gently, uncovered, for 5 minutes, stirring frequently. Season to taste with salt
and pepper. Serve hot.

SERVING SUGGESTIONS *Serve with broiled good-quality sausages, home-made burgers, or pan-fried
liver and bacon, and mashed potatoes.*
VARIATION *Use red onions or shallots in place of regular onions.*

116 RED WINE GRAVY

PREPARATION TIME *10 minutes* **COOKING TIME** *25 minutes* **SERVES 4–6** *Makes about 1¼ cups*

2 tbsp butter, softened
2 tbsp all-purpose flour
1 small onion, roughly
  chopped

1¼ cups beef or lamb
  stock *(see recipe on page
  11)*
½ cup full-bodied red wine

Pan juices from roast meat
  (such as beef, lamb or
  pork)
Sea salt & freshly ground
  black pepper

1 Put 1 tbsp butter and the flour in a small bowl and mix together until well blended to
make beurre manié. Set aside.
2 Melt the remaining butter in a small saucepan, add the onion and sauté gently for about
8–10 minutes, or until softened.
3 Stir the stock, wine, and the juices from the roast meat into the onions and bring to a
boil. Reduce the heat, cover, and simmer for 5 minutes.
4 Remove the onion from the pan using a fine slotted spoon and discard (or strain the
mixture through a sieve and return the liquid to the pan).
5 Bring the liquid back to a boil, then add the beurre manié a little at a time, whisking
continuously to blend in well with the liquid, until all the beurre manié has been added.
Continue to cook, whisking, until the gravy thickens.
6 Simmer gently for 5 minutes, stirring continuously. Season to taste with salt (if required)
and black pepper. Serve hot.

SERVING SUGGESTIONS *Serve with roast beef, lamb, or pork.*
VARIATION *To make a chicken gravy, use chicken stock and white wine in place of beef or lamb stock
and red wine.*

117 RUBY PORT AND CRANBERRY SAUCE

PREPARATION TIME *5 minutes* **COOKING TIME** *30 minutes* **SERVES 6–8** *Makes about 1¼ cups*

2 cups fresh (or frozen, defrosted) cranberries (or use fresh blueberries if cranberries are not available)

Finely grated zest & juice of 1 small orange
⅔ cup light soft brown sugar
½ cup ruby port wine

A good pinch of ground mixed spice
Freshly ground black pepper, to taste

1 Place the cranberries in a saucepan with the orange zest and juice, sugar, port wine, mixed spice, and black pepper. Heat gently, stirring, until the sugar has dissolved.
2 Bring the mixture to a boil, then reduce the heat and simmer, uncovered, for 20–30 minutes, or until the cranberries are really soft, stirring frequently.
3 Remove the pan from the heat and add a little more mixed spice and/or black pepper to taste. Serve hot, or set aside to cool and serve cold.

SERVING SUGGESTIONS *Serve with hot or cold roast turkey, chicken, or pork and all the trimmings.*

118 MADEIRA SAUCE

PREPARATION TIME *5 minutes* **COOKING TIME** *10 minutes* **SERVES 4**

1 tbsp olive oil
6 shallots, sliced
4 tbsp vegetable stock *(see recipe on page 10)*

4 tbsp Madeira
1 tsp dried herbes de Provence
2 tbsp crème fraîche

Sea salt & freshly ground black pepper

1 Heat the oil in a saucepan, add the shallots and sauté for 5 minutes, or until softened.
2 Stir in the stock, Madeira, and dried herbs, then bring the mixture to a boil and simmer, uncovered, for 2 minutes, stirring occasionally.
3 Stir in the crème fraîche and heat gently until hot, stirring continuously. Season to taste with salt and pepper. Serve hot.

SERVING SUGGESTIONS *Serve with pan-fried lamb's liver or kidneys, or chicken livers.*
VARIATIONS *Use 1 onion in place of shallots. Use ruby port wine or red wine in place of Madeira.*

119 SWEET AND SOUR SAUCE

PREPARATION TIME *10 minutes* **COOKING TIME** *20 minutes* **SERVES 4–6** *Makes about 2¼ cups*

1 tbsp cornstarch
4 tbsp red wine
14-oz can chopped tomatoes, puréed

⅔ cup unsweetened apple juice
2 tbsp red wine vinegar
2 tbsp light soft brown sugar

1 tbsp sun-dried tomato paste
Sea salt & freshly ground black pepper

1 In a small bowl, blend the cornstarch with the red wine until smooth, then place it in a pan with the tomatoes, apple juice, vinegar, sugar, and tomato paste, and stir to mix.
2 Bring to a boil, stirring continuously, then reduce the heat and simmer gently, uncovered, for about 15 minutes, or until the sauce is thickened slightly, stirring occasionally. Season to taste with salt and pepper. Serve hot.

SERVING SUGGESTIONS *Serve with cooked meatballs, or with broiled or pan-fried pork steaks or chicken breasts.*

120 PLUM AND GINGER SAUCE

PREPARATION TIME *20 minutes* **COOKING TIME** *25 minutes* **SERVES 6** *Makes about 1¾ cups*

1 tbsp sunflower oil
1 small red onion, finely
chopped
1 clove garlic, crushed

2 tsp (peeled) grated fresh
root ginger
6 red dessert plums, halved,
pitted, & chopped

⅔ cup red wine
2 tbsp light soft brown
sugar
1 tbsp brandy or sherry
(optional)

1 Heat the oil in a saucepan, add the onion, garlic, and ginger and sauté for 5 minutes.
Add the plums and sauté for 1 minute, stirring.

2 Stir in the wine and sugar, and heat gently, stirring continuously, until the sugar has
dissolved. Bring slowly to a boil, then reduce the heat, cover, and simmer for about 10
minutes, or until the plums are soft.

3 Remove the pan from the heat and cool slightly, then purée the mixture in a blender or
food processor until smooth.

4 Return the sauce to the rinsed-out pan and stir in the brandy or sherry, if using. Reheat
gently until hot, stirring continuously. Serve hot or cold.

5 If serving the sauce cold, remove the pan from the heat and set aside to cool completely
before serving.

SERVING SUGGESTIONS *Serve with crispy duck and scallions in Chinese pancakes. Alternatively, serve
with broiled beef, pork, or lamb steaks.*

121 BLACK BEAN SAUCE

PREPARATION TIME *10 minutes* **COOKING TIME** *10–15 minutes* **SERVES 4–6** *Makes about 2 cups*

1 tbsp sunflower oil
3 shallots, finely chopped
1–2 cloves garlic, crushed
1-inch piece of fresh root
   ginger, peeled & finely
   chopped

2 tbsp salted or fermented
   black beans
2 tbsp light soy sauce
2 tbsp dry sherry
1 tsp light soft brown sugar

1¼ cups vegetable stock
   (see recipe on page 10)
2 tsp toasted sesame oil
2–3 tsp cornstarch
Sea salt & freshly ground
   black pepper

1 Heat the oil in a wok or large skillet over a high heat, add the shallots, garlic, and
  ginger and stir-fry for 1–2 minutes, or until softened. Add the black beans and stir-fry
  for 30 seconds, then add the soy sauce, sherry, sugar, and stock and mix well.
2 Bring to a boil, then cook over a high heat for 3–4 minutes, stirring occasionally. Stir
  in the sesame oil.
3 Blend the cornstarch with 1 tbsp cold water in a small bowl until smooth. Stir the
  cornstarch mixture into the hot bean sauce and bring to a boil, stirring continuously,
  until the sauce thickens. Simmer gently for 2–3 minutes, stirring. Season to taste with
  salt and pepper, if necessary. Serve hot.

SERVING SUGGESTIONS *Serve with stir-fried strips of beef, pork, or chicken.*
VARIATIONS *Add 1 seeded and finely chopped fresh red or green chili with the shallots, if desired. Use 4–6 scallions or 1 small onion in place of shallots.*

122 RED PLUM SAUCE

PREPARATION TIME *15 minutes, plus cooling* **COOKING TIME** *15–20 minutes* **SERVES 6–8**

6 red dessert plums, halved
  & pitted
⅔ cup water
Finely grated zest & juice of
  1 orange

¼ cup superfine sugar or
  light soft brown sugar
½ tsp ground cinnamon
1–2 tbsp brandy or sherry

1 Place the plums in a saucepan with the water. Bring slowly to a boil, then cover and simmer
  until the plums are soft, stirring occasionally. Remove the pan from the heat and set aside to
  cool. Once cool, purée the plums and juices in a blender or food processor until smooth.
2 Return the plum purée to a saucepan and stir in the orange zest and juice, sugar, cinnamon,
  and brandy or sherry, mixing well.
3 Reheat the sauce gently until hot, stirring occasionally. Serve hot.
4 Alternatively, remove the saucepan from the heat, let cool completely, then chill before serving.

SERVING SUGGESTIONS *Serve with broiled, roast, or pan-fried lamb or pork chops, or beef steaks.*
VARIATION *Use ground ginger or freshly grated nutmeg, to taste, in place of cinnamon.*
COOK'S TIP *To pit plums, cut around the middle of a firm plum, across the indentation, then twist the two halves apart and remove the pit.*

123 MUSHROOM AND MUSTARD SAUCE

PREPARATION TIME *10 minutes* **COOKING TIME** *10 minutes* **SERVES 4**

3 tbsp butter
3 cups closed cup or
   button mushrooms,
   chopped or sliced
2 tbsp all-purpose flour

⅔ cup milk
⅔ cup vegetable or chicken
   stock *(see recipes on
   pages 10–11),* cooled

1–2 tbsp wholegrain
   mustard, or to taste
Sea salt & freshly ground
   black pepper

1 Melt 2 tbsp butter in a skillet, add the mushrooms and sauté quickly over a fairly high
heat for about 3–5 minutes, or until tender.

2 Using a slotted spoon, remove the mushrooms from the pan to a plate, set aside and
keep hot. Discard any mushroom juices. Alternatively, reserve the juices and add to the
sauce later with the mushrooms, if desired.

3 Meanwhile, place the remaining butter, the flour, milk, and stock in a saucepan and
heat gently, whisking continuously, until the sauce comes to a boil and thickens. Simmer
gently for 3–4 minutes, stirring.

4 Stir the reserved mushrooms (and cooking juices, if desired) and mustard into the
sauce. Reheat gently until hot, stirring continuously. Season to taste with salt and
pepper. Serve hot.

SERVING SUGGESTIONS *Serve with roast chicken, turkey, or pork, or with pan-fried chicken breasts
or pork chops.*

124 CHILI AND TOMATO SAUCE

PREPARATION TIME *10 minutes* **COOKING TIME** *20 minutes* **SERVES 6** *Makes about 2¼ cups*

14-oz can chopped
   tomatoes
½ cup vegetable stock
   (see recipe on page 10)
1 small onion, finely chopped

1 fresh red or green chili,
   seeded & finely chopped
1 tbsp tomato paste
1 clove garlic, crushed
5 tbsp red wine

Sea salt & freshly ground
   black pepper

1 Place the tomatoes, stock, onion, chili, tomato paste, garlic, red wine, and seasoning
in a saucepan and stir to mix.

2 Bring to a boil, then reduce the heat and cook, uncovered, over a medium heat for
15–20 minutes, or until the sauce is cooked and thickened, stirring occasionally.
Adjust the seasoning to taste, and serve hot.

SERVING SUGGESTIONS *Serve with broiled or grilled lamb, beef, or pork kebabs or steaks.*
VARIATIONS *Use beef stock in place of vegetable stock. Use dry white wine or unsweetened apple juice
in place of red wine. Add a little hot chili powder with the fresh chili for a more pronounced spicy
flavor, if desired.*
COOK'S TIP *When preparing fresh chilies, avoid touching your eyes and wash your hands thoroughly
afterwards (or wear disposable gloves), as chilies contain volatile oils in the flesh and seeds which
can irritate skin and eyes.*

125 HERBY TOMATO SAUCE

PREPARATION TIME *5 minutes* **COOKING TIME** *25–35 minutes* **SERVES 4**

1 tbsp olive oil
3 shallots, finely chopped
8-oz can chopped tomatoes

⅔ cup vegetable stock
  (see recipe on page 10)
1 tbsp tomato catsup
A dash of Worcestershire
  sauce

1–2 tbsp chopped fresh
  mixed herbs
Sea salt & freshly ground
  black pepper

1 Heat the oil in a saucepan, add the shallots and sauté for about 5 minutes, or until
  softened.
2 Add the tomatoes, stock, tomato catsup, and Worcestershire sauce and mix well. Bring
  to a boil, then reduce the heat slightly, cover and simmer for 15–20 minutes, stirring
  occasionally.
3 Uncover, stir in the chopped herbs and seasoning, then simmer for a further 5–10
  minutes, or until the sauce has reduced and thickened slightly, stirring occasionally.
  Serve hot.

SERVING SUGGESTIONS *Serve with cooked home-made meatballs, or with broiled good-quality
sausages.*
VARIATIONS *Use 1 small red onion in place of shallots. Use fresh basil or flat-leaf parsley in place of
mixed herbs.*
COOK'S TIP *The cooked tomato sauce may be cooled slightly, puréed in a blender or food processor,
then reheated gently before serving, if desired.*

126 SPICY TOMATO SAUCE

PREPARATION TIME *15 minutes* **COOKING TIME** *35 minutes* **SERVES 6–8**

1½ lb tomatoes, skinned,
  seeded, & chopped
6 shallots, thinly sliced
1 small leek, washed &
  thinly sliced
2 sticks of celery, finely

  chopped
1 clove garlic, crushed
⅔ cup red wine
2 tbsp sun-dried tomato
  paste
2 tsp ground cumin

1 tsp ground coriander
1 tsp hot chili powder
Sea salt & freshly ground
  black pepper

1 Place the tomatoes, shallots, leek, celery, garlic, wine, tomato paste, ground spices,
  and seasoning in a saucepan and mix well.
2 Bring to a boil, stirring occasionally, then reduce the heat, cover and simmer for
  about 25 minutes, or until the sauce is cooked and the vegetables are tender, stirring
  occasionally.
3 Remove the pan from the heat and set aside to cool slightly, then purée the sauce in
  a blender or food processor until smooth.
4 Return the sauce to the rinsed-out saucepan and reheat gently until hot, stirring
  occasionally. Adjust the seasoning to taste, and serve hot.

SERVING SUGGESTIONS *Serve with beef, lamb, or chicken and vegetable kebabs.*
VARIATION *Use unsweetened apple juice or white wine in place of red wine.*

127 BARBECUE BASTING SAUCE

PREPARATION TIME *15 minutes* **COOKING TIME** *15 minutes* **SERVES 4**

1 tbsp olive oil
1 onion, finely chopped
⅔ cup passata

3 tbsp light beer or lager
(such as Budweiser)
2 tbsp light soft brown sugar
2 tbsp Worcestershire sauce

1 tbsp tomato paste
1 tbsp lemon juice
2 tsp smooth English
mustard

1 Heat the oil in a saucepan, add the onion and cook gently for 10 minutes.
2 Remove the pan from the heat, add all the remaining ingredients, and stir to mix well.
3 Transfer the mixture to a blender or food processor and blend until smooth.
4 Return the sauce to the rinsed-out pan and reheat gently, stirring occasionally. Serve hot.

SERVING SUGGESTIONS *Use as a baste for chicken portions or pork chops on a grill, and serve remaining hot sauce separately.*

128 CREAMY CURRY SAUCE

PREPARATION TIME *10 minutes* **COOKING TIME** *25 minutes* **SERVES 4–6**

3 tbsp butter
1 onion, finely chopped
1 clove garlic, crushed
2 tbsp all-purpose flour
3 tbsp medium-hot curry
paste

1 tbsp tomato paste
1¼ cups vegetable or
chicken stock *(see recipes
on pages 10–11)*
1 cup light cream

Sea salt & freshly ground
black pepper

1 Melt the butter in a saucepan, add the onion and sauté gently for 8–10 minutes.
2 Add the garlic and sauté for 1 minute, then add the flour and cook for 1 minute, stirring.
Stir in the curry paste and tomato paste. Remove the pan from the heat and gradually
stir or whisk in the stock.
3 Return the pan to the heat and heat gently, stirring or whisking continuously, until the
sauce comes to a boil and thickens. Simmer gently for 2–3 minutes, stirring.
4 Stir in the cream and reheat gently until hot but not boiling, stirring continuously.
Season to taste with salt and pepper. Serve hot.

SERVING SUGGESTIONS *Serve with broiled or pan-fried pork or lamb chops, or chicken thighs.*

129 CREAMY CAPER SAUCE

PREPARATION TIME *5 minutes* **COOKING TIME** *10 minutes* **SERVES 4** *Makes about 1½ cups*

2 tbsp butter
¼ cup all-purpose flour
1¼ cups full-fat milk

2 tbsp capers, drained &
chopped
1 tbsp vinegar from jar
of capers

Sea salt & freshly ground
black pepper

1 Place the butter, flour, and milk in a saucepan and heat gently, whisking continuously,
until the sauce comes to a boil and is thickened and smooth. Simmer gently for 3–4
minutes, stirring.
2 Stir in the capers and vinegar, and reheat gently until almost boiling. Season to taste
with salt and pepper. Serve hot.

SERVING SUGGESTIONS *Serve with roast or broiled lamb chops or chicken breast joints.*

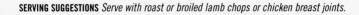

LEMON CAPER SAUCE

PREPARATION TIME *5 minutes* **COOKING TIME** *10 minutes* **SERVES 4** *Makes about 1½ cups*

2 tbsp butter
¼ cup all-purpose flour
1¼ cups milk
2 tbsp capers, drained
  (& chopped, if desired)

1 tbsp vinegar from jar
  of capers
Finely grated zest of 1
  small lemon

Sea salt & freshly ground
  black pepper

1 Place the butter, flour, and milk in a saucepan and heat gently, whisking continuously, until the sauce comes to a boil and is thickened and smooth. Simmer gently for 3–4 minutes, stirring.
2 Stir in the capers, vinegar, and lemon zest and reheat gently until almost boiling. Season to taste with salt and pepper. Serve hot.

SERVING SUGGESTIONS *Serve with char-grilled turkey breast, pork, or lamb steaks.*
VARIATIONS *Use half milk and half vegetable stock in place of the milk. Use white wine vinegar or fresh lemon juice in place of caper vinegar.*

131 WATERCRESS SAUCE

PREPARATION TIME *10 minutes* **COOKING TIME** *10 minutes* **SERVES 4–6** *Makes about 2¼ cups*

1 large bunch watercress
2 tbsp butter
¼ cup all-purpose flour

1¼ cups vegetable or chicken
stock *(see recipes on
pages 10–11)*

⅔ cup heavy cream
Sea salt & freshly ground
black pepper

1 Trim the watercress, then blanch it in a saucepan of boiling water for 30 seconds. Refresh under cold running water, drain well, and pat dry with paper towels. Chop the watercress finely, then set aside.

2 Melt the butter in a small saucepan, then stir in the flour and cook gently for 1 minute, stirring. Remove the saucepan from the heat and gradually stir or whisk in the stock and cream.

3 Return the pan to the heat and bring slowly to a boil, stirring or whisking continuously, until the sauce is thickened and smooth. Simmer gently for 2–3 minutes, stirring.

4 Stir in the chopped watercress and cook gently for 1 minute, stirring. Season to taste with salt and pepper. Serve hot.

SERVING SUGGESTIONS *Serve with broiled or oven-baked chicken portions or turkey breast steaks.*
VARIATIONS *Use milk in place of either stock or cream. Use fresh aragula leaves in place of water-cress.*
COOK'S TIPS *Once cooked, let the sauce cool slightly, then purée it in a blender or food processor, if desired. Reheat gently before serving.*
To retain its wonderful color and flavor, watercress only needs to be cooked very briefly.

132 WHOLEGRAIN MUSTARD SAUCE

PREPARATION TIME *5 minutes* **COOKING TIME** *10 minutes* **SERVES 4** *Makes about 1⅓ cups*

1 tbsp butter
2 tbsp all-purpose flour
1¼ cups full-fat milk
1–2 tbsp wholegrain mustard,
or to taste

Sea salt & freshly ground
black pepper

1 Melt the butter in a saucepan, add the flour and cook gently for 1 minute, stirring. Remove the pan from the heat and gradually stir or whisk in the milk.

2 Return the pan to the heat and heat gently, stirring or whisking continuously, until the sauce comes to a boil and thickens. Simmer gently for 2–3 minutes, stirring.

3 Stir in the mustard and reheat gently until hot, stirring. Season to taste with salt and pepper. Serve hot.

SERVING SUGGESTIONS *Serve with broiled or pan-fried chicken or turkey breast portions, good-quality sausages, pork chops, or steaks, or braised rabbit portions.*
VARIATION *Use Dijon mustard in place of wholegrain mustard.*
COOK'S TIP *Wholegrain or Meaux mustard is a coarse-grained mustard prepared from mixed mustard seeds. It has a grainy texture and a fairly hot, fruity, spicy taste.*

133 CREAMY TARRAGON SAUCE

PREPARATION TIME *5 minutes* **COOKING TIME** *10 minutes* **SERVES 4** *Makes about 1½ cups*

4 tsp butter
3 tbsp all-purpose flour
1¼ cups full-fat milk
4 tbsp heavy cream

1½ tsp French or Dijon
  mustard
1 tbsp chopped fresh
  tarragon

Sea salt & freshly ground
  black pepper

1 Melt the butter in a small saucepan, stir in the flour and cook, stirring, for 1 minute. Remove the pan from the heat and gradually stir or whisk in the milk and cream.

2 Return the pan to the heat and heat gently, stirring or whisking continuously, until the sauce comes to a boil and thickens. Simmer gently for 2–3 minutes, stirring.

3 Stir in the mustard and chopped tarragon, and season to taste with salt and pepper. Serve hot.

SERVING SUGGESTIONS *Serve with broiled or pan-fried lamb steaks, chicken breasts, or turkey breast steaks, or with roast or braised pheasant or partridge.*

VARIATIONS *Use vegetable stock in place of ⅔ cup milk. Use wholegrain mustard in place of French or Dijon mustard. Use 2–3 tbsp chopped fresh parsley in place of tarragon. Stir ½ cup finely grated cheddar cheese into the sauce just before serving, if desired.*

COOK'S TIP *Fresh tarragon has a sweet and spicy flavor which is well suited to serving with chicken, turkey, and lamb. Choose French tarragon, which is the more common type, rather than Russian tarragon; French tarragon has a much better flavor.*

134 CREAMY BLUE CHEESE SAUCE

PREPARATION TIME *10 minutes* **COOKING TIME** *20 minutes* **SERVES 4** *Makes about 1⅓ cups*

1 tbsp butter
1 small onion, finely chopped
1 stick of celery, finely
  chopped
2 tbsp medium-dry sherry
scant 1 cup crème
  fraîche or heavy cream

¾ cup blue cheese, such
  as Stilton, crumbled
1–2 tbsp chopped fresh
  parsley or snipped
  fresh chives
Sea salt & freshly ground
  black pepper

1 Melt the butter in a small saucepan, add the onion and celery and cook gently for about 10 minutes, or until softened.

2 Stir in the sherry and boil until reduced slightly. Stir in the crème fraîche or heavy cream, then bring gently to a boil and bubble for about 5 minutes, or until thickened slightly, stirring occasionally.

3 Stir in the blue cheese until melted, then stir in the chopped parsley or snipped chives. Season to taste with salt and pepper. Serve hot.

SERVING SUGGESTIONS *Serve with broiled or grilled beef or pork steaks, chicken drumsticks or thighs, or turkey breast steaks.*

135 SAGE AND RED ONION SAUCE

PREPARATION TIME *10 minutes* **COOKING TIME** *15 minutes* **SERVES 4–6** *Makes about 2¼ cups*

¼ cup butter
2 red onions, finely chopped
¼ cup all-purpose flour
⅔ cup milk

⅔ cup vegetable stock
*(see recipe on page
10)*, cooled
A squeeze of fresh lime juice
(optional)

1–2 tbsp chopped fresh sage
Sea salt & freshly ground
black pepper

1 Melt 2 tbsp butter in a skillet, add the onions and cook gently for about 10
minutes, or until softened. Remove the pan from the heat, set aside, and keep hot.
2 Meanwhile, place the remaining butter in a saucepan with the flour, milk, stock and
lime juice, if using. Heat gently, whisking continuously, until the sauce comes to a
boil and thickens. Simmer gently for 3–4 minutes, stirring.
3 Stir in the sautéed onions and chopped sage, and reheat gently until hot, stirring
continuously. Season to taste with salt and pepper. Serve hot.

SERVING SUGGESTIONS *Serve with pan-fried or roast chicken, duck, pheasant, or rabbit.*
VARIATION *Use regular onions in place of red onions.*

136 MUSTARD AND HORSERADISH SAUCE

PREPARATION TIME *5 minutes* **COOKING TIME** *10 minutes* **SERVES 4** *Makes about 1¼ cups*

1 tbsp butter
1 tbsp all-purpose flour
1¼ cups milk

2 tsp wholegrain mustard
2 tsp hot horseradish sauce

Sea salt & freshly ground
black pepper

1 Place the butter, flour, and milk in a saucepan. Heat gently, whisking continuously, until
the sauce comes to a boil and thickens. Simmer gently for 3–4 minutes, stirring.
2 Remove the pan from the heat and stir in the mustard, horseradish sauce, and
seasoning. Return the pan to the heat and reheat gently until hot, stirring. Serve hot.

SERVING SUGGESTIONS *Serve with pan-fried beef olives, or with broiled good-quality sausages, or
chicken or turkey breast portions.*

137 MUSTARD HERB SAUCE

PREPARATION TIME *5 minutes* **COOKING TIME** *10 minutes* **SERVES 4–6** *Makes about 1½ cups*

2 tbsp cornstarch
1 cup milk
⅔ cup vegetable stock
*(see recipe on page
10)*, cooled

1 tbsp wholegrain mustard
1 tsp dried mixed herbs
1 tsp clear honey
Sea salt & freshly ground
black pepper

1 In a saucepan, blend the cornstarch with a little of the milk until smooth. Stir in the
remaining milk and stock, then heat gently, stirring continuously, until the sauce comes
to a boil and thickens. Simmer gently for 2–3 minutes, stirring.
2 Stir in the mustard, dried herbs, honey, and seasoning and heat gently until hot, stirring.
Serve hot.

SERVING SUGGESTIONS *Serve with broiled or pan-fried bacon steaks or chicken drumsticks.*

138 SPICED GREEN LENTIL SAUCE

PREPARATION TIME *15 minutes* **COOKING TIME** *1 hour 20 minutes* **SERVES 6–8**

1 tbsp olive oil
1 onion, finely chopped
1 carrot, finely chopped
2 sticks of celery, finely
  chopped
1 tsp *each* of ground cumin,
  ground coriander, ground
  allspice, & cayenne pepper

1 cup green lentils
2¼ cups vegetable stock
  (see recipe on page 10)
3 tbsp medium sherry
Sea salt & freshly ground
  black pepper
2 tbsp chopped fresh
  flat-leaf parsley

1 Heat the oil in a saucepan, add the onion, carrot, and celery and cook gently for about
  10 minutes, or until softened.
2 Stir in the ground spices and cook for 1 minute, stirring. Add the lentils, stock, sherry,
  and seasoning and mix well.
3 Bring gently to a boil, then cover and simmer for about 1 hour, or until the lentils are
  cooked and soft, stirring occasionally.
4 Stir in the chopped parsley, and adjust the seasoning to taste. Serve hot.

SERVING SUGGESTIONS *Serve with North African-style grilled lamb or beef and vegetable kebabs.*
COOK'S TIP *If you prefer a smoother sauce, once the lentils are cooked and soft, remove the pan from
the heat and stir in the chopped parsley. Set aside to cool slightly, then purée briefly in a blender or
food processor. Return the sauce to the rinsed-out pan and reheat gently until hot, stirring.*

139 TOMATO AND GARLIC SAUCE

PREPARATION TIME *5 minutes* **COOKING TIME** *20 minutes* **SERVES 4**

14-oz can chopped tomatoes
1 small onion, finely chopped
2 cloves garlic, crushed
1 tbsp tomato paste

1 tbsp chopped fresh mixed
herbs, or 1 tsp dried
mixed herbs
A pinch of superfine sugar

Sea salt & freshly ground
black pepper

1 Place the tomatoes, onion, garlic, tomato paste, chopped or dried herbs, sugar, and seasoning in a saucepan and mix well.
2 Bring to a boil, then reduce the heat and simmer, uncovered, for 15–20 minutes, or until the sauce is reduced and fairly thick, stirring occasionally.
3 Adjust the seasoning to taste. Serve hot.

SERVING SUGGESTIONS *Serve with char-grilled or grilled lamb, beef, or pork kebabs.*
VARIATION *Use 1 small red onion or 2–3 shallots in place of regular onion.*

140 WILD MUSHROOM AND LEEK SAUCE

PREPARATION TIME *10 minutes* **COOKING TIME** *10 minutes* **SERVES 4**

¼ cup butter
1 small leek, washed &
finely chopped
2 cloves garlic, crushed

4 cups fresh mixed wild
mushrooms, sliced
2 cups chestnut or brown
cap mushrooms, sliced

2 tbsp dry sherry
3 tbsp chopped fresh parsley
Sea salt & freshly ground
black pepper

1 Melt the butter in a skillet, add the leek and garlic and sauté for 2 minutes. Add all the mushrooms and sauté for 4–5 minutes.
2 Add the sherry and cook over a fairly high heat for 2–3 minutes, stirring frequently, until some of the liquid has evaporated and the mushrooms are thoroughly cooked.
3 Stir in the chopped parsley and season to taste with salt and pepper. Serve hot.

SERVING SUGGESTIONS *Serve with pan-fried or roast chicken, turkey, duck, pheasant, or partridge.*
VARIATIONS *Use closed cup or button mushrooms in place of wild mushrooms. Use 2 tbsp chopped fresh cilantro or oregano in place of parsley.*

141 CRIMSON CRANBERRY SAUCE

PREPARATION TIME *5 minutes, plus cooling* **COOKING TIME** *25–30 minutes* **SERVES 4–6**

2 cups fresh (or frozen,
defrosted) cranberries

1 apple, peeled,
cored, & finely chopped
⅔ cup water

1 cup light soft
brown sugar
1–2 tbsp ruby port wine

1 Place the cranberries and chopped apple in a saucepan with the water. Bring to a boil, then reduce the heat, cover, and simmer for 15–20 minutes, or until the fruit is soft, stirring once or twice.
2 Add the sugar, then cook gently, stirring continuously, until the sugar has dissolved. Stir in the port wine, remove the pan from the heat and set aside to cool. Serve warm or cold.

SERVING SUGGESTIONS *Serve with roast or broiled pork, chicken, or turkey.*
VARIATIONS *Use brandy or sherry in place of port. Use 1 ripe pear in place of apple.*

SAUCES FOR MEAT, POULTRY, AND GAME

142 ARAGULA PESTO

PREPARATION TIME *10 minutes* **COOKING TIME** *N/A* **SERVES 4–6** *Makes about 1 cup*

2 cups aragula leaves
½ cup flaked (blanched)
  almonds
1 clove garlic, crushed
  (optional)

7 tbsp extra-virgin olive oil
½ cup fresh Parmesan
  cheese, finely grated

Sea salt & freshly ground
  black pepper

1 Place the aragula in a mortar with the almonds, garlic, if using, and 1 tbsp of the oil.
  Pound or grind with a pestle to make a paste. Gradually work in the remaining oil,
  then stir in the Parmesan cheese and season to taste with salt and pepper.
2 Alternatively, put the aragula, almonds, garlic, if using, and olive oil in a small blender
  or food processor, and blend to form a fairly smooth paste. Add the Parmesan and
  seasoning, and process briefly to mix.
3 Store the pesto in a screw-topped jar, covered with a thin layer of oil, in the refrigerator
  for up to 1 week. Serve cold.

SERVING SUGGESTIONS *Serve with broiled or pan-fried pork chops, or chicken, or turkey breast portions.*

143 THAI-SPICED ~~DIPPING~~ SAUCE

MARINATE (handwritten)

PREPARATION TIME *10 minutes* **COOKING TIME** *N/A* **SERVES 4** *Makes about ⅔ cup*

-or maple syrup (handwritten)

3 scallions, finely chopped
2 tbsp light soy sauce
3 tbsp fresh lemon or
  lime juice
2 tbsp medium chili sauce
  THAI (handwritten)

~~½ tsp Thai 7-spice~~
~~seasoning, or to taste~~
1 tbsp chopped fresh
  cilantro
½ TSP GARLIC (handwritten)
½ TSP GINGER (handwritten)

1–2 tsp light soft brown
  sugar, or to taste
Freshly ground black pepper
  (optional)

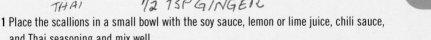

1 Place the scallions in a small bowl with the soy sauce, lemon or lime juice, chili sauce,
  and Thai seasoning and mix well.
2 Stir in the chopped cilantro, then stir in the sugar. Season to taste with black pepper, if
  using. Serve cold as a dipping sauce.

- BLEND ALL TOGETHER. MARINATE BEEF FOR 1HR (handwritten)

SERVING SUGGESTIONS *Serve with cooked Thai beef, pork, chicken, or turkey dishes.*

144 FRESH HERB BUTTER

PREPARATION TIME *10 minutes, plus chilling* **COOKING TIME** *N/A* **SERVES 4–6**

½ cup unsalted butter
  (at room temperature)
2 tbsp finely chopped fresh
  parsley

2 tbsp finely snipped fresh
  chives
2 tsp fresh lemon juice

Sea salt & freshly ground
  black pepper, to taste

1 Place the butter in a small bowl and beat until softened. Add the chopped herbs, lemon
  juice, and salt and pepper to taste and beat until well mixed.
2 Turn the flavored butter onto a piece of plastic wrap and shape into a log. Wrap the
  flavored butter in the plastic wrap, then chill in the refrigerator for at least 1 hour before
  serving. Cut into 4–6 even slices to serve. Serve chilled.

SERVING SUGGESTIONS *Serve a slice of flavored butter on top of char-grilled or pan-fried beef, lamb or
pork steaks, chicken breasts, or turkey breast steaks.*

145 GARLIC BUTTER

PREPARATION TIME *10 minutes, plus chilling* **COOKING TIME** *N/A* **SERVES 4–6**

½ cup unsalted butter (at room temperature)

2 cloves garlic, crushed

2–3 tsp finely chopped fresh parsley or finely snipped fresh chives

2 tsp fresh lemon juice

Sea salt & freshly ground black pepper, to taste

1 Place the butter in a small bowl and beat until softened. Add the crushed garlic, chopped herbs, lemon juice, and salt and pepper to taste, and beat until well mixed.

2 Turn the flavored butter onto a piece of plastic wrap and shape into a log. Wrap the flavored butter in the plastic wrap, then chill in the refrigerator for at least 1 hour before serving. Cut into 4–6 even slices to serve. Serve chilled.

SERVING SUGGESTIONS *Serve a slice of flavored butter on top of broiled, grilled or pan-fried beef, lamb, chicken, or turkey.*

146 LEMON BUTTER

PREPARATION TIME *10 minutes, plus chilling* **COOKING TIME** *N/A* **SERVES 4–6**

½ cup unsalted butter (at room temperature)

Finely grated zest of 1 lemon

2 tsp fresh lemon juice

Freshly ground black pepper, to taste

1 Place the butter in a small bowl and beat until softened. Add the lemon zest, lemon juice, and black pepper to taste, and beat until well mixed.

2 Turn the flavored butter onto a piece of plastic wrap and shape into a log. Wrap the flavored butter in the plastic wrap, then chill in the refrigerator for at least 1 hour before serving. Cut into 4–6 even slices to serve. Serve chilled.

SERVING SUGGESTIONS *Serve a slice of flavored butter on top of char-grilled or pan-fried beef steaks or chicken breasts.*

VARIATION *Use lime zest and juice in place of lemon zest and juice.*

147 SUN-DRIED TOMATO AND BASIL BUTTER

PREPARATION TIME *10 minutes, plus chilling* **COOKING TIME** *N/A* **SERVES 4–6**

½ cup unsalted butter (at room temperature)

⅓ cup sun-dried tomatoes in oil (drained weight), drained, patted dry, & finely chopped

2 tbsp finely chopped fresh basil

Garlic salt & freshly ground black pepper, to taste

1 Place the butter in a small bowl and beat until softened. Add the sun-dried tomatoes, chopped basil, and garlic salt and black pepper to taste, and beat until well mixed.

2 Turn the flavored butter onto a piece of plastic wrap and shape into a log. Wrap the flavored butter in the plastic wrap, then chill in the refrigerator for at least 1 hour before serving. Cut into 4–6 even slices to serve. Serve chilled.

SERVING SUGGESTIONS *Serve a slice of flavored butter on top of broiled pork steaks or chops.*

148 CAJUN-SPICED BUTTER

PREPARATION TIME *10 minutes, plus chilling* **COOKING TIME** *N/A* **SERVES 4–6**

½ cup unsalted butter
(at room temperature)

2 tsp Cajun seasoning mix,
or to taste

Freshly ground black pepper,
to taste

1 Place the butter in a small bowl and beat until softened. Add the Cajun seasoning, and black pepper to taste, and beat until well mixed.
2 Turn the flavored butter onto a piece of plastic wrap and shape into a log. Wrap the flavored butter in the plastic wrap, then chill in the refrigerator for at least 1 hour before serving. Cut into 4–6 even slices to serve. Serve chilled.

SERVING SUGGESTIONS *Serve a slice of flavored butter on top of broiled or pan-fried home-made burgers, chicken breasts, or turkey breast steaks.*

149 HOT HORSERADISH BUTTER

PREPARATION TIME *10 minutes, plus chilling* **COOKING TIME** *N/A* **SERVES 4–6**

½ cup unsalted butter
(at room temperature)
1½ tbsp hot horseradish
sauce

2 tbsp finely snipped
fresh chives
Freshly ground black pepper,
to taste

1 Place the butter in a small bowl and beat until softened. Add the horseradish sauce, snipped chives, and black pepper to taste, and beat until well mixed.
2 Turn the flavored butter onto a piece of plastic wrap and shape into a log. Wrap the flavored butter in the plastic wrap, then chill in the refrigerator for at least 1 hour before serving. Cut into 4–6 even slices to serve. Serve chilled.

SERVING SUGGESTIONS *Serve a slice of flavored butter on top of broiled or pan-fried beef, pork, or venison steaks, or turkey breast steaks.*

150 MAITRE D'HOTEL (PARSLEY) BUTTER

PREPARATION TIME *10 minutes, plus chilling* **COOKING TIME** *N/A* **SERVES 4–6**

½ cup unsalted butter
(at room temperature)
2 tbsp finely chopped
fresh parsley

2 tsp fresh lemon juice
Sea salt & freshly ground
black pepper, to taste

1 Place the butter in a small bowl and beat until softened. Add the chopped parsley, lemon juice, and salt and pepper to taste, and beat until well mixed.
2 Turn the flavored butter onto a piece of plastic wrap and shape into a log. Wrap the flavored butter in the plastic wrap, then chill in the refrigerator for at least 1 hour before serving. Cut into 4–6 even slices to serve. Serve chilled.

SERVING SUGGESTIONS *Serve a slice of flavored butter on top of char-grilled or pan-fried lamb or pork steaks, or chicken or turkey breast portions.*

SALSAS AND RELISHES

Salsas and relishes not only add that wonderful finishing touch to many meals, they also add delicious texture, flavor, and color to broiled, pan-fried or oven-baked meat, poultry, fish, and shellfish.

In addition, they make great summertime foods, ideal for barbecues and eating al fresco. Simple to prepare, many are best made in advance and then let stand for a while before serving, so the flavors develop. This in turn gives you the time to relax and mingle with your friends.

Choose from a wide variety of flavorful recipes, including Salsa Verde, Red Onion Salsa, Hot and Spicy Salsa, Mango Chutney Salsa, Exotic Peach Salsa, Chunky Chili Salsa, Beet and Horseradish Salsa, Red Hot Relish, Chunky Corn Relish, Sweet Chili Relish, and Red Onion Marmalade.

151 SALSA VERDE

PREPARATION TIME *10 minutes, plus standing* **COOKING TIME** *N/A* **SERVES 4**

1 small onion, finely chopped
2 cloves garlic, crushed
4 tbsp chopped fresh parsley
2 tbsp chopped fresh mint
1 tbsp snipped fresh chives

1 tbsp capers, drained
  & chopped
4 tbsp extra-virgin olive oil
2 tbsp fresh lemon or lime
  juice

1 tsp Dijon mustard
A few drops of Tabasco
  sauce, or to taste
Sea salt & freshly ground
  black pepper

1 Place the onion, garlic, chopped herbs, and capers in a small bowl and stir to mix. Add the olive oil, lemon or lime juice, and mustard, and mix well. Add the Tabasco sauce and salt and pepper to taste.

2 Cover and let stand at room temperature for about 30 minutes before serving, so the flavors develop.

SERVING SUGGESTIONS *Serve with broiled lamb, pork, or beef steaks. Alternatively, serve with broiled monkfish or rainbow trout, and roast mixed vegetables.*

VARIATION *Omit the Tabasco sauce and add 1 seeded and finely chopped fresh red or green chili, if preferred.*

COOK'S TIP *If you prefer a smoother salsa, simply process all the ingredients together in a small blender or food processor until thoroughly combined.*

152 PLUM TOMATO AND BASIL SALSA

PREPARATION TIME *15 minutes, plus standing* **COOKING TIME** *N/A* **SERVES 4**

1½ lb ripe plum tomatoes,
  skinned, seeded,
  & finely chopped
2 scallions, chopped
1 large clove garlic, crushed

1 tbsp olive oil
1 tbsp sun-dried tomato
  paste
1–2 tsp balsamic vinegar
2–3 tbsp chopped fresh basil

Sea salt & freshly ground
  black pepper

1 Place the tomatoes, scallions, garlic, oil, tomato paste, balsamic vinegar, chopped basil, and seasoning in a bowl and stir to mix well.

2 Cover and let stand at room temperature for about 30 minutes before serving, so the flavors develop.

SERVING SUGGESTIONS *Serve with broiled or grilled lamb chops, beef kebabs, or chicken drumsticks, or with char-grilled salmon or tuna steaks.*

VARIATIONS *Use 1–2 shallots in place of scallions. Use regular tomato paste in place of sun-dried tomato paste. Use chopped fresh flat-leaf parsley or cilantro in place of basil.*

COOK'S TIPS *Choose ripe plum tomatoes for this recipe to achieve the best flavor. Alternatively, use ripe vine-ripened tomatoes if plum tomatoes are not available.*

See recipe 155 on page 104 for instructions on how to skin and seed tomatoes.

153 MINT SALSA

PREPARATION TIME *15 minutes, plus standing* **COOKING TIME** *N/A* **SERVES 4**

1 lb vine-ripened tomatoes, skinned, seeded, & finely chopped

2 shallots, finely chopped

1 clove garlic, crushed

1 tbsp olive oil

1 tsp balsamic vinegar

2 tbsp chopped fresh mint

Sea salt & freshly ground black pepper

1 Place the tomatoes, shallots, garlic, oil, vinegar, and chopped mint in a bowl and mix well. Season to taste with salt and pepper.

2 Cover and let stand at room temperature for about 30 minutes before serving, so the flavors develop.

SERVING SUGGESTIONS *Serve with broiled lamb and vegetable kebabs, or with broiled or grilled beef steaks, pork chops, or lamb sausages.*

VARIATIONS *Use 1 small red onion or 2–3 scallions in place of shallots. Use chopped fresh basil or cilantro in place of mint.*

COOK'S TIP *Remove fresh mint leaves from their stems, then shake the leaves quickly under cold running water. Pat dry on paper towels, then chop finely on a chopping board using either a sharp kitchen knife or a mezzaluna – a curved, crescent-shaped blade with two handles which rocks backward and forward over the herbs, chopping them in the process.*

154 HOT AND SPICY SALSA

PREPARATION TIME *15 minutes, plus cooling & standing* **COOKING TIME** *15 minutes* **SERVES 6**

2 red bell peppers

2 yellow bell peppers

1 large fresh red chili

1 small red onion, finely chopped

2 tbsp extra-virgin olive oil

2 tsp red wine vinegar

2 tbsp chopped fresh cilantro

1–2 tsp Tabasco sauce, or to taste

Sea salt & freshly ground black pepper

1 Preheat the broiler to high. Cut the bell peppers and chili in half lengthwise and place them, cut-side down, on the rack in a broiler pan. Place under the hot broiler for about 10–15 minutes, or until the skins are blackened and charred.

2 Remove the broiler pan from the heat, cover the bell peppers and chili with a clean, damp dish towel and let cool.

3 Once cool, remove and discard the skin, core, and seeds from the bell peppers and chili, then finely chop the flesh, and place it in a bowl.

4 Add the onion, olive oil, vinegar, and chopped cilantro and mix well. Stir in the Tabasco sauce and salt and pepper to taste, mixing well.

5 Cover and let stand at room temperature for about 1 hour before serving, so the flavors develop.

SERVING SUGGESTIONS *Serve with broiled or oven-baked cod or haddock steaks, or monkfish tail. Alternatively, serve with broiled or grilled chicken breast joints, or pan-fried polenta slices.*

155 RED ONION SALSA

PREPARATION TIME *15 minutes, plus standing* **COOKING TIME** *N/A* **SERVES 4**

3 ripe tomatoes
2 tbsp tomato juice or
   passata

1 tbsp olive oil
1 red onion, finely chopped
2 tsp horseradish sauce

1 tbsp chopped fresh parsley
Sea salt & freshly ground
   black pepper

1 Using a sharp knife, cut a small cross in the base of each tomato. Place the tomatoes
in a bowl, cover them with boiling water and leave for about 30 seconds, or until the
skins split.

2 Using a slotted spoon, remove the tomatoes from the bowl and plunge into cold water,
then drain well.

3 Peel off and discard the skins, then halve the tomatoes and remove and discard
the seeds. Finely chop the flesh and place it in a bowl.

4 Add the tomato juice or passata, olive oil, onion, horseradish sauce, and chopped
parsley to the tomato flesh, and stir to mix well. Season to taste with salt and pepper.

5 Cover and let stand at room temperature for about 1 hour before serving, so the flavors
develop.

SERVING SUGGESTIONS *Serve with broiled good-quality pork or lamb sausages. Alternatively, serve with
broiled or grilled salmon or tuna steaks, or with broiled or pan-fried field (portobello) mushrooms.*
VARIATIONS *Use plum or vine-ripened tomatoes in place of regular tomatoes. Use a regular onion in
place of red onion. Add ½ seeded red bell pepper, finely chopped, with the onion, if desired.*
COOK'S TIP *For extra heat and flavor, choose hot horseradish sauce for this recipe.*

156 MANGO CHUTNEY SALSA

PREPARATION TIME *25 minutes, plus standing* **COOKING TIME** *N/A* **SERVES 6**

2 ripe mangoes
4 scallions, finely chopped
2–3 tsp fresh lime juice
3 tbsp sweet mango chutney

2 tbsp chopped fresh
  cilantro
Freshly ground black pepper,
  to taste

1 Peel, pit, and finely chop the mangoes. Put the mango flesh in a bowl, add the scallions and lime juice, and mix well.
2 Add the mango chutney, cilantro, and black pepper to taste, and stir to mix well.
3 Cover and let stand at room temperature for about 1 hour before serving, so the flavors develop.

SERVING SUGGESTIONS *Serve with pan-fried or oven-baked chicken breast joints or turkey breast steaks.*

157 TASTY TOMATO SALSA

PREPARATION TIME *15 minutes, plus standing* **COOKING TIME** *N/A* **SERVES 4**

1 lb vine-ripened tomatoes,
  skinned, seeded, & finely
chopped

4 sun-dried tomatoes in oil,
  drained, patted dry, &
  finely chopped
2 shallots, finely chopped
1 clove garlic, crushed

1 tbsp olive oil
1–2 tbsp chopped fresh basil
Sea salt & freshly ground
  black pepper

1 Place the fresh tomatoes, sun-dried tomatoes, shallots, garlic, olive oil, chopped basil, and seasoning in a bowl, and stir to mix well.
2 Cover and let stand at room temperature for about 1 hour before serving, so the flavors develop.

SERVING SUGGESTIONS *Serve with broiled or pan-fried cod steaks, monkfish tail, tiger prawns, or scallops. Alternatively, serve with broiled halloumi or goat's cheese.*

158 SPICED TOMATO SALSA

PREPARATION TIME *10 minutes, plus standing* **COOKING TIME** *N/A* **SERVES 4**

2 shallots, finely chopped
1 clove garlic, crushed
1 fresh red chili, seeded
  & finely chopped

1 lb ripe plum tomatoes,
  skinned, seeded, & finely
  chopped
1 tbsp olive oil
1 tbsp chopped fresh
  cilantro

1 tbsp chopped fresh parsley
A squeeze of fresh lime juice
A pinch of superfine sugar
Sea salt & freshly ground
  black pepper

1 Place the shallots, garlic, chili, tomatoes, olive oil, chopped herbs, lime juice, and sugar in a bowl, and stir until thoroughly mixed. Season to taste with salt and pepper.
2 Cover and let stand at room temperature for about 30 minutes before serving, so the flavors develop.

SERVING SUGGESTIONS *Serve with broiled chicken drumsticks or stir-fried turkey strips. Alternatively, serve with broiled cod or haddock fillets or goujons.*

159 CHUNKY CHILI SALSA

PREPARATION TIME *15 minutes, plus cooling* **COOKING TIME** *15 minutes* **SERVES 4**

1 tbsp olive oil
4 shallots, finely chopped
1 clove garlic, crushed
1 small fresh red chili,
   seeded & finely chopped

1 lb ripe tomatoes, skinned,
   seeded, & chopped
6 sun-dried tomatoes in oil,
   drained, patted dry, &
   finely chopped

1 tsp dried herbes
   de Provence
Sea salt & freshly ground
   black pepper

1 Heat the oil in a saucepan, add the shallots, garlic, and chili and cook gently for about 10 minutes, or until softened.

2 Add the fresh tomatoes, sun-dried tomatoes, dried herbs, and seasoning, and stir to mix. Cook gently for a further 5 minutes.

3 Remove the pan from the heat and set aside to cool. Adjust the seasoning to taste. Serve at room temperature, or cover and chill before serving, if desired.

SERVING SUGGESTIONS *Serve with baked stuffed bell peppers or zucchini. Alternatively, serve with broiled haddock or salmon steaks, or chicken kebabs.*

160 ROASTED BELL PEPPER SALSA

PREPARATION TIME *15 minutes, plus cooling & standing* **COOKING TIME** *20 minutes* **SERVES 4–6**

2 red bell peppers
1 yellow bell pepper
1 small red onion, thinly
   sliced
3 plum or vine-ripened
   tomatoes, skinned, seeded,
   & finely chopped

1 clove garlic, crushed
⅓ cup pitted black olives,
   finely chopped
2–3 tsp olive oil
1 tbsp chopped fresh basil
1 tbsp chopped fresh
   flat-leaf parsley

Sea salt & freshly ground
   black pepper

1 Preheat the broiler to high. Cut the bell peppers in half and place them, cut-side down, on the rack in a broiler pan. Place the bell peppers under the broiler for 10–15 minutes, or until the skin is blackened and charred.

2 Remove from the broiler, cover the bell peppers with a clean, damp dish towel, and set aside to cool.

3 Meanwhile, place the onion slices on the rack in the broiler pan. Broil for about 5 minutes, or until softened, turning once. Remove from the broiler and cool slightly.

4 Remove and discard the skin, core, and seeds from the bell peppers and finely chop the flesh. Finely chop the onion slices.

5 Place the chopped bell pepper flesh, onion, tomatoes, garlic, and olives in a bowl, and stir to mix. Add the olive oil and chopped herbs and mix well. Season to taste.

6 Cover and let stand at room temperature for about 1 hour before serving, so the flavors develop.

SERVING SUGGESTIONS *Serve with broiled or pan-fried beef kebabs or good-quality sausages, or with broiled haddock or tuna steaks.*
VARIATIONS *Use 2–3 shallots in place of red onion. Use chopped fresh oregano, marjoram, or cilantro in place of basil.*

161 PINEAPPLE AND GINGER SALSA

PREPARATION TIME *25 minutes, plus standing* **COOKING TIME** *N/A* **SERVES 4**

2 cups prepared fresh
   pineapple, finely chopped
2 tsp finely chopped (peeled)
   fresh root ginger

1 tbsp clear honey
1 tsp fresh lime juice
2 tbsp chopped fresh
   cilantro

Freshly ground black pepper,
   to taste

1 Place the pineapple and ginger in a bowl and stir to mix. Add the honey and lime juice
and toss to mix. Stir in the chopped cilantro, and season to taste with black pepper.
2 Cover and let stand at room temperature for about 30 minutes before serving, so the
flavors develop. Drain off any excess juices before serving, if desired.

SERVING SUGGESTIONS *Serve with char-grilled chicken or duck breasts, or salmon or tuna steaks.*
VARIATION *Use prepared fresh mango in place of pineapple.*

162 APRICOT AND GINGER SALSA

PREPARATION TIME *20 minutes, plus standing* **COOKING TIME** *N/A* **SERVES 4**

1⅓ cups ready-to-eat dried
   apricots, finely chopped
Finely grated zest & juice
   of ½ lime
2 tsp finely chopped (peeled)
   fresh root ginger

1 tbsp clear honey, or to taste
2 tsp olive oil
2 tbsp chopped fresh
   cilantro
Sea salt & freshly ground
   black pepper

4 scallions, finely chopped

1 Place the apricots in a bowl with the lime zest and juice and mix well. Add the ginger,
honey, olive oil, and chopped cilantro, and stir to mix. Season to taste.
2 Cover and leave to stand at room temperature for about 30 minutes, so the flavors
develop. Just before serving, stir in the scallions.

SERVING SUGGESTIONS *Serve with broiled or pan-fried pork or ham steaks, or chicken thighs.*

163 EXOTIC PEACH SALSA

PREPARATION TIME *15 minutes, plus standing* **COOKING TIME** *N/A* **SERVES 4**

3 ripe peaches, peeled,
   pitted, & finely chopped
   *(see Cook's Tip on recipe
   164)*
4 scallions, finely chopped

½ seeded yellow bell pepper,
   finely chopped
1 tbsp fresh lime juice
1 tbsp chopped fresh
   cilantro

Freshly ground black pepper,
   to taste

1 Place the peaches, scallions, yellow bell pepper, lime juice, and chopped coriander in a
small bowl and mix well. Season to taste with black pepper.
2 Cover and let stand at room temperature for about 1 hour before serving, so the
flavors develop.

SERVING SUGGESTIONS *Serve with pan-fried or roast chicken, duck, or pheasant.*

164 PEACH AND MELON SALSA

PREPARATION TIME *25 minutes, plus standing* **COOKING TIME** *N/A* **SERVES 6**

3 ripe peaches, peeled,
  pitted, & finely chopped
  (see Cook's Tip)
1½ cups honeydew melon
  (peeled, seeded weight),
  finely chopped

½ red bell pepper, seeded &
  finely chopped
1 small fresh red chili,
  seeded & finely chopped
1 tbsp fresh lemon juice
2 tsp clear honey

2 tbsp chopped fresh
  cilantro
Freshly ground black pepper,
  to taste

1 Place the peaches, melon, red bell pepper, and chili in a bowl, and stir to mix. Add the lemon juice and honey and toss to mix well. Stir in the chopped cilantro, and season to taste with black pepper.

2 Cover and let stand at room temperature for about 1 hour before serving, so the flavors develop.

SERVING SUGGESTIONS *Serve with broiled or grilled pork, chicken, or turkey kebabs, or haddock or tuna steaks.*

COOK'S TIP *To peel fresh peaches, place the peaches in a heatproof bowl and cover with boiling water. Let stand for about 1 minute, then remove the peaches using a slotted spoon, and plunge them into cold water. Drain well, then peel off the skins using a small, sharp knife.*

165 PINEAPPLE AND CORIANDER SALSA

PREPARATION TIME *25 minutes, plus standing* **COOKING TIME** *N/A* **SERVES 6**

1¾ cups prepared fresh
  pineapple, finely chopped
6 scallions, finely chopped
½ small orange or yellow bell
  pepper, seeded & finely
  chopped

2 tsp finely grated (peeled)
  fresh root ginger
1 tbsp freshly squeezed
  orange or pineapple juice
1 tbsp olive oil
1 tsp clear honey

1 tbsp chopped fresh
  cilantro
Freshly ground black pepper,
  to taste

1 Place the pineapple, scallions, and orange or yellow bell pepper in a bowl, and mix well. Place the fresh ginger, orange or pineapple juice, olive oil, honey, and chopped coriander in a separate small bowl, and whisk together until well mixed.

2 Pour the fruit juice mixture over the chopped pineapple and vegetables and toss to mix well. Season to taste with black pepper.

3 Cover and let stand at room temperature for about 30 minutes before serving, so the flavors develop.

SERVING SUGGESTIONS *Serve with broiled or grilled pork, chicken, or lamb kebabs, or chicken or duck portions.*

VARIATIONS *Use canned (drained) pineapple in place of fresh pineapple. Use 1 small red onion or 2–3 shallots in place of scallions.*

166 MANGO SALSA

PREPARATION TIME *10 minutes, plus standing* **COOKING TIME** *N/A* **SERVES 4**

1 large ripe mango, peeled,
pitted, & finely chopped
¼ small cucumber, finely
chopped

2–3 scallions, finely
chopped
1–2 tbsp chopped fresh
cilantro

Sea salt & freshly ground
black pepper

1 Place the mango, cucumber, scallions, and chopped coriander in a bowl, and stir to mix
thoroughly. Season to taste with salt and pepper.

2 Cover and let stand at room temperature for about 30 minutes before serving, so the
flavors develop.

SERVING SUGGESTIONS *Serve with broiled or grilled chicken drumsticks. Alternatively, serve with
char-grilled salmon or tuna steaks.*

VARIATION *Use 1 small fresh pineapple in place of mango.*

COOK'S TIPS *When buying mangoes, choose sweet-smelling fruits with tight, smooth, unblemished
skins, that give slightly when pressed gently.*

*For this recipe, the cucumber can be peeled, if preferred. However, leaving the peel on the cucumber
will add extra texture and color to this salsa.*

167 RUBY GRAPEFRUIT SALSA

PREPARATION TIME *25 minutes, plus standing* **COOKING TIME** *N/A* **SERVES 4**

1 ruby (or pink) grapefruit
1 large ripe mango, peeled, pitted, & finely chopped
Juice of 1 lime
4 tsp clear honey
1 small fresh red chili, seeded & finely chopped
1 tbsp extra-virgin olive oil
2 scallions, finely chopped
2–3 tbsp snipped fresh chives
Freshly ground black pepper (optional), to taste

1 Peel and segment the grapefruit, then chop the segments and place in a bowl.
2 Add the mango, lime juice, honey, chili, and olive oil, and stir to mix well.
3 Cover and let stand at room temperature for about 1 hour, so the flavors develop.
4 Just before serving, drain off the excess juices, then stir the scallions and snipped chives into the salsa. Season to taste with black pepper, if desired.

SERVING SUGGESTIONS *Serve with roast beef, lamb, turkey, or chicken. Alternatively, serve with broiled beef kebabs, or good-quality beef or lamb sausages.*
VARIATIONS *Use 1–2 oranges in place of grapefruit. Use 1 small fresh pineapple in place of mango. Use chopped fresh cilantro or flat-leaf parsley in place of chives.*

168 TROPICAL SALSA

PREPARATION TIME *20 minutes, plus standing* **COOKING TIME** *N/A* **SERVES 6**

1⅓ cups prepared fresh pineapple, finely chopped
1 ripe nectarine or peach, peeled, pitted, & finely chopped
1 small ripe papaya, peeled, seeded, & finely chopped
1 small yellow or red bell pepper, seeded, & finely chopped
1 tbsp clear honey
1 tbsp fresh lime or lemon juice
2 tbsp chopped fresh cilantro
Freshly ground black pepper, to taste

1 Place the pineapple, nectarine or peach, papaya, and yellow or red bell pepper in a bowl, and stir to mix well.
2 Combine the honey and lime or lemon juice in a separate small bowl. Drizzle the honey mixture over the chopped fruit, add the chopped cilantro, and toss together to mix well. Season to taste with black pepper.
3 Cover and let stand at room temperature for 30 minutes before serving, so the flavors develop.

SERVING SUGGESTIONS *Serve with broiled or oven-baked gammon steaks, chicken or duck breasts, or cod or salmon fillets.*
VARIATIONS *Use ripe mango in place of pineapple. Use chopped flat-leaf parsley in place of cilantro.*

169 SPICY MELON SALSA

PREPARATION TIME *20 minutes, plus standing* **COOKING TIME** *N/A* **SERVES 6**

1 cantaloupe or Galia melon
4 scallions, finely chopped
1 small yellow bell pepper,
  seeded & finely chopped
1 fresh green chili, seeded
  & finely chopped
Juice of ½ lime

2 tsp hot chili sauce, or
  to taste
1 tbsp chopped fresh
  cilantro
1 tbsp chopped fresh mint
Freshly ground black pepper,
  to taste

1 Peel, seed, and finely chop the melon and place it in a bowl. Add the scallions,
yellow bell pepper, and green chlli, and stir to mix.

2 Add the lime juice, chili sauce, and chopped herbs, and toss to mix well. Season to taste
with black pepper.

3 Cover and let stand at room temperature for about 1 hour before serving, so the
flavors develop.

SERVING SUGGESTIONS *Serve with char-grilled tuna or salmon steaks, or with broiled or grilled chicken
or turkey drumsticks. This salsa is also good served with cold cooked sliced cuts.*

COOK'S TIP *When preparing fresh chilies, wear disposable gloves or wash your hands thoroughly afterwards, as the volatile oils in chilies may irritate the skin and eyes.*

170 AVOCADO SALSA

PREPARATION TIME *20 minutes, plus standing* **COOKING TIME** *N/A* **SERVES 6**

Juice of 1 lime
1 tbsp olive oil
2 ripe avocados

1 small fresh red or green
  chili, seeded & finely
  chopped
1 small red onion, finely
  chopped

2–3 tbsp chopped fresh
  cilantro
Sea salt & freshly ground
  black pepper

1 Place the lime juice and olive oil in a bowl, and whisk together to mix, then set aside.
Halve, pit, and peel the avocados, then finely chop the flesh. Add the avocado flesh to
the lime juice and oil mixture and toss gently to mix.

2 Add the chlli, red onion, and chopped cilantro and toss gently to mix, then season to
taste with salt and pepper.

3 Serve immediately, or cover and let stand at room temperature for no more than 30
minutes before serving.

SERVING SUGGESTIONS *Serve with broiled or pan-fried haddock cutlets, monkfish tail, or king prawns.*

COOK'S TIP *To test whether an avocado is ripe, cup the avocado lightly in your hand and squeeze it
very gently. If it gives slightly, it is ready to eat. Do not press the avocado with your fingertips, as this
will cause bruising.*

171 BEET AND HORSERADISH SALSA

PREPARATION TIME *20 minutes, plus standing* **COOKING TIME** *N/A* **SERVES 4–6**

12 oz cooked beet
1 small red onion, finely
   chopped

2 tbsp hot horseradish
   sauce, or to taste
3 tbsp finely snipped
   fresh chives

Sea salt & freshly ground
   black pepper

1 Peel the beet and finely chop the flesh. Place the beet flesh in a bowl with the red onion, and stir to mix.

2 Add the horseradish sauce and toss to mix well, then stir in the snipped chives. Season to taste with salt and pepper.

3 Cover and let stand at room temperature for about 30 minutes before serving, so the flavors develop.

SERVING SUGGESTIONS *Serve with broiled or grilled beef or lamb steaks, good-quality sausages, or chicken drumsticks or thighs.*

COOK'S TIP *There are two types of beet – long and globe-shaped. To prepare fresh beet, cut off the stalk approximately 1 inch above the root, and wash the beet carefully, avoiding tearing the skin. Cook in a pan of lightly salted, boiling water until tender – this may take from 40 minutes up to 1½ hours, depending on the size of the beets. Alternatively, beet can be baked in a preheated oven at 180°C/350°F/gas mark 4 for 2–3 hours. Peel, then slice or dice and serve hot; or let cool, then peel and use as required.*

172 TOMATO AND OLIVE SALSA

PREPARATION TIME *15 minutes, plus cooling* **COOKING TIME** *15 minutes* **SERVES 4**

1 tbsp olive oil
1 onion, finely chopped
1 clove garlic, crushed
1 lb ripe tomatoes, skinned,
   seeded, & finely chopped

2 sun-dried tomatoes in oil,
   drained, patted dry, &
   finely chopped
1 tbsp chopped fresh mixed
   herbs, or 1 tsp dried
   herbes de Provence

⅓ cup pitted black olives,
   finely chopped
Sea salt & freshly ground
   black pepper

1 Heat the oil in a saucepan, add the onion and garlic, and cook gently for about 10 minutes, or until softened.

2 Stir in the fresh tomatoes and sun-dried tomatoes, chopped fresh herbs or dried herbs, olives, and seasoning and cook gently for 2–3 minutes.

3 Remove the pan from the heat and let cool. Serve warm or at room temperature, or cover and chill in the refrigerator before serving.

SERVING SUGGESTIONS *Serve with broiled or pan-fried tuna or salmon steaks, or whole mackerel.*

VARIATION *Add 1 finely chopped (seeded) fresh red chili with the garlic, if desired.*

173 SPICED (BLACK-EYED) PEA SALSA

PREPARATION TIME *20 minutes, plus standing* **COOKING TIME** *N/A* **SERVES 4–6**

1 tbsp olive oil

1 tbsp clear honey

Finely grated zest & juice
of 1 lemon

2 tsp hot chili sauce, or
to taste

14-oz can black-eyed peas,
rinsed & drained

1 small red onion, finely
chopped

½ small yellow bell pepper,
seeded & finely chopped

1 fresh red chili, seeded
& finely chopped

1 clove garlic, crushed

2 tbsp chopped fresh
cilantro

Sea salt & freshly ground
black pepper

1 Place the olive oil, honey, lemon zest and juice, and chili sauce in a bowl, and whisk
together until thoroughly mixed.

2 Add the peas, onion, yellow bell pepper, chili, garlic, and chopped cilantro, and toss to
mix well. Season to taste with salt and pepper.

3 Cover and let stand at room temperature for about 1 hour before serving, so the
flavors develop.

SERVING SUGGESTIONS *Serve with broiled or grilled king prawns, or char-grilled salmon steaks.*

174 CUCUMBER RELISH

PREPARATION TIME *10 minutes* **COOKING TIME** *N/A* **SERVES 4–6**

½ cucumber, finely chopped
2 shallots, finely chopped
1 clove garlic, crushed

⅔ cup natural yogurt
1–2 tbsp chopped fresh mint

Sea salt & freshly ground
black pepper

1 Place the cucumber, shallots, garlic, yogurt, and chopped mint in a bowl and mix well.
2 Season to taste with salt and pepper. Serve immediately, or set aside for no more than 20 minutes before serving.

SERVING SUGGESTIONS *Serve with char-grilled whole sardines or mackerel.*
VARIATIONS *Use fresh basil in place of mint. Use 3–4 scallions in place of shallots.*

175 CUCUMBER AND MINT RELISH

PREPARATION TIME *10 minutes, plus chilling* **COOKING TIME** *N/A* **SERVES 4**

½ cucumber
1 shallot, finely chopped

2 tbsp chopped fresh mint
5 tbsp natural Greek yogurt

Sea salt & freshly ground
black pepper

1 Deseed and finely chop the cucumber and place it in a bowl.
2 Add the shallot, chopped mint, Greek yogurt, and seasoning and mix well. Add a little more yogurt, if desired.
3 Cover and chill for about 1 hour before serving, so the flavors develop.

SERVING SUGGESTIONS *Serve with thin slices or fillets of cold-smoked fish such as smoked salmon, trout, or mackerel.*
VARIATIONS *Use other chopped fresh herbs such as mixed herbs or cilantro in place of mint. Add 1 clove crushed garlic and a dash of fresh lime juice to the relish before chilling and serving, if desired.*

176 RED HOT RELISH

PREPARATION TIME *15 minutes, plus standing* **COOKING TIME** *N/A* **SERVES 4**

1 lb plum or vine-ripened
tomatoes, skinned, seeded,
& finely chopped
2 shallots, finely chopped
1 fresh red or green chili,
finely chopped
1 clove garlic, crushed

2 sun-dried tomatoes in oil,
drained, patted dry, &
finely chopped
1 tbsp olive oil
1 tbsp chopped fresh oregano
or marjoram

A few drops of Tabasco
sauce (optional)
Sea salt & freshly ground
black pepper

1 Place the tomatoes, shallots, chili, garlic, and sun-dried tomatoes in a bowl and stir well.
2 Add the olive oil, chopped oregano or marjoram, and Tabasco, if using, and mix well. Season to taste with salt and pepper.
3 Cover and let stand at room temperature for about 1 hour before serving, so the flavors develop.

SERVING SUGGESTIONS *Serve with broiled or oven-baked tuna or salmon steaks, or chicken wings.*

177 CHAR-GRILLED BELL PEPPER RELISH

PREPARATION TIME *20 minutes, plus cooling & standing* **COOKING TIME** *15 minutes* **SERVES 4**

2 yellow bell peppers
½ small red onion, finely
   chopped
1 fresh red chili, seeded &
   finely chopped

4 tsp olive oil
2 tbsp chopped fresh
   cilantro
2 tsp medium chili sauce,
   or to taste

Sea salt & freshly ground
   black pepper

1 Preheat the broiler to high. Cut the bell peppers in half lengthwise and place them, cut-side down, on the rack in a broiler pan.
2 Place the bell peppers under the hot broiler for about 10–15 minutes, or until the skins are blackened and charred.
3 Remove the broiler pan from the heat, cover the bell peppers with a clean, damp dish towel and let cool.
4 Once cool, remove the skin, core and seeds from the bell peppers, then finely chop the flesh, and place it in a bowl.
5 Add the onion, chili, olive oil, and chopped cilantro to the bell pepper flesh, and mix well. Stir in the chili sauce and salt and pepper to taste, mixing well.
6 Cover and let stand at room temperature for about 1 hour before serving, so the flavors develop.

SERVING SUGGESTIONS *Serve with grilled beef, pork, or turkey steaks or kebabs, or with cold cuts such as beef, ham, or pork. Alternatively, serve with broiled goat's cheese.*
VARIATIONS *Use 2 red bell peppers or 1 yellow and 1 red bell pepper in place of yellow bell peppers. Use 1 fresh green chili in place of red chili.*

178 SWEET CHILLI RELISH

PREPARATION TIME *10 minutes, plus cooling* **COOKING TIME** *50 minutes* **SERVES 4–6**

2 tbsp light soft
   brown sugar
¾ cup red wine
½ cup water

2 apples, peeled, cored, &
   diced
2 plum tomatoes, skinned
   & chopped

½–1 tsp ready-prepared
   chopped fresh red chilies,
   or to taste
A pinch of cayenne pepper
   (optional)

1 Place the sugar in a saucepan with the red wine and water, and heat gently, stirring, until the sugar has dissolved. Stir in the apples, tomatoes, prepared fresh chilies, and cayenne pepper, if using.
2 Bring the mixture to a boil, stirring, then cook, uncovered, over a medium heat for about 45 minutes, or until most of the liquid has evaporated and the mixture is thickened, stirring occasionally.
3 Serve hot or cold. If serving cold, remove the pan from the heat and let cool completely before serving.

SERVING SUGGESTIONS *Serve hot with roast or grilled beef, lamb or pork, or cold with cold cuts such as beef, pork, or ham.*
COOK'S TIP *Jars of ready-prepared chopped fresh red chilies are readily available in supermarkets and delicatessens. Use these chilies sparingly as they are very hot.*

179 CHUNKY CORN RELISH

PREPARATION TIME *10 minutes, plus standing* **COOKING TIME** *N/A* **SERVES 4–6**

4 scallions, finely chopped

8 red radishes, finely chopped

1 small red bell pepper, seeded & finely chopped

7-oz can corn kernels, drained

1 tbsp olive oil

2 tsp fresh lemon juice

1 tsp Dijon mustard

2–3 tbsp snipped fresh chives

Sea salt & freshly ground black pepper

1 Place the scallions, radishes, and red bell pepper in a bowl. Add the corn kernels and stir to mix.

2 In a separate small bowl, whisk together the olive oil, lemon juice, mustard, snipped chives, and salt and pepper to taste. Pour the mustard mixture over the corn and toss to mix well.

3 Cover and let stand at room temperature for about 30 minutes before serving, so the flavors develop.

SERVING SUGGESTIONS *Serve with broiled home-made beef burgers. Alternatively, serve with broiled or grilled beef, pork, or chicken kebabs, or good-quality beef or pork sausages.*

VARIATIONS *Use 2–3 shallots or 1 small red onion in place of scallions. Use chopped fresh flat-leaf parsley or 1–2 tbsp chopped fresh mixed herbs in place of chives.*

180 CRUNCHY PINEAPPLE RELISH

PREPARATION TIME *30 minutes, plus standing* **COOKING TIME** *N/A* **SERVES 4–6**

1 tbsp freshly squeezed
  orange juice
1 tbsp olive oil
1 tbsp clear honey
1 clove garlic, crushed

2 tbsp chopped fresh
  cilantro
1¾ cups prepared fresh
  pineapple, finely chopped
1 small red onion, finely
  chopped

½ small yellow bell pepper,
  seeded & finely chopped
Freshly ground black pepper,
  to taste
2 tbsp toasted sesame
  seeds (optional)

1 Place the orange juice, olive oil, honey, garlic, and chopped cilantro in a bowl and whisk together to mix. Add the pineapple, red onion, and yellow bell pepper, and toss to mix well. Season to taste with black pepper.

2 Cover and let stand at room temperature for about 1 hour before serving.

3 Drain off the excess juices before serving, if desired. Sprinkle the sesame seeds over the top, if using, and toss gently to mix.

SERVING SUGGESTIONS *Serve with broiled or grilled pork or chicken, or tuna steaks.*

181 EXOTIC FRUIT RELISH

PREPARATION TIME *25 minutes, plus standing* **COOKING TIME** *N/A* **SERVES 6**

1 ripe mango, peeled, pitted,
  & finely chopped
1 ripe papaya, peeled, pitted,
  & chopped
1 ripe nectarine, peeled,
  pitted, & finely chopped

2 tsp finely chopped (peeled)
  fresh root ginger
1 tbsp clear honey
1 tsp finely grated lime zest
Juice of ½ lime
2 tbsp chopped fresh mint

Freshly ground black pepper,
  to taste

1 Combine the mango, papaya, and nectarine flesh in a bowl. Add the ginger, honey, lime zest, lime juice, and chopped mint, and stir to mix. Season to taste with black pepper.

2 Cover and let stand at room temperature for about 1 hour before serving.

SERVING SUGGESTIONS *Serve with broiled or grilled tuna or salmon steaks.*

182 RED ONION MARMALADE

PREPARATION TIME *10 minutes* **COOKING TIME** *30 minutes* **SERVES 4**

2 tbsp butter
1 tbsp olive oil
3 red onions, thinly sliced

⅓ cup redcurrant jelly
2 tbsp red wine
1 tbsp red wine vinegar

1 tbsp light soft brown sugar
Sea salt & freshly ground
  black pepper

1 Heat the butter and oil in a saucepan until the butter is melted, then add the onions and cook over a medium heat for about 10 minutes, or until softened.

2 Stir in the redcurrant jelly, red wine, vinegar, sugar, and seasoning and stir to mix. Bring gently to a boil, stirring, then simmer, uncovered, for about 15 minutes, or until the mixture is reduced and thickened, stirring occasionally.

3 Serve hot or cold. If serving cold, remove the pan from the heat and let cool completely before serving.

SERVING SUGGESTIONS *Serve with grilled or char-grilled beef steaks or chicken drumsticks.*

CHAPTER 7

SALAD DRESSINGS AND VINAIGRETTES

Salad dressings, vinaigrettes, and mayonnaises are really what make a salad, bringing together all its separate ingredients to create a delicious combination of flavors.

The best dressings are often the simplest, combining just a few choice ingredients to create a tasty dressing or vinaigrette. There are many ready-made dressings on the market, but home-made dressings are so quick and easy, that you will soon adopt the simple routine of making your own.

Enjoy such classics as French Dressing, Thousand Island Dressing, Hazelnut Dressing, Sweet and Sour Dressing, Waldorf Dressing, Lemon Vinaigrette, Garlic and Herb Mayonnaise, and Fresh Herb Mayonnaise. Alternatively, try warm dressings, such as Orange Cinnamon Dressing, Garlic and Ginger Dressing, Italian Herb Dressing, or Hot Chili Dressing.

183 FRENCH DRESSING

PREPARATION TIME *10 minutes* **COOKING TIME** *N/A* **SERVES 4–6** *Makes about ⅔ cup*

6 tbsp extra-virgin olive oil
2 tbsp white wine vinegar or
cider vinegar or lemon
juice

1–2 tsp Dijon mustard
A pinch of superfine sugar
1 small clove garlic, crushed

1–2 tbsp chopped fresh
mixed herbs
Sea salt & freshly ground
black pepper

1 Place all the ingredients in a small bowl and whisk together until thoroughly mixed.
2 Alternatively, place all the ingredients in a clean screw-top jar, seal, and shake well until thoroughly mixed.
3 Adjust the seasoning to taste, and serve immediately, or keep in a screw-top jar in the refrigerator for up to 1 week. Whisk or shake thoroughly before serving.

SERVING SUGGESTIONS *Serve with a young leaf or mixed green salad.*

184 LIGHT FRENCH DRESSING

PREPARATION TIME *10 minutes* **COOKING TIME** *N/A* **SERVES 8–10** *Makes about 1½ cups*

4 tbsp olive oil
4 tbsp white wine vinegar
4 tbsp tarragon vinegar
⅔ cup white grape juice

2–3 tsp chopped fresh mixed
herbs, such as parsley,
thyme, mint, & rosemary
2 tsp wholegrain mustard
A pinch of superfine sugar

Sea salt & freshly ground
black pepper

1 Place the olive oil, vinegars, grape juice, chopped herbs, mustard, sugar, and seasoning in a small bowl and whisk together until thoroughly mixed.
2 Alternatively, place all the ingredients in a clean screw-top jar, seal, and shake well until thoroughly mixed.
3 Adjust the seasoning to taste and serve immediately, or keep in a screw-top jar in the refrigerator for up to 3 days. Whisk or shake thoroughly before serving.

SERVING SUGGESTIONS *Serve with a fresh mixed garden or green salad, or with a selection of raw, roasted, or char-grilled vegetables.*
VARIATIONS *Use cider vinegar and unsweetened apple juice in place of tarragon vinegar and grape juice. Use Dijon mustard in place of wholegrain mustard.*

185 BALSAMIC MUSTARD DRESSING

PREPARATION TIME *10 minutes* **COOKING TIME** *N/A* **SERVES 4** *Makes about ½ cup*

1 tbsp balsamic vinegar
2–3 tsp Dijon mustard, or
to taste

1 clove garlic, crushed
Sea salt & freshly ground
black pepper

6 tbsp light olive oil

1 Place the vinegar, mustard, garlic, and seasoning in a small bowl and whisk together to mix. Gradually whisk in the oil until well mixed and thickened.
2 Alternatively, place all the ingredients in a clean screw-top jar, seal, and shake well until thoroughly mixed.
3 Adjust the seasoning to taste, and serve immediately, or keep in a screw-top jar in the refrigerator for up to 3 days. Whisk or shake thoroughly before serving.

SERVING SUGGESTIONS *Serve with a young leaf, mixed green, or mixed bean salad.*

186 THOUSAND ISLAND DRESSING

PREPARATION TIME *10 minutes, plus standing* **COOKING TIME** *N/A* **SERVES 6** *Makes about 1 cup*

⅔ cup Mayonnaise
(see recipe on page 37)
2 tbsp plain fromage frais
1 tbsp tomato catsup
1 tbsp seeded & finely
   chopped red bell pepper

1 tbsp seeded & finely
   chopped green bell pepper
1 tbsp finely chopped
   (drained) gherkins
1 tbsp capers (drained),
   finely chopped

1 tbsp snipped fresh chives
Sea salt & freshly ground
   black pepper

1 Place the mayonnaise and fromage frais in a bowl, and stir to mix. Add all the remaining
   ingredients and stir until thoroughly mixed.
2 Cover and leave in a cool place for at least 30 minutes before serving, so the flavors
   develop. Adjust the seasoning to taste. Serve cold. Store in a covered
   container in the refrigerator for up to 1 day, if desired.

SERVING SUGGESTIONS *Serve with cold cooked shrimp or mixed seafood, or with a salad of your choice
such as potato or hard-cooked quail's egg salad.*

187 WALNUT DRIZZLE DRESSING

PREPARATION TIME *10 minutes* **COOKING TIME** *N/A* **SERVES 4** *Makes about ½ cup*

4 tbsp walnut oil
2 tbsp olive oil
2 tbsp white or red wine
   vinegar

1–2 tsp Dijon mustard
   (optional)
Sea salt & freshly ground
   black pepper

1 Place the walnut oil, olive oil, vinegar, mustard, if using, and seasoning in a small bowl
   and whisk together until thoroughly mixed.
2 Alternatively, place all the ingredients in a clean screw-top jar, seal, and shake well until
   thoroughly mixed.
3 Adjust the seasoning to taste, and serve immediately, or keep in a screw-top jar in the
   refrigerator for up to 3 days. Whisk or shake thoroughly before serving.

SERVING SUGGESTIONS *Serve with a warm chicken salad, or cooked vegetables such as green beans.*

188 HAZELNUT DRESSING

PREPARATION TIME *10 minutes* **COOKING TIME** *N/A* **SERVES 4** *Makes about ½ cup*

2 tbsp hazelnut oil
1 tbsp olive oil
1 tbsp lemon juice
1 tbsp clear honey

1 tsp Dijon mustard
2 scallions, finely
   chopped (optional)
1 clove garlic, crushed

1 tbsp chopped fresh
   cilantro
Sea salt & freshly ground
   black pepper

1 Place the oils, lemon juice, honey, mustard, scallions, if using, garlic, chopped cilantro,
   and seasoning in a small bowl and whisk together until thoroughly mixed.
2 Alternatively, place all the ingredients in a clean screw-top jar, seal, and shake well until
   thoroughly mixed.
3 Adjust the seasoning to taste and serve immediately, or keep in a screw-top jar in the
   refrigerator for up to 3 days. Whisk or shake thoroughly before serving.

SERVING SUGGESTIONS *Serve with an avocado or green bean salad sprinkled with chopped hazelnuts.*

189 TOMATO AND BASIL DRESSING

PREPARATION TIME *10 minutes* **COOKING TIME** *N/A* **SERVES 4** *Makes about ½ cup*

5 tbsp passata
1 tbsp extra-virgin olive oil
2 tsp balsamic vinegar

A pinch of superfine sugar
2 tbsp chopped fresh basil

Sea salt & freshly ground
  black pepper

1 Place the passata, olive oil, balsamic vinegar, sugar, chopped basil, and seasoning in a small bowl, and whisk together until thoroughly mixed.

2 Alternatively, place all the ingredients in a clean screw-top jar, seal, and shake well until thoroughly mixed.

3 Adjust the seasoning to taste, and serve immediately, or keep in a screw-top jar in the refrigerator for up to 3 days. Whisk or shake thoroughly before serving.

SERVING SUGGESTIONS *Serve with a mixed Mediterranean-style vegetable salad. Alternatively, serve with a pasta or mixed bean salad.*

190 SPICED TOMATO DRESSING

PREPARATION TIME *10 minutes* **COOKING TIME** *2 minutes* **SERVES 6–8** *Makes about 1 cup*

2 tbsp olive oil
1 tsp *each* of ground cumin,
   ground coriander, &
   hot chili powder

1 clove garlic, crushed
¾ cup tomato juice
2–3 tsp balsamic vinegar
2 tbsp chopped fresh basil

Sea salt & freshly ground
   black pepper

1 Heat the oil in a small saucepan, add the ground spices and garlic and cook gently for
2 minutes.

2 Remove the pan from the heat and whisk in the tomato juice, balsamic vinegar, chopped
basil, and seasoning until thoroughly mixed.

3 Adjust the seasoning to taste. Serve immediately, or set aside to cool, then cover and
chill before serving. Keep in a screw-top jar in the refrigerator for up to 1 day. Whisk well
or shake thoroughly before serving.

SERVING SUGGESTIONS *Serve with a warm chicken or pork salad sprinkled with sunflower seeds.*

191 LEMON AND CUMIN DRESSING

PREPARATION TIME *10 minutes* **COOKING TIME** *N/A* **SERVES 4** *Makes about ½ cup*

1 tbsp fresh lemon juice
1–2 cloves garlic, crushed

½ tsp *each* of ground cumin
   & ground coriander

Sea salt & freshly ground
   black pepper
6 tbsp light olive oil

1 Place the lemon juice, garlic, ground spices, and salt and pepper to taste, in a small
bowl, and whisk together until thoroughly mixed. Gradually whisk in the oil until well
mixed and thickened. Whisk in a little extra lemon juice, if desired.

2 Alternatively, place all the ingredients in a clean screw-top jar, seal, and shake well until
thoroughly mixed.

3 Adjust the seasoning to taste, and serve immediately, or keep in a screw-top jar in the
refrigerator for up to 3 days. Whisk or shake thoroughly before serving.

SERVING SUGGESTIONS *Serve with a mixed leaf or mixed bean salad. Alternatively, serve with a warm
smoked chicken or turkey salad.*

192 FRESH BASIL DRESSING

PREPARATION TIME *10 minutes* **COOKING TIME** *N/A* **SERVES 6** *Makes about 1 cup*

6 tbsp unsweetened white
   grape juice
4 tbsp olive oil

2 tbsp white wine vinegar
   or cider vinegar
2–3 tbsp chopped fresh basil
1 clove garlic, crushed

A pinch of superfine sugar
Sea salt & freshly ground
   black pepper

1 Place the grape juice, olive oil, vinegar, chopped basil, garlic, sugar, and seasoning in a
small bowl and whisk together until thoroughly mixed.

2 Alternatively, place all the ingredients in a clean screw-top jar, seal, and shake well until
thoroughly mixed.

3 Adjust the seasoning to taste, and serve immediately, or keep in a screw-top jar in the
refrigerator for up to 3 days. Whisk or shake thoroughly before serving.

SERVING SUGGESTIONS *Serve with a tomato and mozzarella, or tomato, bell pepper, and onion salad.*

193 GARLIC AND HERB YOGURT DRESSING

PREPARATION TIME *10 minutes* **COOKING TIME** *N/A* **SERVES 4–6** *Makes about ⅔ cup*

⅔ cup natural yogurt or
  natural Greek yogurt
2 tsp fresh lemon juice
1 tsp clear honey
2 small cloves garlic,
  crushed

2 tbsp chopped fresh
  mixed herbs, such as
  parsley, oregano, thyme, &
  chives
Sea salt & freshly ground
  black pepper

1 Place all the ingredients in a small bowl and mix together until well blended.
2 Adjust the seasoning to taste, then serve immediately, or cover and chill for 1–2 hours before serving.

SERVING SUGGESTIONS *Serve with cold cooked small potatoes, sliced tomatoes, crisp crunchy salad leaves, or cold poached salmon.*
VARIATION *Use chopped fresh basil or cilantro in place of mixed herbs.*

194 MINTED YOGURT DRESSING

PREPARATION TIME *10 minutes, plus standing* **COOKING TIME** *N/A* **SERVES 8–10** *Makes about 1½ cups*

1¼ cups natural yogurt
2 tbsp milk

1 clove garlic, crushed
2 tbsp chopped fresh mint

Sea salt & freshly ground
  black pepper

1 Place the yogurt, milk, garlic, chopped mint, and seasoning in a small bowl and whisk together until thoroughly mixed.
2 Cover and leave in a cool place for about 30 minutes before serving, so the flavors develop. Adjust the seasoning to taste, whisk briefly, and serve.

SERVING SUGGESTIONS *Serve with a mixed bean salad, or with a cold broiled chicken, salmon, or tuna salad.*
VARIATIONS *Use natural Greek yogurt in place of ⅔ cup natural yogurt. Add the finely grated zest and juice of 1 lemon or 1 lime in place of garlic and mint.*

195 BASIL YOGURT DRESSING

PREPARATION TIME *10 minutes* **COOKING TIME** *N/A* **SERVES 8–10** *Makes about 1½ cups*

1¼ cups natural yogurt
  or plain fromage frais
2 cloves garlic, crushed
2 scallions, finely
  chopped

A small bunch of fresh
  basil, chopped
1 tsp Dijon or English
  mustard

Sea salt & freshly ground
  black pepper

1 Place all the ingredients in a small bowl, and stir together until thoroughly mixed.
2 Adjust the seasoning to taste, then serve immediately, or cover and chill for 1–2 hours before serving.

SERVING SUGGESTIONS *Serve with a mixed tomato and bell pepper salad, or a mixed green salad.*

196 PARSLEY YOGURT DRESSING

PREPARATION TIME *10 minutes* **COOKING TIME** *N/A* **SERVES 4–6** *Makes about ¼ cup*

6 tbsp natural yogurt
4 tbsp Mayonnaise
  (see recipe on page 37)

2 tsp wholegrain mustard
2–3 tbsp chopped fresh
  parsley

Sea salt & freshly ground
  black pepper

1 Place the yogurt, mayonnaise, mustard, and chopped parsley in a small bowl, and mix together thoroughly.
2 Season to taste with salt and pepper. Serve immediately, or cover and chill for 1–2 hours before serving.

SERVING SUGGESTIONS *Serve with a mixed bell pepper and tomato, or mixed garden vegetable salad.*
VARIATIONS *Use curry paste, chili sauce, or Dijon mustard in place of wholegrain mustard. Add 1 clove crushed garlic to the dressing, if desired.*
COOK'S TIP *To finely chop fresh parsley, wash and dry the parsley and compress the sprigs or leaves into a ball in the palm of your hand. Chop the leaves coarsely, keeping your fingertips tucked well under, then scrape the roughly chopped parsley into a pile using the knife blade. Holding the knife down at its tip, lever the knife handle up and down quickly over the parsley. Keep scraping the parsley into a pile and slicing until it is finely chopped. Use as required.*

197 ORANGE CINNAMON DRESSING

PREPARATION TIME *10 minutes* **COOKING TIME** *5 minutes* **SERVES 8–10** *Makes about 1¼ cups*

⅔ cup unsweetened
  or freshly squeezed
  orange juice
6 tbsp white wine vinegar

4 tbsp sunflower oil
Finely grated zest & juice
  of 1 orange
1 tsp ground cinnamon

Sea salt & freshly ground
  black pepper

1 Place all the ingredients in a small bowl and whisk together until thoroughly mixed.
2 Alternatively, place all the ingredients in a clean screw-top jar, seal, and shake well until thoroughly mixed.
3 Adjust the seasoning to taste, and serve immediately, or keep in a screw-top jar in the refrigerator for up to 3 days. Whisk or shake thoroughly before serving.
4 Alternatively, serve warm, if desired. Whisk all the ingredients together, pour the mixture into a small saucepan and heat gently until warm, whisking continuously, then serve.

SERVING SUGGESTIONS *Serve with mixed salad leaves, pasta salad, cooked or raw vegetables, or a cold cooked pork or ham salad.*
VARIATION *Use ground mixed spice or ginger in place of cinnamon.*
COOK'S TIPS *If citrus fruits such as oranges have been stored in the refrigerator, they will yield the most juice if allowed to come to room temperature before using them.*
  If you need both juice and zest from citrus fruits, as in this recipe, remove the zest before squeezing the fruit.

198 ORANGE AND SESAME SEED DRESSING

PREPARATION TIME *10 minutes* **COOKING TIME** *N/A* **SERVES 4–6** *Makes about ⅔ cup*

4 tbsp unsweetened orange
  juice
1 tbsp olive oil
1 tbsp light soy sauce
1 tbsp red wine vinegar

1 tbsp clear honey
1 tbsp tomato paste
1 tbsp dry sherry
1 clove garlic, crushed

Sea salt & freshly ground
  black pepper
2 tbsp toasted sesame
  seeds (optional)

1 Place the orange juice, olive oil, soy sauce, vinegar, honey, tomato paste, sherry, garlic,
and salt and pepper to taste, in a small bowl and whisk together until thoroughly mixed.
Whisk in the sesame seeds, if using.
2 Alternatively, place all the ingredients in a clean screw-top jar, seal, and shake well
until thoroughly mixed.
3 Adjust the seasoning to taste, and serve immediately, or keep in a screw-top jar in the
refrigerator for up to 3 days. Whisk or shake thoroughly before serving.

SERVING SUGGESTIONS *Serve with a mixed vegetable and cooked egg noodle salad, or with a mixed
bean or dark leaf salad.*

199 LEMON AND HAZELNUT DRESSING

PREPARATION TIME *5 minutes* **COOKING TIME** *N/A* **SERVES 4** *Makes about ½ cup*

2 tbsp hazelnut oil
1 tbsp light olive oil
Juice of 1 lemon

1 tbsp clear honey
1 clove garlic, crushed

Sea salt & freshly ground
  black pepper

1 Place the oils, lemon juice, honey, garlic, and seasoning in a small bowl and whisk
together until thoroughly mixed.
2 Alternatively, place all the ingredients in a clean screw-top jar, seal, and shake well until
thoroughly mixed.
3 Adjust the seasoning to taste, and serve immediately, or keep in a screw-top jar in the
refrigerator for up to 3 days. Whisk or shake thoroughly before serving.

SERVING SUGGESTIONS *Serve with a mixed leaf or shredded vegetable salad. Sprinkle the salad with
toasted chopped hazelnuts just before serving, if desired.*

200 CILANTRO DRIZZLE DRESSING

PREPARATION TIME *5 minutes* **COOKING TIME** *N/A* **SERVES 4–6** *Makes about ¾ cup*

⅔ cup tomato juice
1 clove garlic, crushed
2 tsp balsamic vinegar

½ tsp light soft brown sugar
2 tbsp chopped fresh
  cilantro

Sea salt & freshly ground
  black pepper

1 Place the tomato juice, garlic, balsamic vinegar, sugar, chopped cilantro, and
seasoning in a small bowl and whisk together until thoroughly mixed.
2 Alternatively, place all the ingredients in a clean screw-top jar, seal, and shake well until
thoroughly mixed.
3 Adjust the seasoning to taste, and serve immediately, or keep in a screw-top jar in the
refrigerator for up to 3 days. Whisk or shake thoroughly before serving.

SERVING SUGGESTIONS *Serve with a mixed bean, couscous, or mixed bell pepper and onion salad.*

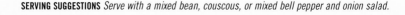

201 FRESH CILANTRO AND LIME DRESSING

PREPARATION TIME *10 minutes* **COOKING TIME** *N/A* **SERVES 8–10** *Makes about 1½ cups*

⅔ cup unsweetened
  white grape juice
6 tbsp white wine vinegar
4 tbsp sunflower oil or
  light olive oil

2 tbsp chopped fresh
  cilantro
Finely grated zest of 1 lime
Juice of 2 limes
1 tsp superfine sugar

Sea salt & freshly ground
  black pepper

1 Put the grape juice, vinegar, oil, chopped cilantro, lime zest, lime juice, sugar, and
seasoning in a small bow,l and whisk together until thoroughly mixed.

2 Alternatively, put all the ingredients in a clean screw-top jar, seal, and shake well until
thoroughly mixed.

3 Adjust the seasoning to taste, and serve immediately, or keep in a screw-top jar in the
refrigerator for up to 3 days. Whisk or shake thoroughly before serving.

SERVING SUGGESTIONS *Serve with a salad of char-grilled or pan-fried halloumi cheese and mixed green
leaves. Alternatively, serve with a cold cooked chicken, pork, or duck salad.*

VARIATIONS *Use lemon zest and juice in place of lime zest and juice. Use chopped fresh mixed herbs
in place of cilantro.*

202 GARLIC AND GINGER DRESSING

PREPARATION TIME *10 minutes* **COOKING TIME** *5 minutes* **SERVES 4–6** *Makes about ¾ cup*

7 tbsp cider vinegar
2 tbsp light soy sauce
1 tbsp sunflower oil
1 tbsp sesame oil

2 cloves garlic, crushed
1-inch piece of fresh root
   ginger, peeled & grated
   or finely chopped

Sea salt & freshly ground
   black pepper

1 Place all the ingredients in a small bowl and whisk together until thoroughly mixed. Alternatively, place all the ingredients in a clean screw-top jar, seal, and shake well until thoroughly mixed.
2 Adjust the seasoning to taste, and serve immediately, or keep in a screw-top jar in the refrigerator for up to 3 days. Whisk or shake thoroughly before serving.
3 Alternatively, serve warm. Simply whisk all the ingredients together, pour the mixture into a small saucepan and heat gently until warm, whisking continuously, then serve.

SERVING SUGGESTIONS *Serve with a char-grilled chicken, shredded vegetable, or mixed bean salad.*

203 MUSTARD AND ORANGE DRESSING

PREPARATION TIME *10 minutes* **COOKING TIME** *N/A* **SERVES 4** *Makes about ½ cup*

4 tbsp olive oil
1 tbsp unsweetened orange
   juice
2 tsp white wine vinegar

1–2 tsp Dijon or wholegrain
   mustard, or to taste
1–2 tbsp chopped fresh
   mixed herbs

Sea salt & freshly ground
   black pepper

1 Place the oil, orange juice, vinegar, mustard, chopped herbs, and seasoning in a small bowl and whisk together until thoroughly mixed.
2 Alternatively, place all the ingredients in a clean screw-top jar, seal, and shake well until thoroughly mixed.
3 Adjust the seasoning to taste, and serve immediately, or keep in a screw-top jar in the refrigerator for up to 3 days. Whisk or shake thoroughly before serving.

SERVING SUGGESTIONS *Serve with a warm mixed seafood, noodle, pasta, rice, or pork salad.*

204 HERBY MUSTARD DRESSING

PREPARATION TIME *10 minutes* **COOKING TIME** *N/A* **SERVES 4** *Makes about ½ cup*

3 tbsp olive oil
3 tbsp cider vinegar
1 tbsp wholegrain mustard

1 clove garlic, crushed
1 tbsp chopped fresh parsley
1 tbsp snipped fresh chives

Sea salt & freshly ground
   black pepper

1 Put the oil, vinegar, mustard, garlic, and chopped herbs in a small bowl and whisk together until thoroughly mixed. Season to taste with salt and pepper.
2 Alternatively, put all the ingredients in a clean screw-top jar, seal, and shake well until thoroughly mixed.
3 Adjust the seasoning, and serve immediately, or keep in a screw-top jar in the refrigerator for up to 3 days. Whisk or shake thoroughly before serving.

SERVING SUGGESTIONS *Serve with a mixed bean, rice, mixed garden vegetable, or mushroom salad.*

205 ITALIAN HERB DRESSING

PREPARATION TIME *10 minutes* **COOKING TIME** *5 minutes* **SERVES 4** *Makes about ½ cup*

6 tbsp extra-virgin olive oil
1 tbsp cider vinegar
1 tsp Dijon mustard

1–2 tbsp chopped fresh
mixed Italian herbs, such
as basil, oregano, & flat-
leaf parsley

Sea salt & freshly ground
black pepper

1 Place all the ingredients in a small bowl and whisk together until thoroughly mixed.
Alternatively, place all the ingredients in a clean screw-top jar, seal, and shake well until
thoroughly mixed.
2 Adjust the seasoning to taste, and serve immediately, or keep in a screw-top jar in the
refrigerator for up to 3 days. Whisk or shake thoroughly before serving.
3 Alternatively, serve warm, if desired. Whisk all the ingredients together, pour the mixture
into a small saucepan and heat gently until warm, whisking continuously, then serve.

SERVING SUGGESTIONS *Serve with a warm pasta or rice salad, or a mixed dark leaf salad.*

206 TOMATO AND HERB DRESSING

PREPARATION TIME *10 minutes* **COOKING TIME** *N/A* **SERVES 4** *Makes about ½ cup*

4 tbsp tomato juice
2 tbsp olive oil
1 tsp balsamic vinegar

1–2 tbsp chopped fresh
mixed herbs
½ tsp superfine sugar

Sea salt & freshly ground
black pepper

1 Place the tomato juice, olive oil, vinegar, chopped herbs, sugar, and seasoning in a
small bowl, and whisk together until thoroughly mixed.
2 Alternatively, place all the ingredients in a clean screw-top jar, seal, and shake well
until thoroughly mixed.
3 Adjust the seasoning to taste, and serve immediately, or keep in a screw-top jar in the
refrigerator for up to 3 days. Whisk or shake thoroughly before serving.

SERVING SUGGESTIONS *Serve with a flaked tuna and garbanzo salad. Alternatively, serve with a mixed
young leaf or pasta salad.*

207 TOMATO BALSAMIC DRESSING

PREPARATION TIME *10 minutes* **COOKING TIME** *N/A* **SERVES 6–8** *Makes about 1 cup*

⅔ cup passata
4 tbsp olive oil
1 tbsp balsamic vinegar

1 clove garlic, crushed
2–3 tbsp chopped fresh
flat-leaf parsley

Sea salt & freshly ground
black pepper

1 Place all the ingredients in a small bowl, and whisk together until thoroughly mixed.
2 Alternatively, place all the ingredients in a clean screw-top jar, seal, and shake well until
thoroughly mixed.
3 Adjust the seasoning to taste, and serve immediately, or keep in a screw-top jar in the
refrigerator for up to 3 days. Whisk or shake thoroughly before serving.

SERVING SUGGESTIONS *Serve with a mixed bean, pasta, or rice salad.*

208 HOT CHILI DRESSING

PREPARATION TIME *10 minutes* **COOKING TIME** *5–10 minutes* **SERVES 6** *Makes about 1 cup*

4 tbsp olive oil
2 shallots, finely chopped
1 fresh red chili, seeded &
  finely chopped

6 tbsp passata
2 tbsp red wine vinegar
1 tsp Dijon mustard

Sea salt & freshly ground
  black pepper

1 Heat 1 tbsp oil in a saucepan, add the shallots and chlli and cook for about 5 minutes, or until softened. Remove the pan from the heat.

2 Place the sautéed shallots and chili in a small blender or food processor with the remaining oil, the passata, vinegar, mustard, and seasoning and blend until smooth and well mixed.

3 Adjust the seasoning to taste, and serve immediately, or keep in a screw-top jar in the refrigerator for up to 3 days. Whisk or shake thoroughly before serving.

4 Alternatively, serve the dressing warm, if desired. Simply return the blended mixture to the pan and reheat gently until warm, stirring continuously, then serve.

SERVING SUGGESTIONS *Serve with garbanzo or fava bean falafel and shredded lettuce in pitta bread. Alternatively, serve with a mixed bean or mixed pasta and vegetable salad.*

VARIATIONS *Use 1 small red onion in place of shallots. Use tomato juice in place of passata.*

COOK'S TIP *Use ½–1 tsp ready-prepared chopped fresh red chilies, or to taste, in place of preparing your own fresh chili and to save a little time.*

209 HOT TOMATO DRESSING

PREPARATION TIME *5 minutes* **COOKING TIME** *10 minutes* **SERVES 4–6** *Makes about ¾ cup*

1 tbsp olive oil
1 clove garlic, crushed
1 tsp *each* of garam masala,
   ground coriander, & hot
   chili powder

½ cup tomato juice
2 tbsp balsamic vinegar
A dash of Tabasco sauce
1 tbsp chopped fresh parsley
1 tbsp snipped fresh chives

Sea salt & freshly ground
   black pepper

1 Heat the oil in a small saucepan, add the garlic and ground spices and cook gently for
   1 minute.
2 Stir in the tomato juice, balsamic vinegar, and Tabasco sauce, and heat gently until the
   mixture just comes to a boil, stirring continuously.
3 Remove the pan from the heat and set aside to cool slightly, then whisk in the chopped
   herbs, and season to taste with salt and pepper. Serve warm.

SERVING SUGGESTIONS *Serve with a mixed tuna, garbanzo, and cherry tomato salad.*

210 SWEET AND SOUR DRESSING

PREPARATION TIME *10 minutes* **COOKING TIME** *N/A* **SERVES 6–8** *Makes about 1 cup*

3 tbsp olive oil
3 tbsp unsweetened
   apple juice
2 tbsp red wine vinegar
2 tbsp clear honey

2 tbsp light soy sauce
2 tbsp tomato catsup
2 tbsp medium sherry
1 clove garlic, crushed
1 tsp ground ginger

Sea salt & freshly ground
   black pepper

1 Place all the ingredients in a small bowl and whisk together until thoroughly mixed.
2 Alternatively, place all the ingredients in a clean screw-top jar, seal, and shake well
   until thoroughly mixed.
3 Adjust the seasoning to taste, and serve immediately, or keep in a screw-top jar in the
   refrigerator for up to 3 days. Whisk or shake thoroughly before serving.

SERVING SUGGESTIONS *Serve with a mixed bean or noodle salad, or with a warm stir-fried chicken or
mixed seafood salad.*

211 CREAMY CURRIED DRESSING

PREPARATION TIME *10 minutes* **COOKING TIME** *N/A* **SERVES 6** *Makes about 1 cup*

6 tbsp Mayonnaise *(see
   recipe on page 37)*
4 tbsp natural yogurt

2 tbsp natural Greek yogurt
1 tbsp tomato paste
1 tbsp medium-hot curry
   paste

2 tbsp snipped fresh
   chives
Sea salt & freshly ground
   black pepper

1 Place the mayonnaise, yogurts, tomato paste, curry paste, and snipped chives in a small
   bowl and stir together until well mixed.
2 Season to taste with salt and pepper. Serve cold. Store in a covered container in the
   refrigerator for up to 2 days.

SERVING SUGGESTIONS *Serve with cold cooked potatoes – toss the dressing with the potatoes and let
stand in a cool place for about 1 hour before serving, so the flavors develop. Alternatively, serve the
dressing with a cold char-grilled chicken or pork salad.*

212 HORSERADISH DRESSING

PREPARATION TIME *10 minutes* **COOKING TIME** *N/A* **SERVES 8–10** *Makes about 1½ cups*

⅔ cup crème fraîche
⅔ cup natural yogurt
2 tbsp horseradish sauce

1–2 tbsp chopped fresh
  mixed herbs, such as
  parsley, chives, &
  oregano or marjoram

Sea salt & freshly ground
  black pepper

1 Place the crème fraîche, yogurt, horseradish sauce, and chopped herbs in a small bowl and stir to mix well.
2 Season to taste with salt and pepper. Serve cold. Store in a covered container in the refrigerator for up to 1 day.

SERVING SUGGESTIONS *Serve with a cold cooked beef or small potato salad. Alternatively, serve with thinly sliced smoked salmon, or smoked mackerel fillets.*
VARIATIONS *Use mayonnaise in place of crème fraîche. Use snipped fresh chives or chopped fresh parsley in place of mixed herbs. Use 1–2 tbsp wholegrain or Dijon mustard, or to taste, in place of horseradish sauce.*

213 AVOCADO DRESSING

PREPARATION TIME *15 minutes* **COOKING TIME** *N/A* **SERVES 4–6**

1 large avocado
Finely grated zest & juice
  of 1 lemon

6 tbsp natural yogurt
1 tsp Dijon mustard

Sea salt & freshly ground
  black pepper

1 Halve, pit, and peel the avocado, then chop the flesh. Place the avocado flesh in a small blender or food processor with the lemon zest and juice, and blend until smooth.
2 Add the yogurt, mustard, and seasoning and blend until smooth and well mixed. Add a little extra yogurt, if desired. Adjust the seasoning to taste, and serve immediately.

SERVING SUGGESTIONS *Serve with a mixed green, young leaf, or cold cooked chicken or turkey salad. Sprinkle the salad with chopped walnuts for extra flavor and crunch, if desired.*
VARIATIONS *Use the finely grated zest and juice of 1 lime in place of lemon zest and juice. Use mayonnaise, natural Greek yogurt, or crème fraîche in place of natural yogurt.*

214 WALDORF DRESSING

PREPARATION TIME *10 minutes* **COOKING TIME** *N/A* **SERVES 4–6** *Makes about ⅔ cup*

6 tbsp Mayonnaise
  (see recipe on page 37)

4 tbsp natural yogurt
2 tbsp snipped fresh chives

Sea salt & freshly ground
  black pepper

1 Place the mayonnaise and yogurt in a small bowl and stir to mix well.
2 Stir in the snipped chives, then season to taste with salt and pepper. Serve immediately, or cover and chill until required. Store in a covered container in the refrigerator for up to 2 days. Serve cold.

SERVING SUGGESTIONS *Serve as a dressing for a traditional mixed waldorf salad (a combination of apples, celery, lettuce, and walnuts, with the addition of cold cooked chicken or turkey, if desired). Alternatively, serve the dressing with shredded coleslaw vegetables.*

215 LEMON VINAIGRETTE

PREPARATION TIME *10 minutes* **COOKING TIME** *N/A* **SERVES 4** *Makes about ½ cup*

3 tbsp light olive oil
3 tbsp sunflower oil
Finely grated zest of 1
   small lemon

2–3 tbsp freshly squeezed
   lemon juice
½ tsp superfine sugar
1 tbsp finely chopped fresh
   parsley (optional)

Sea salt & freshly ground
   black pepper

1 Place the oils, lemon zest, 2 tbsp lemon juice, the sugar, and chopped parsley, if using, in a small bowl and whisk together until thoroughly mixed. Season to taste with salt and pepper, and add a little extra lemon juice to taste, if desired.
2 Alternatively, place all the ingredients in a clean screw-top jar, seal, and shake well until thoroughly mixed.
3 Adjust the seasoning to taste, and serve immediately, or keep in a screw-top jar in the refrigerator for up to 1 week. Whisk or shake thoroughly before serving.

SERVING SUGGESTIONS *Serve with a mixed dark leaf, avocado, or cold char-grilled chicken salad.*

216 QUICK ORANGE VINAIGRETTE

PREPARATION TIME *10 minutes* **COOKING TIME** *N/A* **SERVES 8–10** *Makes about 1¼ cups*

⅔ cup unsweetened orange
   juice
3 tbsp cider vinegar
3 tbsp white wine vinegar

3 tbsp extra-virgin olive oil
1 tsp finely chopped fresh
   rosemary
½ tsp superfine sugar

Sea salt & freshly ground
   black pepper

1 Place all the ingredients in a small bowl and whisk together until thoroughly mixed.
2 Alternatively, place all the ingredients in a clean screw-top jar, seal, and shake well until thoroughly mixed.
3 Adjust the seasoning to taste, and serve immediately, or keep in a screw-top jar in the refrigerator for up to 3 days. Whisk or shake thoroughly before serving.

SERVING SUGGESTIONS *Serve with a carrot, cracked wheat, couscous, or mixed dark leaf salad.*
VARIATION *Use freshly-squeezed orange juice, if preferred.*

217 FRESH HERB VINAIGRETTE

PREPARATION TIME *10 minutes* **COOKING TIME** *N/A* **SERVES 4** *Makes about ½ cup*

6 tbsp extra-virgin olive oil
2 tbsp white wine or cider
   vinegar

2 tsp Dijon mustard
1–2 tbsp chopped fresh
   mixed herbs

Sea salt & freshly ground
   black pepper

1 Place all the ingredients in a small bowl and whisk together until thoroughly mixed.
2 Alternatively, place all the ingredients in a clean screw-top jar, seal, and shake well until thoroughly mixed.
3 Adjust the seasoning to taste, and serve immediately, or keep in a screw-top jar in the refrigerator for up to 1 week. Whisk or shake thoroughly before serving.

SERVING SUGGESTIONS *Serve with a mixed young leaf, green, or garden salad.*

218 FRESH LIME VINAIGRETTE

PREPARATION TIME *10 minutes* **COOKING TIME** *N/A* **SERVES 4** *Makes about ½ cup*

3 tbsp light olive oil
3 tbsp sunflower oil
Finely grated zest of 1 lime

2–3 tbsp freshly squeezed
  lime juice
½ tsp superfine sugar

1 tbsp finely chopped fresh
  cilantro (optional)
Sea salt & freshly ground
  black pepper

1 Place the oils, lime zest, 2 tbsp lime juice, the sugar, and chopped cilantro, if using, in a
  small bowl, and whisk together until thoroughly mixed. Season to taste with salt and
  pepper, and add a little extra lime juice to taste, if desired.
2 Alternatively, place all the ingredients in a clean screw-top jar, seal, and shake well until
  thoroughly mixed.
3 Adjust the seasoning to taste, and serve immediately, or keep in a screw-top jar in the
  refrigerator for up to 1 week. Whisk or shake thoroughly before serving.

SERVING SUGGESTIONS *Serve with a mixed dark leaf, young leaf, or green salad.*

219 WALNUT AND PARSLEY VINAIGRETTE

PREPARATION TIME *10 minutes* **COOKING TIME** *N/A* **SERVES 8–10** *Makes about 1¼ cups*

4 tbsp walnut oil
3 tbsp red wine vinegar
3 tbsp cider vinegar
⅔ cup unsweetened
  red grape juice

1 clove garlic, crushed
1 tsp French or Dijon mustard
A good pinch of superfine
  sugar
2 tbsp chopped fresh parsley

Sea salt & freshly ground
  black pepper

1 Place the walnut oil, red wine and cider vinegars, grape juice, garlic, mustard, sugar,
  and chopped parsley in a small bowl, and whisk together until thoroughly mixed. Season
  to taste with salt and pepper.
2 Alternatively, place all the ingredients in a clean screw-top jar, seal, and shake well until
  thoroughly mixed.
3 Adjust the seasoning to taste and serve immediately, or keep in a screw-top jar in the
  refrigerator for up to 3 days. Whisk or shake thoroughly before serving.

SERVING SUGGESTIONS *Serve with a mixed bean or garden salad, or with cooked hot vegetables such as
green beans, asparagus, or artichokes.*

220 STRAWBERRY VINAIGRETTE

PREPARATION TIME *10 minutes* **COOKING TIME** *N/A* **SERVES 4–6** *Makes about ⅔ cup*

6 tbsp light olive oil or
  sunflower oil
2 tbsp lemon juice

5 fresh, ripe strawberries
A pinch of superfine sugar,
  or to taste

Sea salt & freshly ground
  black pepper

1 Place the oil, lemon juice, strawberries, sugar, and seasoning in a small blender or food
  processor and blend until smooth, well mixed and fairly thick.
2 Adjust the seasoning to taste. Serve immediately.

SERVING SUGGESTIONS *Serve with an avocado salad, or a mixed leaf or summer garden salad.*

221 RASPBERRY VINAIGRETTE

PREPARATION TIME *10 minutes* **COOKING TIME** *N/A* **SERVES 12–14** *Makes about 2¼ cups*

14-oz can raspberries in
   fruit juice
8 tbsp red wine vinegar

5 tbsp sunflower oil or
   light olive oil
1 tsp superfine sugar
1 tsp dried sage

Sea salt & freshly ground
   black pepper

1 Put the raspberries and their juice in a blender or food processor and blend until smooth. Push the raspberry purée through a non-reactive sieve into a bowl and discard the pips and pulp.
2 Put the raspberry juice, vinegar, oil, sugar, sage, and seasoning in a small bowl and whisk together until thoroughly mixed.
3 Alternatively, put all the ingredients in a clean screw-top jar, seal, and shake well until thoroughly mixed.
4 Adjust the seasoning to taste, and serve immediately, or keep in a screw-top jar in the refrigerator for up to 3 days. Whisk or shake thoroughly before serving.

SERVING SUGGESTIONS *Serve with strips of char-grilled vegetables such as zucchini or eggplants, sprinkled with toasted chopped walnuts, if desired. Alternatively, serve with a mixed bean or rice salad, or mixed salad leaves.*

VARIATIONS *Use dried oregano, marjoram, or thyme in place of sage. Use white wine or cider vinegar in place of red wine vinegar.*

222 LEMON MAYONNAISE

PREPARATION TIME *10 minutes* **COOKING TIME** *N/A* **SERVES 8** *Makes about 1¼ cups*

1 quantity of Mayonnaise,
made using lemon juice
(see recipe on page 37)

1½ tsp finely grated lemon
zest

Sea salt & freshly ground
black pepper

1 Spoon the mayonnaise into a small bowl. Fold the lemon zest into the mayonnaise just before serving.

2 Stir a little extra squeeze of lemon juice into the mayonnaise, if desired. Adjust the seasoning to taste.

3 Serve immediately, or cover and chill until required. Store in a covered container in the refrigerator for up to 2 days. Serve cold.

SERVING SUGGESTIONS *Serve with vegetable salads, cold cooked seafood or king prawns, or thin slices of smoked salmon.*
VARIATION *Use lime zest and juice in place of lemon zest and juice.*

223 PARSLEY AND LEMON MAYONNAISE

PREPARATION TIME *10 minutes* **COOKING TIME** *N/A* **SERVES 4** *Makes about ½ cup*

4 tbsp Mayonnaise
(see recipe on page 37)
2 tbsp natural yogurt

2 tbsp chopped fresh parsley
1 tsp finely grated lemon zest

Sea salt & freshly ground
black pepper

1 Place the mayonnaise, yogurt, chopped parsley, and lemon zest in a small bowl and stir to mix well. Season to taste with salt and pepper.

2 Serve immediately, or cover and chill until required. Store in a covered container in the refrigerator for up to 2 days. Serve cold.

SERVING SUGGESTIONS *Serve with cold cooked chicken, tiger prawns, or mixed seafood, or with smoked trout or mackerel fillets.*
VARIATIONS *Use chopped fresh cilantro in place of parsley. Use finely grated lime or orange zest in place of lemon zest.*

224 CHIVE AND LEMON MAYONNAISE

PREPARATION TIME *10 minutes* **COOKING TIME** *N/A* **SERVES 4–6** *Makes about ⅔ cup*

½ cup Mayonnaise *(see recipe
on page 37)*
2 tbsp snipped fresh
chives

1 tsp finely grated
lemon zest
Sea salt & freshly ground
black pepper

1 Place the mayonnaise, snipped chives, and lemon zest in a small bowl and stir to mix well. Season to taste with salt and pepper.

2 Serve immediately, or cover and chill until required. Store in a covered container in the refrigerator for up to 2 days. Serve cold.

SERVING SUGGESTIONS *Serve with a cold cooked king prawn, flaked tuna, or chicken pasta salad.*
VARIATION *Use finely grated lime or orange zest in place of lemon zest.*

225 HORSERADISH MAYONNAISE

PREPARATION TIME *10 minutes* **COOKING TIME** *N/A* **SERVES 8** *Makes about 1¼ cups*

1 quantity of Mayonnaise
(see recipe on page 37)

2 tbsp hot horseradish sauce

Sea salt & freshly ground
black pepper

1 Spoon the mayonnaise into a bowl. Fold the horseradish sauce into the mayonnaise just before serving. Adjust the seasoning to taste.
2 Serve immediately, or cover and chill until required. Store in a covered container in the refrigerator for up to 2 days. Serve cold.

SERVING SUGGESTIONS *Serve with cold cooked sliced beef or pastrami, smoked salmon, trout, or mackerel, or with cold cooked vegetables such as beets.*

226 TASTY MUSTARD MAYONNAISE

PREPARATION TIME *10 minutes* **COOKING TIME** *N/A* **SERVES 8** *Makes about 1¼ cups*

1 quantity of Mayonnaise
(see recipe on page 37)

2 tbsp wholegrain or
Dijon mustard

Sea salt & freshly ground
black pepper

1 Spoon the mayonnaise into a bowl. Fold the mustard into the mayonnaise just before serving. Adjust the seasoning to taste.
2 Serve immediately, or cover and chill until required. Store in a covered container in the refrigerator for up to 2 days. Serve cold.

SERVING SUGGESTIONS *Serve with shredded vegetable salads such as coleslaw, a mixed bean or pasta salad, or with cold cooked beef, ham, sausages, or chicken.*
VARIATION *Use 1–2 tbsp medium-hot curry paste, or to taste, in place of mustard.*
COOK'S TIP *For a slightly lighter mayonnaise, replace ½ cup mayonnaise with natural yogurt or plain fromage frais.*

227 MOROCCAN-SPICED MAYONNAISE

PREPARATION TIME *20 minutes* **COOKING TIME** *2 minutes* **SERVES 6** *Makes about 1 cup*

3 tbsp tomato juice
½ tsp *each* of ground cumin,
ground coriander, paprika,
ground turmeric, ground
cinnamon, & ground
ginger

1 clove garlic, crushed
(optional)
6 tbsp Mayonnaise
(see recipe on page 37)
4 tbsp natural yogurt

2–3 tbsp chopped fresh
cilantro
Sea salt & freshly ground
black pepper

1 Place the tomato juice, ground spices, and garlic, if using, in a small saucepan and cook gently for 2 minutes, stirring continuously. Remove the pan from the heat and set aside to cool.
2 Place the mayonnaise, yogurt, spice mixture, and chopped cilantro in a small bowl and stir to mix thoroughly. Season to taste with salt and pepper.
3 Serve immediately, or cover and let stand in a cool place for about 30 minutes before serving. Store in a covered container in the refrigerator for up to 1 day. Serve cold.

SERVING SUGGESTIONS *Serve with cold cooked small potatoes, or with a mixed bean, rice, or pasta salad.*
VARIATION *Increase the ground spices to 1 tsp each for a more pronounced spicy flavor.*

228 FRESH HERB MAYONNAISE

PREPARATION TIME *10 minutes* **COOKING TIME** *N/A* **SERVES 6** *Makes about 1 cup*

½ cup Mayonnaise *(see recipe on page 37)*
4 tbsp natural yogurt

1½ tbsp chopped fresh parsley
1½ tbsp snipped fresh chives

Sea salt & freshly ground black pepper

1 Place the mayonnaise and yogurt in a small bowl and stir to mix well. Stir in the chopped herbs, and season to taste with salt and pepper.

2 Serve immediately, or cover and chill until required. Store in a covered container in the refrigerator for up to 2 days. Serve cold.

SERVING SUGGESTIONS *Serve with shredded raw vegetables (such as coleslaw vegetables), or with cold cooked sliced pastrami, beef, pork, Parma ham, smoked chicken, or turkey.*

229 WATERCRESS MAYONNAISE

PREPARATION TIME *10 minutes* **COOKING TIME** *N/A* **SERVES 4–6** *Makes about ¾ cup*

½ cup Mayonnaise *(see recipe on page 37)*
1 small bunch watercress, finely chopped

½ tsp freshly grated hot horseradish or hot horseradish sauce, or to taste

Sea salt & freshly ground black pepper

1 Place the mayonnaise, chopped watercress, and horseradish in a small bowl and stir to mix well. Season to taste with salt and pepper.

2 Serve immediately, or cover and chill until required. Store in a covered container in the refrigerator for up to 2 days. Serve cold.

SERVING SUGGESTIONS *Serve with char-grilled fish such as sardines or pilchards, or with a cold cooked chicken, turkey, or ham salad.*

230 TUNA MAYONNAISE

PREPARATION TIME *10 minutes* **COOKING TIME** *N/A* **SERVES 6–8** *Makes about 1¼ cups*

7-oz can tuna in spring water or brine, drained & mashed
4 tbsp Mayonnaise *(see recipe on page 37)*

2 tbsp natural yogurt
2 scalions, finely chopped
1 tsp finely grated lemon zest
Sea salt & freshly ground black pepper

1 Place the tuna, mayonnaise, yogurt, scallions, and lemon zest in a small bowl and stir to mix well. Season to taste with salt and pepper.

2 Serve immediately, or cover and chill until required. Store in a covered container in the refrigerator for up to 1 day. Serve cold.

SERVING SUGGESTIONS *Serve with hot poached eggs or cold hard-cooked eggs. Alternatively, serve with a pasta or rice salad, or use as a sandwich or jacket potato filling, or a toast topper.*
VARIATIONS *Add an extra 2 tbsp mayonnaise and 1 tbsp natural yogurt to the mixture, if desired. Add 1 small clove garlic, crushed, if desired. Use canned red or pink salmon in place of tuna. Add 1–2 tbsp chopped fresh parsley or snipped fresh chives, if desired.*

231 GARLIC AND HERB MAYONNAISE

PREPARATION TIME *10 minutes* **COOKING TIME** *N/A* **SERVES 8** *Makes about 1¼ cups*

1 quantity of Mayonnaise
  (see recipe on page 37)
1 clove garlic, crushed

2 tbsp chopped fresh mixed
  herbs, such as parsley,
  chives, basil, & oregano

Sea salt & freshly ground
  black pepper

1 Make the mayonnaise according to the instructions given, adding the crushed garlic with the egg yolks.

2 Fold the chopped herbs into the garlic mayonnaise just before serving. Season to taste with salt and pepper.

3 Serve immediately, or cover and chill until required. Store in a covered container in the refrigerator for up to 2 days. Serve cold.

SERVING SUGGESTIONS *Serve with oven-roasted or char-grilled mixed Mediterranean vegetables. Alternatively, serve with cold cooked sliced pork, ham, salami, or smoked turkey, or with smoked mackerel fillets.*

COOK'S TIP *Garlic is available all year round as it can be dried and stored successfully. A neatly plaited bunch of garlic will keep well for several months in a dry, airy place.*

CHAPTER 8

LIGHT SAUCES

Everyone loves a tasty sauce as an accompaniment to a meal, but some sauces, though very appealing to the tastebuds, are not so good for the waistline.

This chapter enables you to enjoy a good selection of savory sauces, all of which are lighter, healthier options. They taste just as delicious as other sauces but are lower in fat and/or calories, so are ideal if you are watching your weight.

A wide range of tempting sauces are included, from classics such as Light Cheese Sauce, Fresh Parsley Sauce, Light Caper Sauce, Light Watercress Sauce, and Light Espagnole Sauce, to other favorites such as Light Green Peppercorn Sauce, Tasty Barbecue Sauce, Light Creamy Horseradish Sauce, Mediterranean Tomato Sauce, Red Chili Sauce, and Light Blue Cheese Sauce. There is also a selection of lighter pasta sauces, including favorites such as Light Bolognese Pasta Sauce and Light Spaghetti Carbonara.

232 LIGHT BÉCHAMEL SAUCE

PREPARATION TIME *35 minutes* **COOKING TIME** *10 minutes* **SERVES 4** *Makes about 1¼ cups*

1 small onion or 2 shallots,
  peeled & sliced
1 small carrot, sliced
½ stick of celery, roughly
  chopped
1 bay leaf

6 black peppercorns
Several stalks of fresh
  parsley
1¼ cups semi-skimmed
  milk
2 tbsp reduced-fat spread

¼ cup all-purpose flour
Sea salt & freshly ground
  black pepper

1 Place the onion or shallots, carrot, celery, bay leaf, peppercorns, and parsley stalks in a saucepan with the milk and bring slowly to a boil. Remove the pan from the heat and set aside to infuse for 30 minutes.

2 Strain the mixture into a jug, reserving the milk and discarding the contents of the sieve. Melt the reduced-fat spread in a small saucepan over a low heat, then stir in the flour and cook gently for 1 minute, stirring.

3 Remove the pan from the heat and gradually whisk in the flavored milk. Return the pan to the heat, then bring slowly to a boil, whisking continuously, until the sauce is thickened and smooth. Simmer gently for 2–3 minutes, stirring. Season to taste with salt and pepper. Serve hot.

SERVING SUGGESTIONS *Serve with char-grilled skinless chicken or turkey breast portions, broiled cod or haddock fillets, braised celery, or cooked small fava beans.*

VARIATIONS *Just before serving, stir in ½ cup grated reduced-fat mature cheddar cheese or 2–3 tbsp chopped fresh parsley, if desired.*

233 LIGHT BASIC WHITE SAUCE

PREPARATION TIME *5 minutes* **COOKING TIME** *10 minutes* **SERVES 4** *Makes about 1¼ cups*

2 tbsp reduced-fat spread
¼ cup all-purpose flour

1¼ cups semi-skimmed
milk

Sea salt & freshly ground
black pepper

1 Place the reduced-fat spread, flour, and milk in a small saucepan. Heat gently, whisking continuously, until the sauce comes to a boil and is thickened and smooth.
2 Simmer gently for 3–4 minutes, stirring. Season to taste with salt and pepper. Serve hot.

SERVING SUGGESTIONS *Serve with broiled lean gammon or pork steaks, skinless chicken breasts, or with broiled or poached cod or halibut steaks, or cooked leeks or celery hearts.*
COOK'S TIP *For a slightly thinner sauce, follow the recipe above, decreasing the reduced-fat spread to 1 tbsp and the flour to 2 tbsp.*

234 LIGHT CHEESE SAUCE

PREPARATION TIME *5 minutes* **COOKING TIME** *10 minutes* **SERVES 4** *Makes about 1½ cups*

2 tbsp reduced-fat spread
¼ cup all-purpose flour
1¼ cups semi-skimmed milk
1 tsp Dijon mustard

½ cup reduced-fat mature
cheddar cheese, finely
grated

Sea salt & freshly ground
black pepper

1 Place the reduced-fat spread, flour, and milk in a small saucepan. Heat gently, whisking continuously, until the sauce comes to a boil and is thickened and smooth. Simmer gently for 3–4 minutes, stirring.
2 Remove the pan from the heat, then stir in the mustard and cheese until the cheese is melted. Season to taste with salt and pepper. Serve hot.

SERVING SUGGESTIONS *Serve with oven-baked or broiled cod or haddock fillets. Alternatively, serve with baked ham, char-grilled skinless chicken portions, or steamed cauliflower florets, or with small corn cobs.*
VARIATION *Use reduced-fat red leicester cheese in place of cheddar.*

235 FRESH PARSLEY SAUCE

PREPARATION TIME *5 minutes* **COOKING TIME** *10 minutes* **SERVES 4** *Makes about 1¼ cups*

2 tbsp reduced-fat spread
¼ cup all-purpose flour
1¼ cups semi-skimmed milk

2 tbsp finely chopped
fresh parsley
Sea salt & freshly ground
black pepper

1 Place the reduced-fat spread, flour, and milk in a small saucepan. Heat gently, whisking continuously, until the sauce comes to a boil and is thickened and smooth. Simmer gently for 3–4 minutes, stirring.
2 Stir in the chopped parsley, then season to taste with salt and pepper. Serve hot.

SERVING SUGGESTIONS *Serve with broiled or oven-baked whole plaice, sole, or dab, or with baked lean ham, bacon, or smoked pork.*
VARIATION *Use 1–2 tbsp chopped fresh mixed herbs or tarragon in place of parsley.*

236 LIGHT CAPER SAUCE

PREPARATION TIME *5 minutes* **COOKING TIME** *10 minutes* **SERVES 4** *Makes about 1¼ cups*

2 tbsp reduced-fat spread
¼ cup all-purpose flour
1¼ cups semi-skimmed milk

2 tbsp capers, drained
  (& chopped, if desired)
2 tsp vinegar from the
  jar of capers

Sea salt & freshly ground
  black pepper

1 Place the reduced-fat spread, flour, and milk in a small saucepan. Heat gently, whisking continuously, until the sauce comes to a boil and is thickened and smooth. Simmer gently for 3–4 minutes, stirring.
2 Stir in the capers and vinegar and reheat gently until hot, stirring. Season to taste with salt and pepper. Serve hot.

SERVING SUGGESTIONS *Serve with roast or broiled lean lamb, pork, or venison steaks or chops, or with cod or haddock fillets.*

237 LIGHT TARRAGON SAUCE

PREPARATION TIME *5 minutes* **COOKING TIME** *10 minutes* **SERVES 6** *Makes about 2½ cups*

2 tbsp reduced-fat spread
¼ cup all-purpose flour
1¼ cups vegetable or chicken
  stock *(see recipes on pages
  10–11),* cooled

⅔ cup semi-skimmed milk
1 tbsp tarragon vinegar
1 tbsp chopped fresh
  tarragon
2 tsp French or Dijon mustard

½ cup reduced-fat mature
  cheddar cheese, finely
  grated
Sea salt & freshly ground
  black pepper

1 Place the reduced-fat spread, flour, stock, and milk in a small saucepan. Heat gently, whisking continuously, until the sauce comes to a boil and is thickened and smooth. Simmer gently for 3–4 minutes, stirring.
2 Stir in the vinegar, chopped tarragon, and mustard, and reheat gently until hot, stirring.
3 Remove the pan from the heat and stir in the cheese until melted. Season to taste with salt and pepper. Serve hot.

SERVING SUGGESTIONS *Serve with char-grilled or oven-baked skinless chicken breasts.*

238 LIGHT MUSTARD SAUCE

PREPARATION TIME *5 minutes* **COOKING TIME** *10 minutes* **SERVES 4–6** *Makes about 1½ cups*

2 tbsp reduced-fat spread
¼ cup all-purpose flour
1¼ cups semi-skimmed milk

2 tbsp wholegrain mustard,
  or to taste
Sea salt & freshly ground
  black pepper

1 Place the reduced-fat spread, flour, and milk in a small saucepan. Heat gently, whisking continuously, until the sauce comes to a boil and is thickened and smooth. Simmer gently for 3–4 minutes, stirring.
2 Stir in the mustard and reheat gently until hot, stirring. Season to taste with salt and pepper. Serve hot.

SERVING SUGGESTIONS *Serve with broiled or oven-baked lean bacon, low-fat sausages, ham steaks, skinless chicken or turkey breast portions, or whole mackerel or trout.*

239 LIGHT PARSLEY AND CHIVE SAUCE

PREPARATION TIME *5 minutes* **COOKING TIME** *10 minutes* **SERVES 4–6** *Makes about 1½ cups*

2 tbsp reduced-fat spread
¼ cup all-purpose flour
1¼ cups semi-skimmed milk
2 tbsp chopped fresh parsley

2 tbsp snipped fresh chives
Sea salt & freshly ground
   black pepper

1 Place the reduced-fat spread, flour, and milk in a small saucepan. Heat gently, whisking continuously, until the sauce comes to a boil and is thickened and smooth. Simmer gently for 3–4 minutes, stirring.
2 Stir in the chopped parsley and snipped chives, then season to taste with salt and pepper. Serve hot.

SERVING SUGGESTIONS *Serve with broiled or oven-baked lean smoked pork, skinless chicken drumsticks or thighs, or lean pork steaks. Alternatively, serve with poached salmon or broiled cod or halibut fillets.*
COOK'S TIPS *Chives, with their bright green stems, have a fresh oniony flavor. If fresh chives are not available, scallion tops are similar in flavor and color to chives, and can be chopped and used as a substitute.*
Fresh chive flowers also provide an attractive garnish to savory dishes.

240 LIGHT WATERCRESS SAUCE

PREPARATION TIME *15 minutes* **COOKING TIME** *15 minutes* **SERVES 6** *Makes about 2½ cups*

1 small onion, finely chopped
1 clove garlic, crushed
1 bunch watercress, finely
   chopped
⅔ cup vegetable stock
   (see recipe on page 10)
2 tbsp reduced-fat spread

¼ cup all-purpose flour
1¼ cups semi-skimmed milk
½ cup reduced-fat mature
   cheddar cheese, finely
   grated
Sea salt & freshly ground
   black pepper

1 Place the onion, garlic, watercress, and stock in a saucepan and stir to mix. Bring to a boil, then reduce the heat, cover, and cook gently for 5 minutes, stirring occasionally.
2 Remove the pan from the heat and let cool slightly, then purée the mixture in a blender or food processor until smooth.
3 Place the reduced-fat spread, flour, and milk in a separate saucepan and heat gently, whisking continuously, until the sauce comes to a boil and thickens. Simmer gently for 3–4 minutes, stirring.
4 Add the watercress purée and mix well, then reheat gently until hot, stirring. Remove the pan from the heat and stir in the cheese until melted. Season to taste with salt and pepper. Serve hot.

SERVING SUGGESTIONS *Serve with char-grilled or grilled skinless chicken or turkey breast portions or goujons, or with poached salmon or oven-baked monkfish tail.*
VARIATION *Use 2 shallots in place of onion.*
COOK'S TIPS *Reduced-fat hard cheese such as cheddar is available in several varieties, including mild, medium, and mature flavor strengths. Choose a mature cheddar cheese for this sauce and other reduced-fat cheese sauces, to achieve maximum flavor while keeping the fat content down.*
Finely grating hard cheese such as cheddar will ensure that it goes further and melts more quickly in the sauce.

241 FRESH MUSHROOM SAUCE

PREPARATION TIME *40 minutes* **COOKING TIME** *20 minutes* **SERVES 6** *Makes about 2½ cups*

1 small onion, peeled &
   cut into quarters
1 small carrot, sliced
½ stick of celery, roughly
   chopped
1 bay leaf

½ tsp black peppercorns
2 cups semi-skimmed milk
¼ cup reduced-fat spread
3 cups button mushrooms,
   thinly sliced
¼ cup all-purpose flour

Sea salt & freshly ground
   black pepper

1 Put the onion, carrot, celery, bay leaf, and peppercorns in a saucepan with the milk
and bring slowly to a boil. Remove the pan from heat and set aside to infuse for
30 minutes.

2 Strain the mixture into a jug, reserving the milk. Discard the contents of the sieve. Melt
the reduced-fat spread in a saucepan over a low heat, then add the mushrooms and
cook gently for about 5 minutes, or until softened, stirring occasionally. Stir in the flour
and cook gently for 1 minute, stirring.

3 Remove the pan from the heat, and gradually stir in the flavored milk. Return the pan to
the heat, then bring slowly to a boil, stirring or whisking continuously, until the sauce
thickens. Simmer gently for 2–3 minutes, stirring. Season to taste with salt and pepper.
Serve hot.

SERVING SUGGESTIONS *Serve with broiled or oven-baked lean beef or pork, skinless chicken breasts,*
salmon or haddock fillets, or with cooked cauliflower, corn, or green beans.

242 LIGHT ONION SAUCE

PREPARATION TIME *10 minutes* **COOKING TIME** *20 minutes* **SERVES 6** *Makes about 2½ cups*

2 tbsp reduced-fat spread
1 onion, finely chopped
¼ cup all-purpose flour

2 cups semi-skimmed milk
Sea salt & freshly ground
   black pepper

1 Melt the reduced-fat spread in a saucepan over a low heat, then add the onion and cook
gently for 8–10 minutes, or until softened, stirring occasionally. Stir in the flour and cook
for 1 minute, stirring.

2 Remove the pan from the heat and gradually stir in the milk. Return the pan to the heat,
then bring slowly to a boil, stirring or whisking continuously, until the sauce thickens.
Simmer gently for 2–3 minutes, stirring. Season to taste with salt and pepper. Serve hot.

SERVING SUGGESTIONS *Serve with broiled or grilled lean lamb, pork, or turkey steaks or kebabs.*
Alternatively, serve with cooked egg dishes, such as omelets or frittatas.
VARIATION *Use 1 red onion or 3–4 shallots in place of regular onion.*
COOK'S TIPS *When buying onions, choose firm onions which have dry skins and which show no signs of*
sprouting or discoloration.
   Store onions in a cool, dry, dark, airy place. Onions also store well when hung up in strings –
simply put the onions in a nylon stocking, tie a knot between each onion to prevent them touching
each other, then hang in a dry, airy place.

243 LIGHT GREEN PEPPERCORN SAUCE

PREPARATION TIME *5 minutes* **COOKING TIME** *10 minutes* **SERVES 4–6** *Makes about 1½ cups*

1 tbsp reduced-fat spread
2 tbsp all-purpose flour
⅔ cup vegetable stock
   *(see recipe on page
   10)*, cooled

⅔ cup semi-skimmed milk
1 tbsp green peppercorns in
   brine, drained & chopped
   or crushed

¼ cup smoked hard
cheese, finely grated
Sea salt & freshly ground
   black pepper

1 Place the reduced-fat spread, flour, stock, and milk in a small saucepan. Heat gently, whisking continuously, until the sauce comes to a boil and is thickened and smooth. Simmer gently for 3–4 minutes, stirring.

2 Remove the pan from the heat and stir in the peppercorns, then stir in the cheese until melted. Season to taste with salt and pepper. Serve hot.

SERVING SUGGESTIONS *Serve with broiled skinless chicken or turkey breast portions. Alternatively, serve with poached salmon, cod, or haddock steaks.*

VARIATIONS *Use extra milk in place of stock. Use mature cheddar, emmental or gruyère cheese in place of smoked cheese.*

COOK'S TIP *Black, white, and green peppercorns all come from the fruit of the same tropical Asian vine, but they are picked at different stages and processed differently, which in turn affects their flavor. Black peppercorns have the most pungent flavor, followed by white peppercorns, then green.*

244 LIGHT ESPAGNOLE SAUCE

PREPARATION TIME *15 minutes* **COOKING TIME** *1¼ hours* **SERVES 4–6** *Makes about 2 cups*

2 tbsp reduced-fat spread
1 slice of lean back bacon,
 finely chopped
2 shallots, finely chopped
1 small carrot, finely chopped

1 cup chestnut or brown
 cap mushrooms, finely
 chopped
3 tbsp all-purpse flour
2½ cups beef stock *(see
 recipe on page 11)*

1 dried bouquet garni
4 black peppercorns
1 bay leaf
2 tbsp tomato paste
Sea salt & freshly ground
 black pepper

1 Melt the reduced-fat spread in a saucepan over a low heat, then add the bacon and cook gently for 2 minutes, stirring. Add the shallots, carrot, and mushrooms and cook gently for 8–10 minutes, or until lightly browned, stirring occasionally.

2 Stir in the flour and cook gently until lightly browned, stirring continuously, then remove the pan from the heat and gradually stir in the stock.

3 Add all the remaining ingredients, then return the pan to the heat and bring slowly to a boil, stirring continuously, until the mixture thickens. Cover and simmer gently for 1 hour, stirring occasionally.

4 Strain the sauce through a sieve into a bowl, remove and discard the bouquet garni, then rub the pulp through the sieve. Return the sauce to the rinsed-out pan, and discard the contents of the sieve. Reheat the sauce gently until hot, stirring, then adjust the seasoning to taste. Serve hot.

SERVING SUGGESTIONS *Serve with broiled or roast lean beef, lamb, venison, or pheasant.*

245 LIGHT BURGUNDY SAUCE

PREPARATION TIME *10 minutes* **COOKING TIME** *15 minutes* **SERVES 6** *Makes about 2¼ cups*

2 tbsp reduced-fat spread
1 small red onion, coarsely
 grated
1 clove garlic, crushed
¼ cup all-purpose flour

1 cup beef stock *(see recipe
 on page 11)*
1 cup burgundy or red wine
2 tsp chopped fresh thyme
1 tbsp lemon juice

Sea salt & freshly ground
 black pepper

1 Melt the reduced-fat spread in a saucepan over a low heat. Add the onion and garlic, and cook gently for about 5 minutes, or until softened, stirring occasionally.

2 Stir in the flour and cook for 1 minute, stirring, then remove the pan from the heat and gradually stir in the stock and wine. Return to the heat and bring slowly to a boil, stirring or whisking continuously, until the sauce thickens. Simmer gently for 2–3 minutes, stirring.

3 Stir in the chopped thyme and lemon juice, and season to taste with salt and pepper. Reheat gently until hot, stirring. Serve hot.

SERVING SUGGESTIONS *Serve with broiled or roast lean beef, lamb, pork, pheasant, or low-fat sausages.*

VARIATIONS *Use 2 shallots in place of onion. For a white wine sauce, use chicken or fish stock and medium white wine in place of beef stock and red wine, and serve it with broiled chicken breasts.*

246 LIGHT WHITE WINE AND MUSHROOM SAUCE

PREPARATION TIME *10 minutes* **COOKING TIME** *15 minutes* **SERVES 4–6**

3 cups chestnut (brown cap) or button mushrooms, sliced

2 cloves garlic, thinly sliced

2 cups chicken stock *(see recipe on page 11)*, cooled

Sea salt & freshly ground black pepper

2 tbsp reduced-fat spread

¼ cup all-purpose flour

⅔ cup medium-dry white wine

1–2 tbsp chopped fresh tarragon, or 1–2 tsp dried tarragon

1 Place the mushrooms, garlic, ½ cup of the stock, and a little seasoning in a saucepan. Bring to a boil, then reduce the heat, cover, and simmer for 8–10 minutes.

2 Meanwhile, place the remaining stock, the reduced-fat spread, flour, and wine in a separate saucepan and heat gently, whisking continuously, until the sauce comes to a boil and thickens. Simmer gently for 3–4 minutes, stirring.

3 Remove the mushrooms from their cooking liquid using a slotted spoon, and add to the wine sauce. Discard the garlic and mushroom cooking liquid. Add the chopped fresh or dried tarragon to the wine sauce and stir to mix, then reheat gently until hot, stirring. Adjust the seasoning to taste. Serve hot.

SERVING SUGGESTIONS *Serve with oven-baked or char-grilled skinless chicken or turkey breast portions, or with broiled haddock, monkfish, or halibut.*

VARIATION *Use chopped fresh flat-leaf parsley or fresh mixed herbs in place of tarragon.*

247 LIGHT HERBY MUSHROOM SAUCE

PREPARATION TIME *10 minutes* **COOKING TIME** *45–50 minutes* **SERVES 6–8**

2 tsp olive oil

2 shallots, finely chopped

¾ lb chestnut or brown cap mushrooms, finely chopped

1¼ cups vegetable stock *(see recipe on page 10)*

1¼ cups semi-skimmed milk

2 tbsp chopped fresh sage

1 bay leaf

Sea salt & freshly ground black pepper

1 tbsp cornstarch

1 Heat the oil in a non-stick saucepan, add the shallots and mushrooms, and cook gently for about 8–10 minutes, or until softened.

2 Stir in the stock and milk, then add the chopped sage, bay leaf, and a little salt and pepper, mixing well. Bring slowly to a boil, then cover and simmer gently for 25–30 minutes, stirring occasionally. Remove and discard the bay leaf.

3 In a small bowl, blend the cornstarch with 2 tbsp cold water until smooth. Stir the cornstarch mixture into the mushroom sauce, then bring slowly back to a boil, stirring continuously, until the mixture thickens. Simmer gently for 2–3 minutes, stirring. Adjust the seasoning to taste, and serve hot.

SERVING SUGGESTIONS *Serve with broiled or oven-baked lean pork or veal, or skinless chicken or turkey breast portions. Alternatively, serve with broiled cod or haddock fillets, or whole trout.*

248 LIGHT THOUSAND ISLAND SAUCE

PREPARATION TIME *10 minutes, plus standing* **COOKING TIME** *N/A* **SERVES 8–10**

1¼ cups reduced-calorie
  mayonnaise
4 tbsp natural yogurt
2 tbsp tomato catsup
3 tbsp gherkins, drained
  & finely chopped

2 tbsp seeded & finely
  chopped red bell pepper
2 tbsp seeded & finely
  chopped green or yellow
  bell pepper

1 tbsp chopped fresh parsley
  or cilantro
Sea salt & freshly ground
  black pepper

1 Place the mayonnaise, yogurt, and tomato catsup in a bowl and stir to mix. Add the
chopped gherkins, bell peppers, and chopped parsley or cilantro and mix well. Season to
taste with salt and pepper.

2 Cover and leave in a cool place for about 30 minutes before serving, so the flavors
develop. Serve cold.

SERVING SUGGESTIONS *Serve with cold cooked shrimp or a cold cooked mixed seafood salad.*
VARIATIONS *Use chopped (pitted) green or stuffed olives in place of green or yellow bell peppers. Add
1–2 cold hard-cooked eggs, shelled and mashed or finely chopped, to the sauce, if desired.*

249 LIGHT CREAMY HORSERADISH SAUCE

PREPARATION TIME *10 minutes, plus standing* **COOKING TIME** *N/A* **SERVES 4** *Makes about ⅔ cup*

4 tbsp grated (peeled)
  fresh horseradish
1 tsp superfine sugar
2 tsp Dijon or English
  mustard

2 tbsp malt vinegar
3 tbsp reduced-fat light
  or heavy cream, or natural
  yogurt

Sea salt & freshly ground
  black pepper

1 Place the grated horseradish in a bowl, add the sugar and mustard, and stir to mix well.
2 Stir in the vinegar, then gently stir in the cream or yogurt, mixing well. Season to taste with salt and pepper.
3 Cover and let stand in a cool place for about 30 minutes before serving, so the flavors develop. Serve cold.

SERVING SUGGESTIONS *Serve with broiled or oven-baked mackerel or trout fillets, or smoked salmon.*

250 MINTED APPLE SAUCE

PREPARATION TIME *10 minutes* **COOKING TIME** *15 minutes* **SERVES 4–6**

1 small onion, finely chopped
1 lb tart apples, peeled,
  cored, & sliced

A small bunch of fresh mint
  leaves, finely chopped

2 tbsp superfine sugar or
  light soft brown sugar,
  or to taste

1 Place the onion and apples in a saucepan with 2 tbsp water. Cover and cook gently for about 10 minutes, or until the apples and onion are softened, stirring occasionally.
2 Remove the pan from the heat and mash the apples and onion lightly to form a pulp.
3 Stir in the chopped mint and sugar, then reheat gently, stirring continuously, until the sugar has dissolved. Taste, and add a little more sugar, if desired. Serve hot or cold. If serving cold, remove the pan from the heat and set aside to cool completely, then serve.

SERVING SUGGESTIONS *Serve with hot or cold roast or grilled lean ham, or smoked pork.*

251 TASTY BARBECUE SAUCE

PREPARATION TIME *10 minutes* **COOKING TIME** *25–30 minutes* **SERVES 4–6** *Makes about 1¼ cups*

3 tbsp reduced-fat spread
1 onion, finely chopped
⅔ cup tomato juice
2 tbsp red wine vinegar

1 tbsp Worcestershire sauce
1 tbsp light soft brown sugar
2 tsp English mustard
1 tbsp tomato paste

Sea salt & freshly ground
  black pepper

1 Melt the reduced-fat spread in a small saucepan over a low heat, then add the onion and cook gently for 8–10 minutes, or until softened, stirring occasionally.
2 Add the tomato juice, vinegar, Worcestershire sauce, sugar, mustard, tomato paste, and seasoning, and mix well. Bring gently to a boil, then simmer, uncovered, for 10–15 minutes, stirring occasionally. Serve hot.
3 If you would like a smoother sauce, remove the pan from the heat and let the cooked sauce cool slightly, then purée the sauce in a blender or food processor until smooth. Return the sauce to the rinsed-out pan and reheat gently before serving.

SERVING SUGGESTIONS *Serve with grilled or broiled low-fat sausages, or skinless chicken thighs.*

252 RED CHILI SAUCE

PREPARATION TIME *10 minutes* **COOKING TIME** *30–35 minutes* **SERVES 6–8** *Makes about 2 cups*

1 tbsp olive oil
6 scallions, finely
  chopped
1 fresh red chili, finely
  chopped

1 clove garlic, crushed
14-oz can chopped tomatoes
1 tsp fresh lemon juice
1 tbsp light soft brown sugar

Sea salt & freshly ground
  black pepper

1 Heat the oil in a saucepan, add the scallions, chili, and garlic and sauté for 5 minutes, or until softened. Add the tomatoes, lemon juice, sugar, and seasoning and mix well.
2 Bring to a boil, then reduce the heat and simmer gently, uncovered, for 20–25 minutes, or until the sauce is cooked and thickened slightly, stirring occasionally. Adjust the seasoning to taste. Serve hot.

SERVING SUGGESTIONS *Serve with broiled monkfish tail, king prawns, or scallops.*

253 MEDITERRANEAN TOMATO SAUCE

PREPARATION TIME *10 minutes* **COOKING TIME** *30 minutes* **SERVES 8** *Makes about 2½ cups*

2 tsp olive oil
1 red onion, finely chopped
1 clove garlic, crushed
1 lb ripe plum or vine-ripened
  tomatoes, skinned &
  chopped

1 tbsp tomato paste
½ tsp superfine sugar
4 tbsp red or white wine
Sea salt & freshly ground
  black pepper
2 tbsp chopped fresh basil

1 Heat the oil in a saucepan, add the onion and garlic, and sauté for 5 minutes. Add the tomatoes, tomato paste, sugar, wine, and seasoning to taste, and mix well.
2 Bring to a boil, stirring, then reduce the heat, cover, and simmer for 20 minutes, or until thickened, stirring occasionally. Stir in the chopped basil. Serve hot.

SERVING SUGGESTIONS *Serve with char-grilled tuna steaks or lean lamb cutlets.*

254 TASTY BASIL SAUCE

PREPARATION TIME *5 minutes* **COOKING TIME** *15 minutes* **SERVES 4–6** *Makes about 1½ cups*

1 tbsp reduced-fat spread
1 small onion or 2 shallots,
  finely chopped
1 clove garlic, crushed
2 tbsp all-purpose flour

1¼ cups semi-skimmed milk
¼ cup fresh Parmesan
  cheese, finely grated
2–3 tbsp chopped fresh basil

Sea salt & freshly ground
  black pepper

1 Melt the reduced-fat spread in a saucepan over a low heat. Add the onion or shallots, and garlic and cook gently for about 5 minutes, or until softened, stirring occasionally.
2 Stir in the flour and cook for 1 minute, stirring, then remove the pan from the heat and gradually whisk in the milk. Return the pan to the heat, then bring slowly to a boil, whisking continuously, until the sauce thickens. Simmer gently for 2–3 minutes, stirring.
3 Stir or whisk the Parmesan cheese into the sauce until melted, then stir in the chopped basil. Season to taste with salt and pepper. Serve hot.

SERVING SUGGESTIONS *Serve with broiled whole plaice or lemon sole.*

255 QUICK TOMATO SAUCE

PREPARATION TIME *10 minutes* **COOKING TIME** *25 minutes* **SERVES 6** *Makes about 2 cups*

3 tbsp reduced-fat spread
1 onion, finely chopped
14-oz can chopped tomatoes
1 tbsp tomato paste

1 tsp dried herbes de
   Provence
Sea salt & freshly ground
   black pepper
4 tbsp dry white wine

1 Melt the reduced-fat spread in a saucepan over a low heat. Add the onion and cook
gently for 5 minutes, stirring occasionally.

2 Add the tomatoes, tomato paste, dried herbs, and salt and pepper to taste, and mix well.

3 Bring almost to a boil, stir in the wine, then bring to a boil, reduce the heat and
simmer, uncovered, for 15–20 minutes, or until the sauce is cooked and thickened,
stirring occasionally. Serve hot.

SERVING SUGGESTIONS *Serve with char-grilled or grilled tuna or salmon steaks. Alternatively, serve with
poached or oven-baked cod or haddock fillets, skinless chicken breasts, or broiled polenta slices.*
VARIATIONS *Add 1 clove of crushed garlic to the tomato sauce, if desired. Cook the garlic with the
onion and continue as above. Use 1 red onion or 4 shallots in place of regular onion. Use 1 tbsp
chopped fresh mixed herbs in place of dried herbs.*
COOK'S TIP *If you prefer a smoother sauce, remove the pan from the heat and let the cooked sauce
cool slightly, then purée the sauce in a blender or food processor until smooth. Return the sauce to
the rinsed-out pan, and reheat gently before serving.*

256 LIGHT BLUE CHEESE SAUCE

PREPARATION TIME *10 minutes* **COOKING TIME** *N/A* **SERVES 4–6**

½ cup low-fat cream cheese
    with garlic & herbs
½ cup whole-milk natural
    yogurt or half-fat
    crème fraîche

½ cup mature Danish
    blue cheese, crumbled

1 Place the cream cheese and yogurt or crème fraîche in a small bowl.
2 Add the Danish blue cheese and blend the ingredients together until smooth and well combined. Serve immediately.

SERVING SUGGESTIONS *Serve with sliced (cored) pears or apples. Alternatively, serve with slices of (peeled and seeded) charantais or Galia melon.*
VARIATIONS *Use plain low-fat cream cheese in place of flavored cream cheese. Use other blue cheeses such as Stilton or gorgonzola in place of Danish blue. Use plain fromage frais in place of yogurt or crème fraîche.*
COOK'S TIPS *Danish blue cheese is a blue-veined, semi-soft cheese made from cow's milk, with a buttery, crumbly texture. It is a white cheese which is densely veined and has a rich, strong, quite salty flavor.*

To store cheese such as Danish blue, wrap it loosely in baking parchment or foil and store in an airtight container in the refrigerator.

257 LIGHT CHEESY BROCCOLI SAUCE

PREPARATION TIME *15 minutes* **COOKING TIME** *10 minutes* **SERVES 6–8**

2 cups small broccoli
    florets
1 small onion, chopped
1 tbsp reduced-fat spread
2 tbsp all-purpose flour

⅔ cup semi-skimmed milk
⅔ cup vegetable stock *(see
    recipe on page 10)*,
    cooled

½ cup reduced-fat mature
    cheddar cheese, finely
    grated
Sea salt & freshly ground
    black pepper

1 Cook the broccoli and onion in a saucepan of boiling water for about 6–7 minutes, or until cooked and very tender. Drain, rinse under cold running water, drain again, then place in a blender or food processor with 3 tbsp water, and blend until smooth. Set aside.
2 Place the reduced-fat spread, flour, milk, and stock in a small saucepan and heat gently, whisking continuously, until the sauce comes to a boil and thickens. Simmer gently for 3–4 minutes, stirring.
3 Stir in the broccoli purée and reheat gently until hot, stirring continuously. Remove the pan from the heat, stir in the cheese until melted, then season to taste with salt and pepper. Serve hot.

SERVING SUGGESTIONS *Serve with broiled or oven-baked haddock or cod steaks, or whole trout.*

258 LIGHT BOLOGNESE PASTA SAUCE

PREPARATION TIME *10 minutes* **COOKING TIME** *1 hour 40 minutes* **SERVES 4**

1 onion, chopped
1 clove garlic, crushed
1 lb extra-lean
    ground beef
3 carrots, finely chopped
3 cups chestnut or brown
    cap mushrooms, sliced

3 sticks of celery, finely
    chopped
14 oz can chopped tomatoes
1 tbsp tomato paste
2 tsp dried mixed herbs
1¼ cups beef stock *(see
    recipe on page 11)*

1¼ cups dry white wine or
    red wine
Sea salt & freshly ground
    black pepper

1 Place the onion and garlic in a large, non-stick saucepan with the ground beef. Cook
  gently until the ground beef is browned all over, stirring occasionally.
2 Add the carrots, mushrooms, and celery and cook for 5 minutes, stirring occasionally.
3 Stir in the tomatoes, tomato paste, mixed herbs, stock, wine, and salt and pepper to
  taste, and mix well. Bring to a boil, then reduce the heat, cover, and simmer for 1 hour,
  stirring occasionally.
4 Uncover the pan, increase the heat slightly and simmer for a further 20–30 minutes to
  thicken the sauce. Serve hot.

SERVING SUGGESTIONS *Serve with hot pasta such as spaghetti, spaghettini, tagliatelle, or fettucine.*
VARIATIONS *Use 1 red onion or 4 shallots in place of regular onion. Use lean ground turkey or pork in
place of ground beef.*

259 LIGHT SPAGHETTI CARBONARA

PREPARATION TIME *10 minutes* **COOKING TIME** *15 minutes* **SERVES 4–6**

12 oz dried spaghetti
Sea salt & freshly ground
    black pepper
2 tsp olive oil
1 onion, finely chopped
1 clove garlic, crushed

½ lb cooked lean smoked or
    unsmoked ham, cut into
    strips
3 eggs, beaten
6 tbsp reduced-fat heavy
    cream

¾ cup fresh Parmesan
    cheese, finely grated
2 tbsp chopped fresh parsley
    or snipped fresh chives
    (optional)

1 Cook the spaghetti in a large saucepan of lightly salted, boiling water for 10–12
  minutes, or until just cooked or al dente.
2 Meanwhile, heat the oil in a non-stick saucepan, add the onion and garlic and cook
  gently for 8–10 minutes, or until softened. Add the ham and mix well. Remove the pan
  from the heat and set aside.
3 Mix the eggs, cream, Parmesan cheese, chopped parsley or snipped chives, if using, and
  seasoning together in a bowl.
4 Drain the pasta thoroughly and return to a clean pan. Add the ham mixture and toss to
  mix. Add the egg mixture and cook gently over a very low heat, tossing continuously,
  until the eggs are lightly cooked. Serve immediately.

SERVING SUGGESTIONS *Serve with spaghetti, as above, or with tagliatelle, if preferred.*

260 LIGHT TOMATO, BASIL, AND OLIVE PASTA SAUCE

PREPARATION TIME *10 minutes* COOKING TIME *30–35 minutes* SERVES 4

2 tsp olive oil
3 shallots, finely chopped
1 clove garlic, crushed
14-oz can chopped tomatoes
8-oz can chopped tomatoes

⅔ cup dry white wine or
   dry vermouth
2 tbsp tomato catsup
Sea salt & freshly ground
   black pepper

⅔ cup pitted black olives,
   halved
3 tbsp chopped fresh basil

1 Heat the oil in a non-stick saucepan, add the shallots and garlic and sauté for about 5 minutes, or until softened. Add all the tomatoes, the wine or vermouth, tomato catsup, and salt and pepper to taste, and mix well.

2 Bring to a boil, then reduce the heat, cover and simmer for 15 minutes, stirring occasionally.

3 Uncover the pan, increase the heat slightly and simmer for a further 5–10 minutes, or until the sauce is thickened, stirring occasionally. Stir in the olives and chopped basil and mix well. Serve hot.

SERVING SUGGESTIONS *Serve with hot pasta such as fusilli, farfalle, or spirali.*
VARIATIONS *Use 1 small regular or red onion in place of shallots. Use vegetable stock (see recipe on page 10) in place of white wine or vermouth. Use char-grilled or roasted bell peppers in oil (drained, patted dry, and chopped) in place of olives. Use 1–2 tbsp chopped fresh mixed herbs in place of basil.*

261 GARLIC MUSHROOM PASTA SAUCE

PREPARATION TIME *10 minutes* COOKING TIME *25 minutes* SERVES 4–6

2 tbsp reduced-fat spread
1 onion, finely chopped
4 cloves garlic, crushed
1 lb closed cup
   mushrooms, sliced
¼ cup all-purpose flour

¾ cup semi-skimmed milk
½ cup vegetable stock *(see
   recipe on page 10)*
2 tbsp reduced-fat light
   cream
1 tbsp chopped fresh parsley

Sea salt & freshly ground
   black pepper

1 Melt the reduced-fat spread in a saucepan over a low heat. Add the onion and garlic, and cook gently for 5 minutes, stirring occasionally. Stir in the mushrooms, then cover the pan and cook gently for 8–10 minutes, or until softened, stirring occasionally.

2 Stir in the flour and cook for 1 minute, stirring, then remove the pan from the heat and gradually stir in the milk and stock. Return the pan to the heat. Bring slowly to a boil, stirring or whisking continuously, until the sauce thickens. Simmer gently for 2–3 minutes, stirring.

3 Remove the pan from the heat and stir in the cream and chopped parsley, then season to taste with salt and pepper. Serve hot.

SERVING SUGGESTIONS *Serve with hot pasta such as tagliatelle, linguine, or fettucine.*
VARIATIONS *Use 3–4 shallots in place of onion. Use half-fat crème fraîche in place of cream.*

262 CREAMY LEEK AND MUSHROOM PASTA SAUCE

PREPARATION TIME *10 minutes* **COOKING TIME** *20 minutes* **SERVES 4**

4 cups leeks (trimmed
 weight), washed & sliced
10 oz closed cup mushrooms,
 sliced
1 bay leaf

3 tbsp reduced-fat spread
⅓ cup all-purpose flour
2¼ cups semi-skimmed milk
2 tbsp snipped fresh chives

Sea salt & freshly ground
 black pepper

1 Steam the leeks and mushrooms with the bay leaf over a saucepan of boiling water for
 10–15 minutes, or until cooked and tender. Remove and discard the bay leaf, then drain
 the vegetables thoroughly, set aside, and keep hot.
2 Meanwhile, make the sauce. Place the reduced-fat spread, flour, and milk in a
 saucepan. Heat gently, whisking continuously, until the sauce comes to a boil and is
 thickened and smooth. Simmer gently for 3–4 minutes, stirring.
3 Stir in the steamed vegetables and snipped chives, and reheat gently until hot, stirring.
 Season to taste with salt and pepper. Serve hot.

SERVING SUGGESTIONS *Serve with hot pasta such as linguine, pappardelle, or fettucine.*
VARIATIONS *Use chopped fresh parsley or 1–2 tbsp chopped fresh tarragon in place of chives. Use
zucchini in place of mushrooms.*
COOK'S TIP *When buying leeks, choose those that are crisp, fresh and bright in color. Avoid dry or soft
leeks, or those with slimy leaves.*

263 FLAKED SALMON AND ZUCCHINI PASTA SAUCE

PREPARATION TIME *10 minutes* **COOKING TIME** *20 minutes* **SERVES 4**

2 tbsp reduced-fat spread
2 shallots, finely chopped
2 zucchini, cut into
 matchstick strips
¼ cup all-purpose flour

1¼ cups semi-skimmed milk
7½-oz can red salmon,
 drained, boned & flaked
A dash of Tabasco sauce

1–2 tbsp snipped fresh
 chives
Sea salt & freshly ground
 black pepper

1 Melt the reduced-fat spread in a saucepan over a low heat. Add the shallots and
 zucchini and cook gently for about 8–10 minutes, or until softened, stirring occasionally.
2 Stir in the flour and cook for 1 minute, stirring, then remove the pan from the heat and
 gradually stir in the milk.
3 Return the pan to the heat and bring slowly to a boil, stirring or whisking continuously,
 until the sauce thickens. Simmer gently for 2–3 minutes, stirring.
4 Stir in the salmon, Tabasco sauce, and snipped chives and reheat gently until hot,
 stirring. Season to taste with salt and pepper. Serve hot.

SERVING SUGGESTIONS *Serve with hot pasta such as farfalle, conchiglie, or penne.*
VARIATIONS *Use 1 small regular or red onion in place of shallots. Use about 4 cups sliced or chopped
mushrooms in place of zucchini. Use canned pink salmon or tuna in place of red salmon. Use
chopped fresh parsley or cilantro in place of chives.*

CHAPTER 9

SAVORY AND SWEET DIPS

A great way to entertain family and friends at a party is to serve a tempting selection of flavorful home-made dips. Dips encourage your guests to circulate and mingle, and they are easy to serve and sample. Most are quick and easy to make, and many can be made in advance – ideal for parties, barbecues, and get-togethers.

Accompany savory dips with an assortment of fresh vegetable crudités, warm pitta bread fingers, roast potato wedges, breadsticks, tortilla chips, thick-cut crisps, or small crackers. For sweet dips, try serving a selection of prepared, assorted fresh fruit, fingers of chocolate brownies or sponge cakes, marshmallows, small squares of fudge, lady fingers, dried fruit, and whole nuts.

Choose from a delicious selection of savory and sweet dips, including Guacamole, Houmous, Tzatziki, Honey Mustard Dip, Sour Cream and Chive Dip, Roast Garlic Dip, Blue Cheese Dip, Italian Tomato Dip, and Creamy Crab Dip. Or try some sweet delights such as Honey Yogurt Dip, Lemon Cream Swirl, Raspberry Cream Dip, Wicked Chocolate Fondue, and Velvety Chocolate Dip.

264 GUACAMOLE

PREPARATION TIME *10 minutes* **COOKING TIME** *N/A* **SERVES 4–6**

2 ripe avocados
Juice of 1 small lime
3 shallots, finely chopped
2 plum tomatoes, skinned,
   seeded, & finely chopped

1 fresh green chili, seeded
   & finely chopped
1 clove garlic, crushed
1 tbsp chopped fresh
   cilantro

Sea salt & freshly ground
   black pepper
Fresh cilantro sprigs,
   to garnish

1 Halve, pit, and peel the avocados and place the flesh in a bowl. Mash the avocado flesh with the lime juice until smooth.

2 Stir in the shallots, tomatoes, chili, garlic, chopped cilantro, and salt and pepper to taste. Mix well.

3 Transfer the mixture to a bowl, garnish with cilantro sprigs, and serve immediately.

SERVING SUGGESTIONS *Serve with a selection of raw vegetable crudités such as carrot, cucumber, and bell pepper sticks, and scallions. Guacamole is also good served with tortilla chips or pitta bread.*

265 HOUMOUS

PREPARATION TIME *10 minutes* **COOKING TIME** *N/A* **SERVES 4**

15-oz can garbanzos,
   rinsed & drained
Juice of 1 lemon
3 tbsp extra-virgin olive oil

2 tbsp light tahini paste
1 clove garlic, crushed
½ tsp ground coriander
½ tsp ground cumin

Sea salt & freshly ground
   black pepper
Fresh cilantro sprigs,
   to garnish

1 Place the garbanzos in a blender or food processor with the lemon juice, olive oil, tahini paste, garlic, ground coriander, ground cumin, and salt and pepper to taste. Blend until smooth and thoroughly mixed. Adjust the seasoning to taste.

2 Transfer the mixture to a bowl. Garnish with cilantro sprigs and serve.

SERVING SUGGESTIONS *Serve with a selection of fresh raw vegetable crudités, such as bell pepper, carrot and zucchini sticks, button mushrooms and small ears of corn, or with warm pitta bread.*

266 TARAMASALATA

PREPARATION TIME *15 minutes* **COOKING TIME** *N/A* **SERVES 6–8**

1 thick slice of white bread,
   crusts removed
¼ lb fresh smoked cod's roe,
   soaked, drained
   & skinned

Juice of ½ lemon
1 clove garlic, crushed
5 tbsp sunflower oil
5 tbsp olive oil

Freshly ground black pepper,
   to taste

1 Hold the bread slice under cold running water to soak it, then drain and squeeze out the excess liquid. Place the bread, cod's roe, lemon juice, and garlic in a small blender or food processor, and process briefly to mix.

2 With the motor running and blades turning, gradually add the sunflower oil in a thin, steady stream, followed by the olive oil in a thin, steady stream, until the mixture becomes smooth, light, and creamy.

3 Transfer to a bowl, and season to taste with black pepper. Serve immediately.

SERVING SUGGESTIONS *Serve with warm small pitta breads, or fingers of hot toast.*

267 TAPENADE

PREPARATION TIME *10 minutes* COOKING TIME *N/A* SERVES 4–6

⅔ cup pitted black olives
1 tbsp capers, rinsed
   & drained

1¾-oz can anchovy
   fillets in oil, drained
1 clove garlic, peeled
1 tbsp white wine vinegar

1 tbsp chopped fresh parsley
6 tbsp olive oil
Freshly ground black pepper,
   to taste

1 Place the olives, capers, and anchovy fillets in a small blender or food processor and process briefly to chop. Add the garlic, vinegar, and chopped parsley and process briefly to mix.
2 With the motor running and blades turning, gradually add the oil in a slow, steady stream, until it is all incorporated.
3 Transfer the mixture to a bowl and season to taste with black pepper. Serve immediately, or cover and refrigerate for up to 3 days.

SERVING SUGGESTIONS *Serve with a selection of char-grilled vegetables, fingers of toast, warm small pitta breads or breadsticks.*
VARIATION *Add 1 tsp finely grated lemon zest with the garlic, if desired.*

268 TZATZIKI

PREPARATION TIME *10 minutes, plus chilling* COOKING TIME *N/A* SERVES 6–8

1 cucumber
1¼ cups natural Greek yogurt
1 tbsp light olive oil

2 cloves garlic, crushed
2 tbsp chopped fresh mint

Sea salt & freshly ground
   black pepper

1 Halve, seed, and finely chop the cucumber. Place the cucumber in a bowl, add the yogurt and olive oil, and stir to mix well.
2 Add the garlic and chopped mint and mix well, then season to taste with salt and pepper. Cover and chill until ready to serve.

SERVING SUGGESTIONS *Serve with warm whole wheat pitta bread fingers, breadsticks, or a selection of fresh vegetable crudités.*

269 AVOCADO DIP

PREPARATION TIME *10 minutes* COOKING TIME *N/A* SERVES 6–8

2 ripe avocados
A squeeze of fresh lemon
   juice, or to taste

1 clove garlic, crushed
2 scallions, finely
   chopped

1 tbsp snipped fresh chives
Sea salt & freshly ground
   black pepper

1 Halve, pit, and peel the avocados. Place the flesh in a bowl with the lemon juice and mash until smooth and mixed.
2 Stir in the garlic, scallions, and snipped chives, and season to taste with salt and pepper. Serve immediately, or cover and leave at room temperature for about 30 minutes before serving.

SERVING SUGGESTIONS *Serve with broiled vegetable crudités such as small zucchini, bell pepper sticks, baby carrots, or small ears of corn.*

270 CREAMY GARLIC AND CHIVE DIP

PREPARATION TIME *5 minutes* **COOKING TIME** *N/A* **SERVES 6**

⅔ cup sour cream
⅔ cup plain fromage frais
2 cloves garlic, crushed
2 shallots, finely chopped
  (optional)

2–3 tbsp snipped fresh
  chives
Sea salt & freshly ground
  black pepper

Additional snipped fresh
  chives, to garnish
  (optional)

1 Place the sour cream and fromage frais in a bowl and mix together until well blended.
2 Add the garlic, shallots, if using, and snipped chives and mix well. Season to taste with
  salt and pepper.
3 Transfer the mixture to a bowl and serve immediately, or cover and chill until ready to
  serve. Garnish with a sprinkling of snipped chives, if desired, just before serving.

SERVING SUGGESTIONS *Serve with broiled or pan-fried goujons of breaded white fish or chicken.*
Alternatively, serve with oven-baked potato wedges.
VARIATIONS *Use crème fraîche or natural Greek yogurt in place of sour cream. Use half a small red*
onion or 2 scallions in place of shallots. Use other chopped fresh herbs such as parsley or mixed
herbs in place of chives.
COOK'S TIP *Fresh chive flowers also create an attractive garnish for this dip.*

271 HONEY MUSTARD DIP

PREPARATION TIME *10 minutes* **COOKING TIME** *N/A* **SERVES 8–10**

1 cup crème fraîche
½ cup Mayonnaise *(see recipe on page 37)*

3 tbsp wholegrain mustard, or to taste
2 tbsp clear honey, or to taste

Sea salt & freshly ground black pepper (optional)

1 Place the crème fraîche and mayonnaise in a bowl and stir gently until well blended.

2 Stir in the mustard and honey to taste, until well mixed. Season to taste with salt and pepper, if desired.

3 Serve immediately, or cover and chill for about 1 hour before serving, so the flavors develop a little more.

SERVING SUGGESTIONS *Serve with roasted sweet potato wedges, or with a selection of fresh raw vegetable crudités such as carrot and cucumber sticks, and cherry tomatoes.*
VARIATION *Use Dijon mustard in place of wholegrain mustard.*

272 SOUR CREAM AND CHIVE DIP

PREPARATION TIME *10 minutes* **COOKING TIME** *N/A* **SERVES 6**

1¼ cups thick sour cream or crème fraîche
1 clove garlic, crushed

2–3 scallions, finely chopped (optional)
3–4 tbsp snipped fresh chives

Sea salt & freshly ground black pepper
Fresh chive flowers, to garnish (optional)

1 Place the sour cream or crème fraîche in a bowl. Add the garlic, scallions, if using, and snipped chives, and mix well. Season to taste with salt and pepper.

2 Transfer the mixture to a bowl and serve immediately, or cover and chill until ready to serve. Garnish with chive flowers just before serving, if desired.

SERVING SUGGESTIONS *Serve with a selection of fresh vegetable crudités, or with cold cooked baby new potatoes, or cold broiled cocktail sausages.*
VARIATION *Use chopped fresh mixed herbs in place of chives.*

273 WATERCRESS CHEESE DIP

PREPARATION TIME *10 minutes, plus chilling* **COOKING TIME** *N/A* **SERVES 6–8**

1 cup full-fat cream cheese
3 tbsp crème fraîche

1 bunch watercress, finely chopped
1 clove garlic, crushed

Sea salt & freshly ground black pepper

1 Place the cream cheese in a bowl and stir until softened a little more. Stir in the crème fraîche until well combined.

2 Stir in the watercress and garlic, then season to taste with salt and pepper.

3 Cover and chill for at least 1 hour before serving, so the flavors develop.

SERVING SUGGESTIONS *Serve with breadsticks, crackers, or a selection of raw vegetable crudités.*

274 FRESH HERB DIP

PREPARATION TIME *10 minutes* **COOKING TIME** *N/A* **SERVES 8–10**

¾ cup plain fromage frais
¾ cup Mayonnaise *(see recipe on page 37)*
2 scallions, finely chopped

3 tbsp chopped fresh parsley
2 tbsp snipped fresh chives
1 tsp fresh lemon juice

Sea salt & freshly ground black pepper

1 Place the fromage frais and mayonnaise in a bowl and gently fold together to mix well.
2 Stir in the scallions, chopped herbs, and lemon juice and mix well. Season to taste.
3 Serve immediately, or cover and chill for about 1 hour before serving.

SERVING SUGGESTIONS *Serve with cheese breadsticks and fresh vegetable crudités such as small carrots, bell pepper sticks, and broccoli florets.*

275 ROASTED GARLIC DIP

PREPARATION TIME *15 minutes* **COOKING TIME** *45 minutes* **SERVES 6–8**

2 whole heads of garlic, unpeeled
1 tbsp olive oil

1 cup full-fat cream cheese
3 tbsp snipped fresh chives

Sea salt & freshly ground black pepper

1 Preheat the oven to 200°C/400°F/gas mark 6. Slice the top quarter off each garlic head to expose the garlic cloves (but do not separate the cloves).
2 Place the garlic heads in a small roasting pan or baking dish, then drizzle the oil over the top. Cover with foil, then bake in the oven for about 45 minutes, or until the garlic is soft and golden brown. Remove from the oven and set aside to cool completely.
3 Once cool, gently squeeze the garlic heads from the root ends to remove the garlic from the papery skins. Place the garlic flesh in a small bowl and mash with a fork.
4 Add the cream cheese and mix well, then stir in the snipped chives. Season to taste with salt and pepper. Serve immediately, or cover and chill before serving.

SERVING SUGGESTIONS *Serve with warm small pitta breads, breadsticks, or fingers of hot toast.*

276 RED BELL PEPPER HOUMOUS

PREPARATION TIME *10 minutes* **COOKING TIME** *N/A* **SERVES 8–10**

15-oz can garbanzos, rinsed & drained
4 oz roasted red bell peppers in oil (drained weight), drained & patted dry

1 large clove garlic, crushed
1 tbsp fresh lemon juice
4 tbsp extra-virgin olive oil, plus extra for drizzling
2 tbsp light tahini paste

½ tsp hot chili powder, or to taste
Sea salt & freshly ground black pepper

1 Place the garbanzos, red bell peppers, and garlic in a small blender or food processor and blend to mix.
2 Add the lemon juice, 4 tbsp olive oil, the tahini paste, chili powder, and salt and pepper, and blend until smooth and well mixed. Adjust the seasoning to taste.
3 Transfer the mixture to a bowl and drizzle with a little extra olive oil, if desired. Serve.

SERVING SUGGESTIONS *Serve with breadsticks or fresh vegetable crudités such as zucchini and celery sticks, scallions, and baby corn.*

SAVORY AND SWEET DIPS

277 BLUE CHEESE DIP

PREPARATION TIME *10 minutes* **COOKING TIME** *N/A* **SERVES 8**

½ lb dolcelatte or Stilton
  cheese
1 tbsp fresh lemon juice

1 small clove garlic, crushed
  (optional)
1 cup crème fraîche

2 tbsp snipped fresh
  chives (optional)
Sea salt & freshly ground
  black pepper

1 Place the dolcelatte or Stilton cheese in a bowl and mash until smooth and softened.
2 Stir in the lemon juice and garlic, if using, then gradually beat in the crème fraîche until
  the mixture is smooth, creamy, and well combined.
3 Stir in the snipped chives, if using, then season to taste with salt and pepper.
  Serve immediately.

SERVING SUGGESTIONS *Serve with sesame or whole wheat breadsticks, or with fresh vegetable crudités
such as celery sticks and broccoli florets.*

278 SOFT CHEESE, CHIVE, AND SCALLION DIP

PREPARATION TIME *5 minutes* **COOKING TIME** *N/A* **SERVES 6–8**

1 cup full-fat cream cheese
3 tbsp sour cream

2 scallions, finely
  chopped
3 tbsp snipped fresh chives

Sea salt & freshly ground
  black pepper

1 Place the cream cheese in a small bowl and beat until softened a little more. Stir in the
  sour cream until smooth and well mixed.
2 Stir in the scallions and snipped chives, then season to taste with salt and pepper.
3 Serve immediately, or cover and chill for about 1 hour before serving.

SERVING SUGGESTIONS *Serve with cold, cooked cocktail sausages or chipolatas, or with a selection of
fresh vegetable crudités such as radishes, small carrots, and small plum tomatoes.*

279 HERBY LIMA BEAN DIP

PREPARATION TIME *15 minutes, plus chilling* **COOKING TIME** *N/A* **SERVES 4–6**

1 cup plain cottage cheese
14-oz can lima beans, rinsed
  & drained
1 bunch of scallions,
  chopped

1 small bunch of watercress,
  chopped
4 tbsp Mayonnaise
  (see recipe on page 37)
3 tbsp chopped fresh
  mixed herbs

Sea salt & freshly ground
  black pepper
Fresh herb sprigs, to garnish

1 Place the cottage cheese, lima beans, scallions, watercress, mayonnaise, and chopped
  herbs in a blender or food processor and blend together until well mixed and smooth.
2 Transfer the mixture to a bowl and season to taste with salt and pepper, mixing well.
  Cover and chill until ready to serve. Garnish with herb sprigs.

SERVING SUGGESTIONS *Serve with warm mini naan breads, or with a selection of fresh vegetable
crudités such as carrot and bell pepper sticks, celery sticks, and baby ears of corn.*
VARIATION *Use other canned pulses such as cannellini or black-eyed peas in place of lima beans.*

280 ITALIAN TOMATO DIP

PREPARATION TIME *15 minutes* **COOKING TIME** *N/A* **SERVES 6–8**

1 cup full-fat cream cheese
4 tbsp Mayonnaise
 (see recipe on page 37)

4-oz sun-dried tomatoes in
 oil (drained weight),
 drained, patted dry, &
 finely chopped

3 tbsp chopped fresh basil
Sea salt & freshly ground
 black pepper

1 Place the cream cheese in a small bowl and beat until softened a little more. Stir in the mayonnaise until well combined.
2 Stir in the tomatoes and chopped basil, then season to taste with salt and pepper.
3 Serve immediately, or cover and chill for about 1 hour before serving.

SERVING SUGGESTIONS *Serve with small breadsticks, cheese straws, or small crackers.*

281 QUICK SALSA DIP

PREPARATION TIME *10 minutes, plus chilling* **COOKING TIME** *N/A* **SERVES 8–10**

1 cup full-fat cream cheese
2 tbsp sour cream
1¼ cups chilled fresh
 ready-made tomato salsa
2 tbsp chopped fresh basil

Sea salt & freshly ground
 black pepper
Small fresh basil leaves or
 shredded fresh basil
 leaves, to garnish (optional)

1 Place the cream cheese in a small bowl and beat until softened a little more. Stir in the sour cream until smooth and well combined.
2 Stir in the tomato salsa and chopped basil, mixing well, then season to taste.
3 Cover and chill for about 1 hour before serving, so the flavors develop.
4 Garnish with small basil leaves or shredded basil leaves just before serving, if desired.

SERVING SUGGESTIONS *Serve with baked potato and sweet potato wedges, or chicken nuggets or goujons.*

282 RICH CHEESE FONDUE

PREPARATION TIME *10 minutes* **COOKING TIME** *10 minutes* **SERVES 6–8**

1 large clove garlic, peeled
 & halved
2 cups gruyère cheese,
 grated
2 cups emmental cheese,
 grated

1 tbsp cornstarch
2 tbsp Kirsch
1 cup dry white wine
A pinch of freshly grated
 nutmeg (optional)

Freshly ground black pepper,
 to taste
Chopped fresh parsley, to
 garnish (optional)

1 Rub the garlic halves around the inside of a fondue pan or heavy-based saucepan. Place the gruyère and emmental cheeses in the pan. Blend the cornstarch with the Kirsch until smooth and add to the pan together with the wine. Stir to mix.
2 Bring slowly to a boil over a very low heat, stirring continuously, until the mixture is melted and combined. Simmer gently for 3–4 minutes, stirring. Season to taste with nutmeg, if using, and black pepper.
3 Set the pan over the fondue burner (or over a heated serving tray) at the table. Serve immediately, sprinkled with chopped parsley, if desired. Serve with forks for dipping.

SERVING SUGGESTIONS *Serve with chunks of crusty bread and a selection of raw vegetable crudités.*

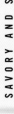

283 SPICY ROASTED EGGPLANT DIP

PREPARATION TIME *20 minutes, plus cooling & chilling* **COOKING TIME** *30–45 minutes* **SERVES 6**

2 eggplant, cut into
  chunks or large dice
1 onion, sliced
2 cloves garlic, thinly sliced

⅔ cup tomato juice
1 tsp *each* of hot chili
  powder, ground coriander,
  & ground cumin

2 tbsp olive oil
Juice of 1 lemon
Sea salt & freshly ground
  black pepper, to taste

1 Preheat the oven to 200°C/400°F/gas mark 6. Place all the ingredients in a non-stick
roasting pan and toss together to mix well. Cover with foil and bake in the oven for
30–45 minutes, or until the vegetables are cooked and tender, stirring one or two times.

2 Remove from the oven and set aside to cool, leaving the foil cover on.

3 Once cool, purée the mixture in a blender or food processor until smooth and well mixed.
Adjust the seasoning to taste, then transfer the mixture to a bowl, cover, and chill until
ready to serve.

SERVING SUGGESTIONS *Serve with a selection of warm Middle-Eastern flatbreads cut into fingers or
triangles, and fresh vegetable crudités such as carrot and bell pepper sticks.*

VARIATIONS *Use 1 fresh red chili, seeded and finely chopped, in place of chili powder. Use 2 leeks,
trimmed and washed, in place of onion. Use lime or orange juice in place of lemon juice.*

284 CREAMY RED BELL PEPPER DIP

PREPARATION TIME *10 minutes* **COOKING TIME** *N/A* **SERVES 6–8**

⅔ cup sour cream
5 tbsp Mayonnaise *(see recipe on page 37)*

6 oz roasted red bell peppers in oil (drained weight), drained, patted dry & finely chopped
1 clove garlic, crushed

2 tbsp chopped fresh basil
A dash of Tabasco sauce, or to taste
Sea salt & freshly ground black pepper

1 Place the sour cream and mayonnaise in a small bowl and stir gently to combine well. Add the red bell peppers, garlic, and chopped basil and stir to mix. Add the Tabasco sauce, and season to taste with salt and pepper.

2 Serve immediately, or cover and chill for about 1 hour before serving.

SERVING SUGGESTIONS *Serve with cheese straws, small breadsticks, chicken nuggets, or a selection of fresh vegetable crudités such as cucumber sticks, baby ears of corn, and button mushrooms.*
VARIATIONS *Use crème fraîche in place of sour cream. Use 1–2 tbsp chopped fresh Italian mixed herbs in place of basil.*
COOK'S TIP *Jars of roasted red bell peppers preserved in oil or brine and vinegar are readily available in supermarkets and delicatessens.*

285 ROASTED BELL PEPPER AND BROWN LENTIL DIP

PREPARATION TIME *30 minutes, plus cooling & chilling* **COOKING TIME** *40 minutes* **SERVES 6**

1 cup brown lentils
Vegetable stock *(see recipe on page 10)*, for cooking lentils
1 bay leaf
2 red bell peppers

1 onion, finely chopped
1 clove garlic, crushed
2 cups button mushrooms, finely chopped
¾ cup mature cheddar cheese, finely grated

2 tbsp chopped fresh · cilantro
Sea salt & freshly ground black pepper
2 tbsp natural yogurt or crème fraîche (optional)

1 Place the lentils in a saucepan and cover with plenty of vegetable stock. Add the bay leaf and stir to mix. Bring to a boil, then reduce the heat, cover, and simmer gently for 30–40 minutes, or until the lentils are cooked and tender, stirring occasionally. Drain the lentils, reserving the lentils and discarding the bay leaf.

2 Meanwhile, preheat the broiler to high. Cut each bell pepper in half and place them, cut-side down, on the rack in a broiler pan. Place under the hot broiler for about 10–15 minutes, or until the skin is blackened and charred. Remove from the heat, cover the bell peppers with a clean, damp dish towel and let cool slightly, then remove and discard the skin, core, and seeds from the bell peppers and dice the flesh.

3 Place the onion, garlic, mushrooms, and bell pepper flesh in a saucepan with 2 tbsp vegetable stock. Cover and cook gently for about 10 minutes, or until the vegetables are tender, stirring occasionally. Remove the pan from the heat and add the cooked lentils, cheese, chopped cilantro and seasoning, mixing well.

4 Place the mixture in a blender or food processor and blend until smooth, then transfer the mixture to a bowl and set aside to cool. Once cool, stir in the yogurt or crème fraîche, if using, then cover and chill until ready to serve.

SERVING SUGGESTIONS *Serve with fresh vegetable crudités such as carrot and celery sticks and small plum tomatoes, warm small pitta or naan breads, and sesame breadsticks.*

286 TARTARE DIP

PREPARATION TIME *15 minutes, plus chilling* **COOKING TIME** *N/A* **SERVES 8–10**

1 cup Mayonnaise *(see recipe on page 37)*
½ cup plain fromage frais
1 tbsp red onion, finely chopped

1½ tsp gherkins (drained weight), drained & finely chopped
1½ tsp capers (drained weight), drained & finely chopped

1 tbsp chopped fresh parsley
1 tbsp snipped fresh chives
Sea salt & freshly ground black pepper

1 Place the mayonnaise and fromage frais in a bowl and stir to mix. Add the onion, gherkins, capers, and chopped herbs, and stir. Season to taste with salt and pepper.
2 Cover and chill for about 1 hour before serving, so the flavors develop.

SERVING SUGGESTIONS *Serve with baked or pan-fried breaded fish, chicken, or turkey goujons or nuggets, or fish fingers.*

287 TUNA AND WATERCRESS DIP

PREPARATION TIME *10 minutes, plus chilling* **COOKING TIME** *N/A* **SERVES 8**

14-oz can tuna in brine or spring water, drained & flaked
15-oz can cannellini beans, rinsed & drained
1 cup natural cottage cheese

1 small bunch watercress, roughly chopped
2 tbsp Mayonnaise *(see recipe on page 37)*
2 tbsp natural Greek yogurt
Finely grated zest of 1 lime

Sea salt & freshly ground black pepper

1 Place the tuna, beans, cottage cheese, watercress, mayonnaise, Greek yogurt, lime zest, and seasoning in a blender or food processor. Blend until the mixture is smooth and thoroughly mixed.
2 Transfer the tuna mixture to a bowl, cover, and chill until ready to serve.

SERVING SUGGESTIONS *Serve with a selection of fresh vegetable crudités such as baby carrots, radishes, cherry tomatoes, scallions, and small corn.*

288 SARDINE AND CHIVE DIP

PREPARATION TIME *10 minutes* **COOKING TIME** *N/A* **SERVES 6–8**

4½oz can sardines in tomato sauce
1 cup full-fat cream cheese

2 tbsp Mayonnaise *(see recipe on page 37)*
1 tbsp fresh lime juice
2 tbsp snipped fresh chives

Sea salt & freshly ground black pepper

1 Place the sardines and tomato sauce in a bowl, and mash with a fork. Add the cream cheese and mash together until well mixed.
2 Stir in the mayonnaise, lime juice, and snipped chives, mixing well. Season to taste with salt and pepper.
3 Serve immediately, or cover and chill for about 1 hour before serving.

SERVING SUGGESTIONS *Serve with breadsticks, small slices of French bread, or fingers of hot toast.*
COOK'S TIP *Remove the bones from the sardines before mashing them, if preferred.*

289 CREAMY CRAB DIP

PREPARATION TIME *20 minutes* **COOKING TIME** *N/A* **SERVES 8–10**

1 cup full-fat cream cheese
2 tbsp Mayonnaise *(see recipe on page 37)*
2 tsp fresh lemon juice
½ small red bell pepper, seeded & finely chopped

2 scallions, finely chopped
1 clove garlic, crushed
1 cup canned white crab meat (drained weight), drained & flaked
2 tbsp chopped fresh parsley

Sea salt & freshly ground black pepper

1 Place the cream cheese in a small bowl and beat until softened a little more. Stir in the mayonnaise and lemon juice until smooth.
2 Add the red bell pepper, scallions, and garlic and mix well. Add the crab meat and chopped parsley and stir to mix. Season to taste with salt and pepper.
3 Serve immediately, or cover and chill for about 1 hour before serving.

SERVING SUGGESTIONS *Serve with breadsticks, small crackers, or a selection of fresh vegetable crudités such as celery and carrot sticks, baby ears of corn, and broccoli florets.*

290 PEANUT BUTTER DIP

PREPARATION TIME *10 minutes* **COOKING TIME** *N/A* **SERVES 8–10**

½ cup creamy smooth peanut butter
¾ cup heavy cream

¾ cup plain fromage frais
½ tsp ground cinnamon

1 Place the peanut butter in a small bowl and beat until smooth and softened. Set aside.
2 Place the cream and fromage frais in a separate bowl, and beat together until the mixture thickens and holds its shape in soft peaks. Gently fold in the peanut butter until well mixed, then stir in the cinnamon.
3 Serve immediately, or cover and chill for about 1 hour before serving.

SERVING SUGGESTIONS *Serve with prepared fresh fruit such as apple or pear slices and chunks of banana (brushed with lemon juice to prevent discoloration).*

291 HONEY YOGURT DIP

PREPARATION TIME *5 minutes* **COOKING TIME** *N/A* **SERVES 6–8**

1 cup natural Greek yogurt

¼ cup thick natural bio yogurt

2 tbsp clear honey, or to taste
½ tsp ground cinnamon

1 Place the Greek and bio yogurts in a bowl and fold gently together.
2 Fold in the honey and cinnamon, mixing gently until well combined. Serve immediately.

SERVING SUGGESTIONS *Serve with prepared fresh fruit such as apple and pear wedges, peach or nectarine slices, chunks of banana (brushed with lemon juice to prevent discoloration), and whole strawberries and raspberries or loganberries.*
VARIATIONS *Use maple syrup or light corn syrup in place of honey. Use ground mixed spice or ginger in place of cinnamon.*
COOK'S TIP *Use clear, runny honey rather than thick honey for this recipe, as it is easier to combine with other ingredients such as yogurt.*

292 VANILLA YOGURT DIP

PREPARATION TIME *5 minutes* **COOKING TIME** *N/A* **SERVES 4**

¾ cup natural Greek yogurt
⅔ cup thick natural bio
   yogurt or fromage frais

1–2 tbsp clear honey, or to
   taste
A few drops of vanilla
   extract

1 Place the Greek yogurt and bio yogurt or fromage frais in a bowl and fold together.
2 Fold in the honey and vanilla extract to taste. Serve immediately.

SERVING SUGGESTIONS *Serve with raw or warm broiled fruit chunks or slices such as apricot, mango, pineapple, apple, and pear.*
VARIATIONS *Use lightly whipped heavy cream in place of bio yogurt or fromage frais. Use almond extract in place of vanilla extract.*

293 LEMON CREAM SWIRL

PREPARATION TIME *10 minutes* **COOKING TIME** *N/A* **SERVES 8–10**

1 cup heavy cream
¾ cup plain fromage frais

Finely grated zest of 1 lemon
5 tbsp luxury lemon curd

1 Place the cream and fromage frais in a bowl and whip together until the mixture
   thickens and holds its shape. Fold in the lemon zest.
2 Transfer the cream mixture to a serving bowl, then spoon the lemon curd over the top.
3 Lightly fold the lemon curd into the whipped cream mixture using a metal spoon to
   create a swirly, marbled effect. Serve immediately.

SERVING SUGGESTIONS *Serve with a selection of prepared fresh mixed berries such as strawberries, raspberries, and blueberries, and lemon shortcake biscuits, or shortbread fingers.*

294 MARMALADE ORANGE DIP

PREPARATION TIME *10 minutes* **COOKING TIME** *N/A* **SERVES 8**

1 cup full-fat cream cheese
3 tbsp crème fraîche

1 tsp finely grated orange
zest

3 tbsp orange marmalade
(total weight about
2½ oz)

1 Place the cream cheese in a bowl and beat until softened a little more. Stir in the crème fraîche until smooth and well mixed, then stir in the orange zest. Fold in the marmalade, mixing well.
2 Serve immediately, or cover and chill for about 1 hour before serving.

SERVING SUGGESTIONS *Serve with prepared fresh fruit dippers such as peach or nectarine wedges, whole strawberries, and mango slices. Alternatively, serve with fingers of chocolate sponge cake or chocolate brownies, or lady fingers.*
VARIATION *Use lime or lemon marmalade and zest in place of orange marmalade and zest.*

295 RASPBERRY CREAM DIP

PREPARATION TIME *15 minutes* **COOKING TIME** *N/A* **SERVES 8–10**

2 cups fresh raspberries
¼ cup superfine sugar

Finely grated zest & juice of
½ orange

1¼ cups heavy cream

1 Place the raspberries, sugar, and orange zest and juice in a blender or food processor and blend until smooth. Press the raspberry mixture through a non-reactive sieve into a bowl. Reserve the raspberry purée, and discard the contents of the sieve.
2 Place the cream in a separate bowl and whip until thick. Gently fold the raspberry purée into the whipped cream until well mixed.
3 Transfer the mixture to a bowl, then serve immediately, or cover and chill for about 2 hours before serving.

SERVING SUGGESTIONS *Serve with prepared fresh fruit such as whole strawberries, apple or pear slices, and peach or apricot wedges. Alternatively, serve with lady fingers or fingers of chocolate brownies.*
VARIATIONS *Use fresh loganberries, tayberries, or blackberries in place of raspberries.*

296 WICKED CHOCOLATE FONDUE

PREPARATION TIME *5 minutes* **COOKING TIME** *10–15 minutes* **SERVES 4**

8 squares good-quality
  semi-sweet chocolate,
  broken into squares

¼ cup butter, diced
⅔ cup heavy cream
2 tbsp light corn syrup

2 tbsp brandy (optional)

1 Place the chocolate, butter, cream, and light corn syrup in a heatproof serving bowl. Place the bowl over a pan of simmering water, and heat until the ingredients are melted, well blended and smooth, stirring occasionally. Stir in the brandy, if using, mixing well.
2 Place the bowl of hot chocolate fondue on a heatproof mat on the table. Alternatively, pour the chocolate fondue into a fondue pan, and set the pan over the fondue burner (on a very low heat) at the table. Serve immediately.

SERVING SUGGESTIONS *Dip prepared fresh fruit such as whole strawberries, cherries, pineapple and apricot halves in the chocolate fondue, either using forks or your fingers. Other foods suitable for dipping include dried fruit, whole nuts, marshmallows, lady fingers, and fingers of sponge cake.*

297 CARAMEL CHOCOLATE DIP

PREPARATION TIME *5 minutes* **COOKING TIME** *5 minutes* **SERVES 8–10**

14oz soft toffees (weight
    includes wrappers)

6-oz can evaporated milk
4 squares semi-sweet
    chocolate chips

½ tsp vanilla extract

1 Unwrap the toffees and place them in a heavy-based saucepan with the evaporated milk
and chocolate chips. Heat gently, stirring continuously, until the mixture is smooth and
well combined.
2 Remove the pan from the heat and stir in the vanilla extract. Serve hot.

SERVING SUGGESTIONS *Serve with a selection of prepared fresh fruit such as apple and pear wedges,
strawberries, cherries, and chunks of banana (brushed with lemon juice to prevent discoloration).
Alternatively, serve with fingers of sponge cake, small cookies, shortbread fingers, or small chunks
of chocolate brownies.*

298 VELVETY CHOCOLATE DIP

PREPARATION TIME *5 minutes* **COOKING TIME** *5 minutes* **SERVES 6–8**

8 squares semi-sweet
    chocolate, broken into

squares
¾ cup heavy cream

½ tsp vanilla extract
½ tsp ground cinnamon

1 Place the chocolate and cream in a heatproof bowl. Place the bowl over a pan of
simmering water and heat until the chocolate mixture is melted, combined, and smooth,
stirring occasionally.
2 Remove the bowl from the pan, then whisk in the vanilla extract and cinnamon. Serve
hot or cold (at room temperature, not chilled).

SERVING SUGGESTIONS *Serve with a selection of prepared fresh fruit such as pineapple chunks, whole
strawberries, peach or nectarine wedges, papaya or mango slices, and lychees.*
VARIATIONS *Use milk or white chocolate in place of semi-sweet chocolate. Use almond or peppermint
extract in place of vanilla extract and omit the cinnamon. Use ground mixed spice or ginger in place
of cinnamon.*

299 CREAMY CHOCOLATE ORANGE DIP

PREPARATION TIME *15 minutes* **COOKING TIME** *8–10 minutes* **SERVES 8**

8 squares semi-sweet
    chocolate, broken into
    squares

1 cup light cream
Finely grated zest of 1 orange

1 tbsp orange-flavored
    liqueur, or to taste
    (optional)

1 Place the chocolate and cream in a small, heavy-based saucepan. Heat gently over a low
heat, stirring frequently, until the chocolate mixture is melted, combined, and smooth.
2 Remove the pan from the heat and stir in the orange zest and liqueur, if using. Serve hot
or cold (at room temperature, not chilled).

SERVING SUGGESTIONS *Serve with prepared fresh fruit such as whole strawberries, cherries, pear,
peach or apricot wedges, and chunks of banana (brushed with lemon juice to prevent discoloration).
Alternatively, serve with lady fingers, small cookies, or shortbread fingers.*
VARIATION *Use brandy or whisky in place of orange-flavored liqueur.*

SWEET SAUCES AND COULIS

Many desserts are just not the same without the addition of an accompanying sauce to tempt your tastebuds. Sweet sauces and fruit coulis often add that special finishing touch to a dessert, providing an extra luscious treat at mealtimes.

In this chapter there is a wide selection of delicious sweet sauces, all of which are sure to impress your family and friends. Choose from old favorites such as Crème Anglaise, Brandy Sauce, Butterscotch Sauce, and Rum and Raisin Sauce, or enjoy delectable delights such as Yummy Chocolate Fudge Sauce, Coffee Drizzle Sauce, Cherry Brandy Sauce, and Caribbean Coconut Sauce. Also included are a colorful collection of flavorful fruit coulis such as Crimson Fruit Coulis, Sweet Strawberry Coulis, Raspberry Vodka Coulis, Exotic Mango Coulis, and Iced Blackcurrant Coulis.

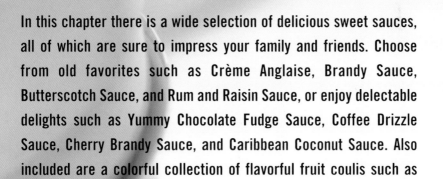

300 BASIC SWEET WHITE SAUCE

PREPARATION TIME *5 minutes* **COOKING TIME** *10 minutes* **SERVES 4** *Makes about 1¼ cups*

5 tsp cornstarch
1¼ cups milk

A knob of butter

5–6 tsp superfine sugar, or
to taste

1 Place the cornstarch in a small bowl, add a little of the milk and stir until smooth.
2 Put the remaining milk in a small saucepan with the butter and heat gently until just boiling. Gradually pour the hot milk onto the cornstarch mixture, stirring continuously.
3 Return the mixture to the saucepan and bring slowly to a boil, stirring continuously, until the sauce is thickened and smooth. Simmer gently for 2–3 minutes, stirring. Stir in the sugar to taste. Serve hot.

SERVING SUGGESTIONS *Serve with steamed or baked puddings such as spotted dick or jam roly-poly, or with fruit pies, tarts, or strudels.*
VARIATIONS *Stir in the finely grated zest of 1 lemon or 1 small orange just before serving. Stir in 1–2 tbsp brandy or ½–1 tsp vanilla extract, or to taste, just before serving.*

301 FRESH LEMON WHITE SAUCE

PREPARATION TIME *5 minutes* **COOKING TIME** *10 minutes* **SERVES 4** *Makes about 1¼ cups*

1 tbsp butter
2 tbsp all-purpose flour

1¼ cups milk
Finely grated zest of 1 small
lemon

5–6 tsp superfine sugar, or
to taste

1 Place the butter, flour, and milk in a small saucepan. Heat gently, whisking continuously, until the sauce comes to a boil and thickens. Simmer gently for 3–4 minutes, stirring.
2 Remove the pan from the heat, then stir in the lemon zest and sugar to taste. Serve hot.

SERVING SUGGESTIONS *Serve with char-grilled mixed fruit kebabs or fresh mixed berries, or with baked fruit puddings or tarts such as apricot or pear upside-down pudding.*
VARIATION *Use the finely grated zest of 1 small orange or 1 lime in place of lemon zest.*

302 QUICK VANILLA WHITE SAUCE

PREPARATION TIME *5 minutes* **COOKING TIME** *10 minutes* **SERVES 4** *Makes about 1¼ cups*

5 tsp cornstarch
1¼ cups milk
A knob of butter

5–6 tsp superfine sugar, or
to taste

½–1 tsp vanilla extract, or
to taste

1 Place the cornstarch in a small bowl, add a little of the milk and stir until smooth.
2 Put the remaining milk in a small saucepan with the butter and heat gently until just boiling. Gradually pour the hot milk onto the cornstarch mixture, stirring continuously.
3 Return the mixture to the saucepan and bring slowly to a boil, stirring continuously, until the sauce is thickened and smooth. Simmer gently for 2–3 minutes, stirring. Stir in the sugar and vanilla extract to taste. Serve hot.

SERVING SUGGESTIONS *Serve with steamed or baked fruit puddings, or with pies or tarts such as pineapple tarte tatin or strawberry tart.*

303 CRÈME ANGLAISE (EGG CUSTARD SAUCE)

PREPARATION TIME *35 minutes* **COOKING TIME** *15 minutes* **SERVES 4–6** *Makes about 1½ cups*

1¼ cups milk
1 vanilla pod, split in half
   lengthwise

3 egg yolks
1 tbsp superfine sugar

1 Pour the milk into a small, heavy-based saucepan, add the vanilla pod and heat gently until almost boiling. Remove the pan from the heat and set aside to infuse for 15 minutes.

2 Remove and discard the vanilla pod. Place the egg yolks and sugar in a bowl and whisk together until thick and creamy. Gradually whisk in the hot infused milk, then strain the mixture back into the saucepan.

3 Cook over a low heat for about 10 minutes, or until the mixture thickens enough to thinly coat the back of a wooden spoon, stirring continuously. Do not allow the mixture to boil or it may curdle. Serve hot or cold. If serving cold, pour the custard sauce into a clean bowl and cover the surface closely with a piece of non-stick baking paper to prevent a skin forming, and let cool.

SERVING SUGGESTIONS *Serve with broiled, baked, or stewed fruit, hot baked or steamed fruit puddings, or with fruit crumbles such as raspberry and apple.*

VARIATIONS *Infuse the milk with the pared zest of 1 lemon or 1 small orange in place of the vanilla pod. For a chocolate crème anglaise sauce, melt 2 squares good-quality bittersweet chocolate with the milk in Step 1.*

304 SABAYON SAUCE

PREPARATION TIME *10 minutes* **COOKING TIME** *10 minutes* **SERVES 6–8**

4 egg yolks
¼ cup superfine sugar
⅔ cup medium
   white wine

Finely grated zest of 1 lemon
⅔ cup heavy cream,
   whipped (optional)

1 Put the egg yolks, sugar, and wine in a large, heatproof bowl and place the bowl over a pan of simmering water. Using an electric whisk, whisk the mixture for about 8–10 minutes, or until thick and frothy.

2 Remove the bowl from the heat and whisk in the lemon zest. Serve at once, or whisk until cool, then serve.

3 Alternatively, whisk the sabayon sauce until cool, then gently fold the whipped cream into the sauce just before serving.

SERVING SUGGESTIONS *Serve with cold fruit desserts such as fruit salads or fruit tarts, or with hot fruit desserts such as apricot strudel or apple tarte tatin.*

VARIATION *Use finely grated zest of 1 small orange in place of lemon zest.*

305 CREAMY ORANGE SAUCE

PREPARATION TIME *10 minutes* **COOKING TIME** *N/A* **SERVES 6–8**

⅔ cup heavy cream
⅔ cup plain fromage
   frais

4 tbsp luxury orange curd
Finely grated zest of 1 small
   orange (optional)

1 Place the cream and fromage frais in a bowl and whip together until the mixture thickens and holds its shape in soft peaks.

2 Gently fold in the orange curd and orange zest, if using, until well combined. Serve cold.

SERVING SUGGESTIONS *Serve with raspberry tartlets or poached figs, or with fresh fruit such as raspberries, sliced strawberries or mixed summer berries.*

VARIATIONS *Use the finely grated zest of 1 lemon in place of orange zest. Use luxury lemon curd in place of luxury orange curd. Fold the orange curd and orange zest into 1¼ cups thick crème fraîche in place of the whipped cream and fromage frais, if desired. Use ⅔ cup extra heavy cream in place of fromage frais for a richer sauce, if desired.*

COOK'S TIPS *Before whipping the cream and fromage frais together, chill the whisk and bowl as well as the cream, to achieve maximum whipped volume.*

Use a balloon or spiral hand whisk or an electric whisk, but be careful not to over-whip the mixture.

306 YUMMY CHOCOLATE FUDGE SAUCE

PREPARATION TIME *5 minutes* **COOKING TIME** *10 minutes* **SERVES 4–6** *Makes about 1½ cups*

⅔ cup light soft brown
   sugar
½ cup superfine sugar
¼ cup butter, diced

2 squares good-quality semi-
   sweet chocolate, broken
   into squares
3 tbsp light corn syrup

A few drops of vanilla
   extract
4 tbsp light cream

1 Place the sugars, butter, chocolate, and syrup in a small, heavy-based saucepan. Heat
  gently until the mixture is well blended and smooth, stirring continuously. Bring to a boil
  and simmer very gently for 5 minutes, stirring.
2 Remove the pan from the heat, add the vanilla extract and cream and mix thoroughly.
  Serve hot.

SERVING SUGGESTIONS *Serve with scoops of vanilla or other flavored ice cream, or with profiteroles or
sliced fruit such as pears, peaches, or bananas.*
VARIATIONS *Use good-quality milk chocolate in place of semi-sweet chocolate. Use evaporated milk in
place of cream.*
COOK'S TIPS *Choose a good-quality semi-sweet chocolate for this recipe, ideally one containing a high
percentage of cocoa solids, often labelled as 'Continental' chocolate.*
   *When storing soft brown sugar, keep it moist by storing in an airtight container with one or two
wedges of apple, or a piece of fresh bread.*

307 BRANDY SAUCE

PREPARATION TIME *5 minutes* **COOKING TIME** *10 minutes* **SERVES 4–6** *Makes about 1½ cups*

1 tbsp cornstarch
1¼ cups full-fat milk

1–2 tbsp superfine sugar or
light soft brown sugar, or
to taste

2 tbsp brandy, or to taste

1 In a small bowl, blend the cornstarch with 2 tbsp milk to form a smooth paste. Set aside.
2 Put the remaining milk in a small saucepan and heat gently until just boiling. Gradually pour the hot milk onto the cornstarch mixture, stirring continuously, until it is thoroughly combined.
3 Return the mixture to the saucepan and bring slowly to a boil, stirring continuously, until the sauce is thickened and smooth. Simmer gently for 2–3 minutes, stirring.
4 Stir in the sugar and brandy to taste and reheat gently until hot, stirring. Serve hot.

SERVING SUGGESTIONS *Serve with Christmas pudding, mince pies, or mincemeat tart.*
VARIATION *Use rum, sherry, or whisky in place of brandy.*

308 SWEET SHERRY SAUCE

PREPARATION TIME *5 minutes* **COOKING TIME** *10 minutes* **SERVES 4–6** *Makes about 1½ cups*

5 tsp cornstarch
1¼ cups milk

5–6 tsp superfine sugar, or
to taste

2–3 tbsp sweet sherry, or
to taste

1 In a small bowl, blend the cornstarch with 2 tbsp milk to form a smooth paste. Set aside.
2 Put the remaining milk in a small saucepan and heat gently until just boiling. Gradually pour the hot milk onto the cornstarch mixture, stirring, until it is thoroughly combined.
3 Return the mixture to the saucepan and bring slowly to a boil, stirring continuously, until the sauce is thickened and smooth. Simmer gently for 2–3 minutes, stirring.
4 Stir in the sugar and sherry to taste, and reheat gently until hot, stirring. Serve hot.

SERVING SUGGESTIONS *Serve with steamed or baked puddings, or with fruit pies or strudels.*

309 QUICK CHOCOLATE SAUCE

PREPARATION TIME *5 minutes* **COOKING TIME** *10 minutes* **SERVES 4–6** *Makes about 1½ cups*

5 tsp cornstarch
1 tbsp unsweetened Dutch-
processed cocoa powder

1¼ cups milk
2 tbsp superfine sugar or
light soft brown sugar,

or to taste

1 Place the cornstarch and cocoa powder in a small saucepan and blend with 3 tbsp milk to form a smooth paste. Gradually blend in the remaining milk.
2 Heat gently, whisking continuously, until the sauce comes to a boil and is thickened and smooth. Simmer gently for 2–3 minutes, stirring.
3 Stir in the sugar to taste, and mix well. Serve hot.

SERVING SUGGESTIONS *Serve with steamed or baked chocolate fruit puddings such as pineapple or pear upside-down pudding, or with chocolate sponge pudding.*

310 CHOCOLATE CUSTARD SAUCE

PREPARATION TIME *5 minutes* **COOKING TIME** *10 minutes* **SERVES 4–6** *Makes about 1½ cups*

1 tbsp cornstarch	processed cocoa powder	to taste
1 tbsp unsweetened Dutch-	1–2 tbsp superfine sugar, or	1¼ cups milk

1 Place the cornstarch, cocoa powder, and sugar in a small bowl. Add a little of the milk and blend together to form a smooth paste, then set aside.

2 Put the remaining milk in a small saucepan and heat gently until almost boiling. Gradually pour the hot milk onto the blended cornstarch mixture, stirring until smooth.

3 Return the mixture to the pan and heat gently, stirring continuously, until the sauce comes to a boil and thickens. Simmer gently for 1–2 minutes, stirring. Serve hot.

SERVING SUGGESTIONS *Serve with chocolate pineapple upside-down pudding, or pear galette, or with poached fruit such as pears, peaches, or apricots.*

311 RICH CHOCOLATE SAUCE

PREPARATION TIME *5 minutes* **COOKING TIME** *10 minutes* **SERVES 4–6** *Makes about 1¼ cups*

6 squres good-quality	½ cup heavy cream	2 tbsp light corn syrup
semisweet chocolate,	⅓ cup light or dark soft	1 tbsp butter
broken into squares	brown sugar	

1 Place the chocolate, cream, sugar, light corn syrup, and butter in a small, heavy-based saucepan. Heat gently, stirring continuously, until the chocolate has melted and the sugar has dissolved.

2 Bring slowly to a boil, stirring continuously, until the mixture is blended and smooth, then simmer very gently for 1–2 minutes, stirring occasionally. Cool slightly before serving, then serve hot.

SERVING SUGGESTIONS *Serve with chocolate profiteroles, or scoops of vanilla ice cream.*

312 CREAMY WHITE CHOCOLATE SAUCE

PREPARATION TIME *5 minutes* **COOKING TIME** *10 minutes* **SERVES 4–6** *Makes about 1¼ cups*

6 squares good-quality white	⅔ cup heavy cream
chocolate, roughly chopped	1 tbsp butter, diced

1 Place the chocolate, cream, and butter in a heatproof bowl. Place the bowl over a pan of simmering water and heat gently, stirring continuously, until the ingredients have melted together, and the sauce is well blended and smooth.

2 Serve hot or cold (at room temperature, not chilled). If serving the sauce cold, stir it well before serving.

SERVING SUGGESTIONS *Serve with steamed sponge puddings, baked fruit puddings, fruit tarts, or with prepared broiled fruit or fresh fruit such as cherries, raspberries, or strawberries.*

VARIATION *Use good-quality milk or semisweet chocolate in place of white chocolate.*

313 BUTTERSCOTCH SAUCE

PREPARATION TIME *5 minutes* **COOKING TIME** *10 minutes* **SERVES 6** *Makes about 1¾ cups*

1 cup light soft brown sugar
⅔ cup heavy cream
¼ cup butter, diced

⅓ cup light corn syrup
A few drops of vanilla
  extract

1 Place the sugar, cream, butter, and light corn syrup in a small, heavy-based saucepan.
2 Bring slowly to a boil, stirring occasionally, until the sauce is well blended and smooth.
3 Just as the sauce reaches a gentle boil, remove the pan from the heat and stir in the vanilla extract.
4 Serve hot or cold (at room temperature, not chilled). If serving the sauce cold, stir it well before serving.

SERVING SUGGESTIONS *Serve with raw or baked sliced bananas, or with baked sponge puddings, or scoops of vanilla or butterscotch ice cream.*

VARIATIONS *Use dark soft brown sugar in place of light soft brown sugar. Use maple syrup in place of light corn syrup.*

COOK'S TIP *If soft brown sugar becomes hard during storage, place the sugar in a microwave-proof dish and add a wedge of apple. Cover and microwave on HIGH for 30 seconds. Remove and discard the apple, and stir the sugar well — it should now be softened.*

314 CHOCOLATE MARSHMALLOW SAUCE

PREPARATION TIME *5 minutes* **COOKING TIME** *10 minutes* **SERVES 4–6** *Makes about 1⅔ cups*

3 squares semisweet
 chocolate, roughly chopped

¼ lb marshmallows,
 snipped into pieces

6 tbsp heavy cream
4 tbsp light corn syrup

1 Put the chocolate, marshmallows, cream, and light corn syrup in a small, heavy-based saucepan. Heat gently, stirring frequently, until the chocolate and marshmallows have melted and the sauce is well blended, smooth, and hot.
2 Serve hot or cold (at room temperature, not chilled). If serving the sauce cold, stir it well before serving.

SERVING SUGGESTIONS *Serve with prepared fresh fruit such as sliced bananas or pears, or with creamy fruit desserts, or scoops of ice cream.*
VARIATION *Use clear honey or maple syrup in place of light corn syrup.*
COOK'S TIP *Snip the marshmallows into pieces using a pair of greased or floured kitchen scissors.*

315 HEAVENLY CHOCOLATE GINGER SAUCE

PREPARATION TIME *10 minutes* **COOKING TIME** *10 minutes* **SERVES 4** *Makes about 1 cup*

6 squares semisweet
 chocolate, broken into
 squares
3 tbsp heavy cream

½ cup preserved stem
 ginger in syrup (drained
 weight), drained & finely
 chopped

2 tbsp syrup from the jar
 of stem ginger
1 tsp ground cinnamon
 (optional)

1 Place the chocolate, cream, chopped ginger, and ginger syrup in a heatproof bowl.
2 Place the bowl over a pan of simmering water and heat gently, stirring continuously, until the chocolate mixture is melted, well combined and smooth.
3 Whisk the cinnamon, if using, into the sauce. Serve immediately.

SERVING SUGGESTIONS *Serve with ice cream, yogurt ice, fresh fruit such as strawberries or cherries, or with individual steamed sponge puddings.*

316 BUTTERSCOTCH HAZELNUT SAUCE

PREPARATION TIME *5 minutes* **COOKING TIME** *10 minutes* **SERVES 4–6** *Makes about 1¼ cups*

¾ cup light soft brown
 sugar
⅓ cup butter, diced
5 tbsp light corn syrup

A few drops of vanilla
 extract
4 tbsp heavy cream

2–3 tbsp finely chopped
 toasted hazelnuts

1 Place the sugar, butter, and light corn syrup in a small, heavy-based saucepan. Heat gently until the mixture is melted and well blended, stirring continuously. Bring slowly to a boil, then simmer very gently for 5 minutes, stirring.
2 Remove the pan from the heat, add the vanilla extract and cream and stir to mix thoroughly. Stir in the chopped hazelnuts. Serve hot.

SERVING SUGGESTIONS *Serve with steamed or baked sponge puddings or hot apple-filled pancakes or crêpes, or with ice cream or ice cream desserts.*

317 CARAMEL SYRUP SAUCE

PREPARATION TIME *5 minutes* **COOKING TIME** *20 minutes* **SERVES 6** *Makes about 2 cups*

⅔ cup light soft brown
  sugar

½ cup superfine sugar
2 cups water

1 tbsp arrowroot

1 Put the soft brown and superfine sugars in a saucepan with the water, then heat gently until the sugar has dissolved, stirring continuously. Bring slowly to a boil and simmer gently for 10 minutes, stirring occasionally.

2 In a small bowl, blend the arrowroot with 2 tbsp cold water until smooth. Whisk the arrowroot mixture into the sugar syrup, mixing well.

3 Reheat the sauce gently until it comes to a boil and thickens, stirring continuously. Serve hot.

SERVING SUGGESTIONS *Serve with poached or baked fruit such as sliced oranges, bananas, or pineapple, or with ice cream or steamed sponge puddings.*
VARIATION *Once the sauce has thickened, stir in 2–3 tbsp brandy or orange-flavored liqueur, or a little chopped preserved stem ginger, if desired, and reheat gently before serving.*

318 STICKY TOFFEE SAUCE

PREPARATION TIME *5 minutes* **COOKING TIME** *10–15 minutes* **SERVES 6** *Makes about 2 cups*

¾ cup butter, diced
⅓ cup light corn syrup

½ cup light soft brown
  sugar

½ tsp vanilla extract, or
  to taste

1 Place the butter, syrup and sugar in a small, heavy-based saucepan. Bring slowly to a boil, stirring continuously, then simmer gently for about 2 minutes, or until syrupy.

2 Stir in the vanilla extract to taste. Serve hot.

SERVING SUGGESTIONS *Serve with individual steamed sponge puddings, or with scoops of ice cream.*

319 COFFEE CUSTARD SAUCE

PREPARATION TIME *5 minutes* **COOKING TIME** *10 minutes* **SERVES 4–6** *Makes about 1½ cups*

1 tbsp cornstarch
3 tbsp light soft brown
  sugar, or to taste

1¼ cups full-fat milk
2 tsp instant coffee granules

1 Place the cornstarch and sugar in a small bowl. Add a little of the milk and blend together to form a smooth paste, then set aside. In a separate small bowl, blend the coffee granules with 1 tbsp hot water and set aside.

2 Put the remaining milk in a small saucepan and heat gently until almost boiling. Gradually pour the hot milk onto the blended cornstarch mixture, stirring until smooth.

3 Return the mixture to the pan and stir in the dissolved coffee, then heat gently, stirring continuously, until the custard sauce comes to a boil and thickens. Simmer gently for 1–2 minutes, stirring. Serve hot.

SERVING SUGGESTIONS *Serve with steamed or baked sponge puddings, or chocolate puddings or tarts, or with scoops of vanilla or chocolate-chip ice cream.*

320 RICH MOCHA SAUCE

PREPARATION TIME *5 minutes* **COOKING TIME** *15 minutes* **SERVES 4–6** *Makes about 1½ cups*

4 tsp cornstarch
1 tbsp light soft brown sugar
  or superfine sugar

1¼ cups full-fat milk
1–2 tsp instant coffee
  granules, or to taste

2 squares semisweet
  chocolate, roughly chopped
A few drops of vanilla
  extract (optional)

1 Place the cornstarch and sugar in a small bowl. Add a little of the milk and blend together to form a smooth paste, then set aside.

2 In a separate small bowl, dissolve the coffee granules in 1 tbsp hot water. Add the dissolved coffee to the cornstarch paste, and stir to mix well. Set aside.

3 Put the remaining milk in a small, heavy-based saucepan, add the chocolate and heat gently until the chocolate has melted and the mixture is almost boiling, stirring occasionally.

4 Gradually pour the hot chocolate milk onto the blended cornstarch mixture, stirring continuously, until smooth.

5 Return the mixture to the pan and heat gently, stirring continuously, until the custard sauce comes to a boil and thickens. Simmer gently for 1–2 minutes, stirring.

6 Stir in the vanilla extract, if using. Serve hot.

SERVING SUGGESTIONS *Serve with steamed or baked sponge puddings, or upside-down fruit puddings, or with poached, baked, or broiled fruit such as pears or peaches.*
COOK'S TIP *Choose full-fat milk for this recipe, to achieve a delicious, creamy flavor. Semi-skimmed milk can be used as an alternative, to create a slightly less rich sauce, if preferred.*

321 COFFEE DRIZZLE SAUCE

PREPARATION TIME *5 minutes* **COOKING TIME** *10 minutes* **SERVES 4–6** *Makes about 1¼ cups*

4 tsp cornstarch
1¼ cups milk

2 tsp instant coffee granules

2 tbsp superfine sugar or
  light soft brown sugar

1 In a bowl, blend the cornstarch with 2 tbsp milk to form a smooth paste, then set aside.

2 Put the remaining milk in a small saucepan and heat gently until just boiling.

3 Pour the hot milk onto the cornstarch mixture, stirring continuously, until it is thoroughly combined.

4 Return the mixture to the saucepan and bring slowly to a boil, stirring continuously, until the sauce is thickened and smooth. Simmer gently for 2–3 minutes, stirring.

5 In a small bowl, dissolve the coffee granules in 2 tbsp hot water.

6 Stir the dissolved coffee and sugar into the sauce, and reheat gently until hot, stirring. Serve hot.

SERVING SUGGESTIONS *Serve with ice cream or ice cream desserts, or with broiled or stewed fruit such as peaches, nectarines, pears, or apples.*
COOK'S TIP *In Step 3, gradually pour the hot milk onto the blended cornstarch mixture, stirring continuously, to ensure a smooth sauce and to prevent lumps forming.*

322 RUM AND RAISIN SAUCE

PREPARATION TIME *5 minutes* **COOKING TIME** *10 minutes* **SERVES 4–6** *Makes about 1⅓ cups*

⅓ cup raisins

1 tbsp cornstarch

1 cup milk

½ cup heavy cream

1 tbsp butter

1 tbsp light soft brown sugar,
. or to taste

2 tbsp rum

1 Roughly chop the raisins, then set aside. In a small bowl, blend the cornstarch with 2 tbsp of the milk, until smooth. Set aside.

2 Heat the remaining milk, cream, and butter in a small, heavy-based saucepan until almost boiling. Gradually pour the hot milk and cream mixture onto the cornstarch mixture, stirring continuously.

3 Return the mixture to the saucepan and bring slowly to a boil, stirring continuously, until the sauce is thickened and smooth. Simmer gently for 2–3 minutes, stirring.

4 Stir in the sugar, rum, and raisins and reheat gently until hot, stirring. Serve hot.

SERVING SUGGESTIONS *Serve with hot pancakes or crêpes and ice cream, or with mince pies.*
VARIATIONS *Use chopped golden raisins, dried cherries, or ready-to-eat dried figs or apricots in place of raisins. Use brandy or whisky in place of rum.*

323 ORANGE MARMALADE SAUCE

PREPARATION TIME *5 minutes* **COOKING TIME** *10 minutes* **SERVES 4** *Makes about 1 cup*

Juice of 1 orange
5 tbsp orange marmalade

2 tsp arrowroot

1–2 tsp brandy or whisky, or
to taste (optional)

1 Pour the orange juice into a measuring jug and make up to ⅔ cup with cold water.
2 Pour the mixed orange juice and water into a small saucepan, add the marmalade and stir to mix.
3 Heat gently, stirring continuously, until the marmalade has dissolved, then bring the mixture slowly to a boil, stirring occasionally.
4 In a small bowl, blend the arrowroot with 1 tbsp cold water until smooth, then stir the arrowroot mixture into the marmalade sauce.
5 Reheat gently, stirring continuously, until the sauce comes to a boil and thickens.
6 Stir in the brandy or whisky, if using. Serve hot.

SERVING SUGGESTIONS *Serve with individual steamed or baked sponge puddings, or with fruit pies or puddings, scoops of vanilla, chocolate, or other flavored ice cream, or broiled fruit such as mango, bananas, or nectarines.*
VARIATIONS *Use lemon and lime marmalade in place of orange marmalade and omit the brandy, if desired. Use orange-flavored liqueur in place of brandy or whisky.*
COOK'S TIP *Use shredless, fine-cut/shred or thick-cut/shred orange marmalade for this recipe.*

324 STEM GINGER SAUCE

PREPARATION TIME *5 minutes* **COOKING TIME** *15 minutes* **SERVES 4** *Makes about 1 cup*

¼ cup superfine sugar
⅔ cup water

⅔ cup preserved stem
ginger in syrup (drained
weight), drained & finely
chopped

4 tbsp syrup from the jar
of stem ginger
2 tbsp fresh lemon juice
1 tsp arrowroot

1 Place the sugar in a saucepan with the water. Heat gently, stirring continuously, until the sugar has dissolved, then bring the mixture to a boil and boil for 5 minutes.
2 Stir the stem ginger into the sugar mixture with the ginger syrup and lemon juice and mix well.
3 In a small bowl, blend the arrowroot with 1 tbsp cold water until smooth, then stir the arrowroot mixture into the sauce.
4 Reheat gently, stirring continuously, until the sauce comes to a boil and thickens. Serve hot.

SERVING SUGGESTIONS *Serve with steamed or baked sponge puddings or fruit puddings, or with scoops of ice cream or yogurt ice, or fresh fruit such as fruit salad, fruit compote,or sliced Galia, charantais, cantaloupe, or honeydew melon.*
VARIATION *Use light soft brown sugar in place of superfine sugar.*
COOK'S TIP *Preserved stem ginger adds a delicious, warming flavor to this sweet sauce. Preserved stem ginger can also be used to add extra flavor and texture to many gingerbread or ginger cake recipes.*

325 QUICK ORANGE CUSTARD SAUCE

PREPARATION TIME *5 minutes* **COOKING TIME** *10 minutes* **SERVES 4–6** *Makes about 1½ cups*

1 tbsp cornstarch
1–2 tbsp superfine sugar, or
   to taste

Finely grated zest of 1 small
   orange
1¼ cups full-fat milk

1 Place the cornstarch, sugar, and orange zest in a small bowl. Add a little of the milk and blend together to form a smooth paste, then set aside.

2 Put the remaining milk in a small saucepan and heat gently until almost boiling. Gradually pour the hot milk onto the blended cornstarch mixture, stirring continuously.

3 Return the mixture to the pan and heat gently, stirring continuously, until the sauce comes to a boil and thickens. Simmer gently for 1–2 minutes, stirring. Serve hot.

SERVING SUGGESTIONS *Serve with steamed or baked sponge puddings, fruit puddings or crumbles, or with pies or tarts such as blueberry pie, or plum or pear tarte tatin.*
VARIATION *Use the finely grated zest of 1 lemon in place of orange.*

326 LEMON HONEY SYRUP

PREPARATION TIME *5 minutes* **COOKING TIME** *5 minutes* **SERVES 4** *Makes about 1 cup*

2½ tsp arrowroot
½ cup water

6 tbsp clear honey

Finely grated zest & juice of
   1 small lemon

1 Blend the arrowroot with the water in a small saucepan until smooth. Stir in the honey and lemon zest and juice.

2 Heat gently, stirring continuously, until the sauce comes to a boil and thickens slightly. Serve hot.

SERVING SUGGESTIONS *Serve with steamed or baked sponge puddings, hot pancakes or crêpes, or scoops of ice cream, or with blueberry tart or apricot galette.*
VARIATION *Use light corn syrup or maple syrup in place of honey.*
COOK'S TIP *Add an extra ½ tsp arrowroot if you prefer a slightly thicker sauce.*

327 CREAMY CITRUS SAUCE

PREPARATION TIME *10 minutes* **COOKING TIME** *10 minutes* **SERVES 6** *Makes about 2 cups*

2 tbsp butter
¼ cup all-purpose flour
2 cups full-fat milk

3 tbsp superfine sugar, or
   to taste
Finely grated zest of 1
   small orange

Finely grated zest of 1
   small lemon
Finely grated zest of 1
   small lime

1 Place the butter, flour, and milk in a saucepan. Heat gently, whisking continuously, until the sauce comes to a boil and thickens. Simmer gently for 3–4 minutes, stirring.

2 Stir in the sugar and citrus fruit zests, then reheat gently until hot, stirring. Serve hot.

SERVING SUGGESTIONS *Serve with broiled or baked fresh fruit such as peaches, pears, or nectarines, scoops of ice cream, fresh mixed berries, or with baked fruit puddings or tarts such as pear crumble or cherry tart.*
COOK'S TIP *Choose unwaxed citrus fruits, or thoroughly wash and dry citrus fruits before use to remove any traces of possible residues.*

328 CALYPSO MANGO SAUCE

PREPARATION TIME *15 minutes* **COOKING TIME** *10 minutes* **SERVES 6–8** *Makes about 2½ cups*

1 ripe mango peeled, pitted, & roughly chopped
3 tbsp butter
⅓ cup all-purpose flour

1¼ cups coconut milk
⅔ cup heavy cream
⅔ cup light soft brown sugar

1 Place the mango flesh in a blender or food processor and blend until smooth. Set aside.
2 Melt the butter in a saucepan, stir in the flour and cook for 1 minute, stirring. Remove the pan from the heat and gradually whisk in the coconut milk and cream.
3 Return the pan to the heat and cook gently, whisking continuously, until the sauce comes to a boil and thickens. Simmer gently for 2–3 minutes, stirring.
4 Remove the pan from the heat and stir in the puréed mango and sugar and mix well. Reheat the sauce gently until hot, stirring. Serve hot.

SERVING SUGGESTIONS *Serve with steamed or baked plain or fruit sponge puddings, broiled mixed tropical fruit, or tropical fruit compote.*

329 FESTIVE ORANGE AND GOLDEN RAISIN SAUCE

PREPARATION TIME *5 minutes* **COOKING TIME** *20 minutes* **SERVES 4**

1¼ cups unsweetened orange juice

packed 1 cup golden raisins

1 tbsp brandy, sherry or whisky (optional)

1 Place the orange juice and golden raisins in a saucepan and stir to mix. Bring slowly to a boil, then cook gently for about 15 minutes, stirring occasionally, until a lot of the liquid has evaporated or been absorbed and the golden raisins have plumped up.
2 Stir in the brandy, sherry or whisky, if using, and reheat gently until hot, stirring. Serve hot.

SERVING SUGGESTIONS *Serve with hot plain or fruit-filled pancakes or crêpes, steamed or baked sponge puddings, or with scoops of vanilla or flavored ice cream.*

330 CHERRY BRANDY SAUCE

PREPARATION TIME *10 minutes* **COOKING TIME** *20 minutes* **SERVES 4–6** *Makes about 1⅔ cups*

½ cup red wine
⅓ cup light soft brown sugar

1¼ cups pitted fresh sweet dark cherries

2 tsp arrowroot
2 tbsp cherry brandy

1 Place the red wine and sugar in a small saucepan and heat gently until the sugar has dissolved, stirring continuously.
2 Add the cherries and cover the pan. Bring the mixture to a boil, then reduce the heat and cook gently for about 10 minutes, or until the cherries are cooked and tender, stirring occasionally.
3 In a small bowl, blend the arrowroot with the cherry brandy until smooth, then stir it into the cherry mixture. Reheat gently, stirring continuously, until the sauce comes to a boil and thickens. Serve hot.

SERVING SUGGESTIONS *Serve with hot pancakes, chocolate crêpes, or waffles, steamed or baked sponge puddings, broiled fresh fruit, or with peach or apple galette or tarte tatin.*

331 STRAWBERRY JAM SAUCE

PREPARATION TIME *5 minutes* **COOKING TIME** *10 minutes* **SERVES 4–6** *Makes about 1½ cups*

6 tbsp seedless strawberry
  jam

2 cups water
2 tsp lemon juice

2 tsp arrowroot
A few drops of red food
  coloring (optional)

1 Place the jam in a saucepan with the water and lemon juice, then bring the mixture
slowly to a boil, stirring continuously.

2 In a small bowl, blend the arrowroot with 2 tbsp cold water until smooth. Stir the
arrowroot mixture into the hot jam sauce, then reheat gently, stirring continuously, until
the sauce comes to a boil and thickens.

3 Remove the pan from the heat and stir in the food coloring, if using. Cool for a few
minutes, then serve hot.

SERVING SUGGESTIONS *Serve with steamed sponge puddings, or with baked cheesecake.*

332 CRUSHED PEACH SAUCE

PREPARATION TIME *10 minutes* **COOKING TIME** *N/A* **SERVES 8–10** *Makes about 3 cups*

14-oz can peach slices
  or peach halves in fruit
  juice

⅔ cup plain fromage frais
⅔ cup heavy cream
2 tbsp clear honey

1 Place the peach slices or halves and their juice in a blender or food processor and mix to
form a smooth purée.

2 Add the fromage frais, cream, and honey and process until well mixed.

3 Pour the peach sauce into a jug, and serve immediately, or cover and chill for about 2
hours before serving. Serve cold.

SERVING SUGGESTIONS *Serve with fresh berries such as strawberries, raspberries, and blackberries.*

333 BLACKBERRY APPLE SAUCE

PREPARATION TIME *40 minutes* **COOKING TIME** *10 minutes* **SERVES 4–6** *Makes about 1½ cups*

2 tart apples, peeled, cored,
  & thinly sliced
2 cups fresh blackberries
¼ cup superfine sugar

½ cup full-fat cream cheese
⅔ cup light or heavy cream

1 Put the apples and blackberries in a saucepan with 3 tbsp cold water. Cover and cook
gently until the fruit is soft, stirring occasionally.

2 Remove the pan from the heat and stir in the sugar. Set aside to cool slightly, then purée
the fruit mixture in a blender or food processor until smooth. Press the fruit purée
through a non-reactive sieve into a bowl. Reserve the fruit sauce and discard the
contents of the sieve.

3 Whisk the cream cheese and cream together until well combined, then add the fruit
sauce and whisk until thoroughly mixed. Serve immediately, or cover and chill before
serving. Serve cold.

SERVING SUGGESTIONS *Serve with fruit strudels, or with broiled fruit such as peaches or pears.*

MELBA SAUCE

PREPARATION TIME *10 minutes* **COOKING TIME** *5 minutes* **SERVES 4** *Makes about 1 cup*

4 tbsp redcurrant or
   blackcurrant jelly
2 cups fresh raspberries

2 tbsp confectioners' sugar,
   sifted

1 tbsp framboise (raspberry)
   liqueur or kirsch (cherry
   eau de vie), or to taste

1 Place the redcurrant or blackcurrant jelly in a small saucepan, and heat gently until
   melted, stirring continuously. Remove the pan from the heat and set aside.
2 Place the raspberries in a small blender or food processor. Add the melted redcurrant or
   blackcurrant jelly, the confectioners' sugar and liqueur, and stir to form a smooth purée.
3 Press the fruit purée through a non-reactive sieve into a bowl, then discard the contents
   of the sieve. Pour the raspberry sauce into a jug, and serve cold.

SERVING SUGGESTIONS *Serve with poached fruit such as peaches, nectarines, or pears, or with
fruit-filled meringues or pavlova.*
VARIATIONS *Use seedless raspberry jam in place of redcurrant or blackcurrant jelly. Use fresh
blackberries, loganberries, or mixed berries in place of raspberries.*

335 RED BERRY CRUSH

PREPARATION TIME *10 minutes* **COOKING TIME** *15 minutes* **SERVES 4** *Makes about 1¼ cups*

1 cup fresh raspberries	1 cup fresh loganberries	2–3 tbsp clear honey
1 cup fresh blackberries	or tayberries	1 tsp ground mixed spice

1 Place the raspberries, blackberries, and loganberries or tayberries in a saucepan with 3 tbsp cold water. Cover and cook gently until the fruit is soft, stirring occasionally.

2 Remove the pan from the heat and set aside to cool slightly, then purée the fruit in a blender or food processor until smooth. Press the fruit purée through a non-reactive sieve into a bowl, then discard the contents of the sieve.

3 Return the fruit purée to the rinsed-out saucepan, and stir in the honey and mixed spice, mixing well, then reheat gently until hot, stirring. Serve hot or cold. If serving cold, remove the pan from the heat and set aside to cool completely, then serve.

SERVING SUGGESTIONS *Serve with summer pudding, streamed sponge puddings or scoops of ice cream.*
VARIATIONS *Use gooseberries or strawberries in place of loganberries or tayberries.*

336 ROSY RHUBARB AND STRAWBERRY SAUCE

PREPARATION TIME *20 minutes* **COOKING TIME** *20 minutes* **SERVES 6–8** *Makes about 2⅓ cups*

1½ cups fresh ripe strawberries, halved	¼ cup butter, diced	1 tbsp amaretto (almond liqueur)
2 cups fresh rhubarb, trimmed & cut into ½-inch pieces	½ cup water	
	¼ cup superfine sugar or light soft brown sugar, or to taste	

1 Place the strawberries and rhubarb in a saucepan with the butter and water and heat gently until the mixture comes to a boil, stirring occasionally. Cover and simmer for about 10 minutes, or until the rhubarb is soft, stirring occasionally.

2 Remove the pan from the heat and cool slightly, then purée the mixture in a blender or food processor until smooth.

3 Return the fruit purée to the rinsed-out saucepan, then stir in the sugar to taste. Reheat gently, stirring until the sugar has dissolved, then bring slowly to a boil, stirring occasionally. Stir in the amaretto. Serve hot or cold. If serving cold, remove the pan from the heat and set aside to cool completely, then serve.

SERVING SUGGESTIONS *Serve with ice cream desserts such as chocolate terrine, or with blancmange.*
VARIATIONS *Use raspberries or loganberries in place of strawberries.*

337 LUSCIOUS LEMON SAUCE

PREPARATION TIME *10 minutes* **COOKING TIME** *N/A* **SERVES 6–8**

⅔ cup heavy cream	4 tbsp luxury lemon curd
⅔ cup plain fromage frais	Finely grated zest of 1 small lemon (optional)

1 Place the cream and fromage frais in a bowl, and whip together until the mixture thickens and holds its shape in soft peaks.

2 Gently fold in the lemon curd and lemon zest, if using, until well combined. Serve cold.

SERVING SUGGESTIONS *Serve with fresh fruit such as mixed berries, strawberries, or fruit compote.*

338 SUNSET ORANGE SAUCE

PREPARATION TIME *10 minutes* **COOKING TIME** *10 minutes* **SERVES 4** *Makes about 1 cup*

2 tsp arrowroot
Finely grated zest & juice
  of 1 orange
2 tbsp light soft brown
  sugar or superfine sugar

½ cup water
⅔ cup preserved stem
  ginger in syrup (drained
  weight), drained & finely
  chopped

1 tbsp syrup from the jar of
  stem ginger

1 In a small bowl, blend the arrowroot with 1 tbsp cold water until smooth, then set aside.
  Place the orange juice, sugar and water in a small, heavy-based saucepan, and heat
  gently, stirring continuously, until the sugar has dissolved, then bring to a boil.
2 Remove the pan from the heat and gradually pour the hot orange liquid onto the
  arrowroot mixture, stirring continuously. Return the sauce to the pan, stir in the orange
  zest, chopped ginger, and ginger syrup and heat gently, stirring continuously, until the
  sauce comes to a boil and thickens. Serve hot.

SERVING SUGGESTIONS *Serve with steamed sponge puddings, or with sliced oranges or pineapple.*

339 GOLDEN APRICOT SAUCE

PREPARATION TIME *20 minutes* **COOKING TIME** *30 minutes* **SERVES 6–8** *Makes about 2½ cups*

¼ cup superfine sugar
⅔ cup water

1⅓ cups ready-to-eat dried
  apricots, roughly chopped

1¼ cups dry white wine
  or unsweetened orange
  juice

1 Place the sugar and water in a saucepan and heat gently, stirring continuously, until the
  sugar has dissolved.
2 Stir in the apricots and wine or orange juice and mix well. Bring slowly to a boil, then
  cover and simmer gently for 20 minutes, stirring occasionally.
3 Remove the pan from the heat and set aside to cool slightly, then purée the mixture in a
  blender or food processor until smooth.
4 Return the sauce to the rinsed-out pan and reheat gently until hot, stirring. Serve hot.

SERVING SUGGESTIONS *Serve with hot pancakes, crêpes or waffles, or with baked pears or peaches.*

340 FRAGRANT FRUIT SAUCE

PREPARATION TIME *5 minutes* **COOKING TIME** *10 minutes* **SERVES 6** *Makes about 2 cups*

2 tbsp arrowroot
scant 1 cup unsweetened
  apple juice

scant 1 cup unsweetened
  orange juice
2 tbsp ginger wine

2 tbsp clear honey

1 In a small bowl, blend the arrowroot with 4 tbsp apple juice until smooth. Set aside.
2 Place the remaining apple juice, the orange juice, ginger wine, and honey in a saucepan
  and heat gently until almost boiling, stirring occasionally. Gradually pour the hot fruit
  juices onto the blended arrowroot mixture and stir well.
3 Return the sauce to the pan and heat gently, stirring continuously, until the sauce comes
  to a boil and thickens. Serve hot.

SERVING SUGGESTIONS *Serve with sliced fresh fruit or hot crêpes, or with fruit compote.*

341 SUMMER STRAWBERRY SAUCE

PREPARATION TIME *10 minutes* **COOKING TIME** *15 minutes* **SERVES 6** *Makes about 2 cups*

2 cups fresh ripe strawberries	Finely grated zest & juice of 2 lemons	1 tsp arrowroot
⅔ cup water	¼ cup superfine sugar, or to taste	

1 Place the strawberries in a blender or food processor and blend until smooth.

2 Pour the strawberry purée into a saucepan and stir in the water, lemon zest and juice, and sugar.

3 Heat gently, stirring continuously, until the sugar has dissolved, then bring the mixture to a boil and simmer gently for 5 minutes, stirring occasionally.

4 In a small bowl, blend the arrowroot with 1 tbsp cold water until smooth. Gradually stir the arrowroot mixture into the hot strawberry purée and mix well.

5 Reheat gently, stirring continuously, until the sauce comes to a boil and thickens slightly. Serve hot.

SERVING SUGGESTIONS *Serve with chilled lemon or vanilla cheesecake, fresh fruit kebabs, fruit jelly, sorbet, or scoops of ice cream or yogurt ice.*

VARIATION *Use 1 orange in place of lemons.*

COOK'S TIP *Add an extra ½–1 tsp arrowroot, if you prefer a slightly thicker sauce.*

342 VERY BERRY SAUCE

PREPARATION TIME *10 minutes* **COOKING TIME** *5 minutes* **SERVES 4–6**

3 tbsp unsweetened red
  grape juice
3 tbsp unsweetened
  apple juice
1 tbsp clear honey

3 cups fresh mixed berries,
  such as raspberries,
  blackberries,
  blueberries, & small
  strawberries (halved or
  quartered)

1 Place the fruit juices and honey in a small saucepan, and heat gently until almost boiling, stirring continuously. Remove the pan from the heat.

2 Place the mixed berries in a serving bowl and pour over the hot fruit juice mixture. Stir gently to mix, then set aside. Serve hot or cold.

SERVING SUGGESTIONS *Serve with cream-filled meringues, small meringues, or meringue nests.*

343 FRESH BLACKCURRANT SAUCE

PREPARATION TIME *10 minutes* **COOKING TIME** *15 minutes* **SERVES 6** *Makes about 2 cups*

2 cups fresh or frozen
  (defrosted) blackcurrants,
  topped & tailed

2–3 tbsp clear honey, or to
  taste
2 tbsp crème de cassis
  (blackcurrant liqueur)

1 tsp arrowroot

1 Place the blackcurrants in a saucepan with the honey and 4 tbsp cold water. Cover and cook gently until the blackcurrants are soft, stirring occasionally.

2 Remove the pan from the heat and stir in the crème de cassis. In a small bowl, blend the arrowroot with 1 tbsp cold water until smooth. Gradually stir the arrowroot mixture into the blackcurrant sauce and mix well.

3 Return the pan to the heat and heat gently, stirring continuously, until the sauce comes to a boil and thickens. Serve hot or cold. If serving cold, remove the pan from the heat, and set aside to cool completely, then serve.

SERVING SUGGESTIONS *Serve with hot pancakes or crêpes, sorbet, or poached fruit such as pears.*

344 BLUEBERRY SYRUP

PREPARATION TIME *5 minutes* **COOKING TIME** *10–15 minutes* **SERVES 6–8** *Makes about 2½ cups*

1 cup superfine sugar
⅔ cup water

2 cups fresh blueberries
Juice of 1 lemon

1 Place the sugar and water in a small, heavy-based saucepan and heat gently until the sugar has dissolved, stirring continuously.

2 Add the blueberries, then bring slowly to a boil, stirring continuously. Simmer gently for 3–5 minutes, stirring.

3 Stir in the lemon juice, then remove the pan from the heat, and set aside for 5 minutes. Serve hot.

SERVING SUGGESTIONS *Serve with steamed plain or fruit sponge puddings, hot pancakes, or crêpes.*

345 CINNAMON-SPICED APRICOT AND DATE SAUCE

PREPARATION TIME *10 minutes* **COOKING TIME** *15 minutes* **SERVES 4**

½ cup ready-to-eat dried
  apricots, finely chopped

½ cup pitted dried dates,
  finely chopped
2 tbsp light soft brown sugar

2 tsp ground cinnamon
⅔ cup water

1 Place the apricots, dates, sugar, and cinnamon in a saucepan with the water.
2 Bring slowly to a boil, stirring continuously, then simmer gently, uncovered, until the
  fruit is soft and the sauce has reduced and thickened slightly. Serve hot.

SERVING SUGGESTIONS *Serve with hot pancakes or crêpes, or with steamed or baked sponge puddings.*
VARIATIONS *Use ready-to-eat dried peaches or pears in place of apricots. Use 1–2 tsp ground mixed
spice or ginger in place of cinnamon.*

346 SWEET PLUM SAUCE

PREPARATION TIME *25 minutes* **COOKING TIME** *20 minutes* **SERVES 6–8** *Makes about 2⅓ cups*

6 large red dessert plums,
  halved & pitted
⅔ cup water
Finely grated zest & juice
  of 1 orange

¼ cup superfine sugar or
  light soft brown sugar,
  or to taste
½ tsp ground cinnamon
1 tbsp brandy

1 Place the plums in a saucepan with the water. Bring slowly to a boil, then cover and
  simmer gently until the plums are soft, stirring occasionally.
2 Remove the pan from the heat and set aside to cool slightly, then purée the plums and
  juices in a blender or food processor until smooth.
3 Return the plum purée to the rinsed-out saucepan, and stir in the orange zest and juice,
  sugar, cinnamon, and brandy and mix well. Reheat the sauce gently until hot, stirring.
  Serve hot or cold. If serving cold, remove the pan from the heat and set aside to cool
  completely, then serve.

SERVING SUGGESTIONS *Serve with fruit pies, tarts, or strudels, ice cream, ice cream desserts, or with
vanilla blancmange or milk jelly.*

347 PASSION FRUIT SAUCE

PREPARATION TIME *5 minutes* **COOKING TIME** *10 minutes* **SERVES 4** *Makes about 1 cup*

2 passion fruit
1½ tsp arrowroot

⅔ cup unsweetened
  orange juice

1 tbsp clear honey, or to taste
½ tsp ground mixed spice

1 Cut each passion fruit in half and scoop out and reserve the flesh and seeds. Set aside.
2 In a saucepan, blend the arrowroot with 2 tbsp orange juice until smooth, then stir in
  the remaining orange juice together with the honey and mixed spice. Heat gently, stirring
  continuously, until the sauce comes to a boil and thickens.
3 Stir the passion fruit flesh and seeds into the sauce and reheat gently until hot, stirring.
  Serve hot.

SERVING SUGGESTIONS *Serve with mixed fruit kebabs, fresh fruit salad or compote, ice cream, or
chocolate desserts, such as chocolate mousse or chocolate terrine.*

348 RUBY RASPBERRY SAUCE

PREPARATION TIME *20 minutes* COOKING TIME *15–20 minutes* SERVES 4 *Makes about 1¼ cups*

2 cups fresh raspberries
¼ cup superfine sugar

⅔ cup medium white wine
1 tsp arrowroot

A few drops of almond
extract

1 Place the raspberries in a saucepan with 2 tbsp cold water and bring slowly to a boil, then cover and simmer gently until the raspberries are soft, stirring occasionally.
2 Remove the pan from the heat and set aside to cool slightly, then purée the raspberry mixture in a blender or food processor until smooth. Press the raspberry purée through a non-reactive sieve into a bowl, then discard the contents of the sieve. Return the raspberry purée to the rinsed-out saucepan, and stir in the sugar and wine, mixing well.
3 In a small bowl, blend the arrowroot with 1 tbsp cold water until smooth. Stir the arrowroot mixture into the raspberry sauce. Heat gently, stirring continuously, until the sauce comes to a boil and thickens.
4 Remove the pan from the heat and stir in the almond extract. Serve hot or cold. If serving cold, remove the pan from the heat and set aside to cool completely, then serve.

SERVING SUGGESTIONS *Serve with steamed or baked sponge puddings or scoops of chocolate or strawberry ice cream, or with prepared fresh fruit such as sliced pears, peaches, or apricots.*
VARIATIONS *Use blackberries or loganberries in place of raspberries. Use unsweetened apple juice in place of white wine.*

349 CLEMENTINE SAUCE

PREPARATION TIME *30 minutes* COOKING TIME *20 minutes* SERVES 6–8 *Makes about 2⅓ cups*

10 clementines, peeled &
segmented (removing the
pith & membranes)
1 tbsp fresh lemon juice

⅔ cup water
⅓ cup light soft brown
sugar
2 tsp arrowroot

1–2 tbsp orange-flavored
liqueur, or to taste

1 Place the clementine segments in a saucepan with the lemon juice and water. Bring to a boil, then reduce the heat, cover and cook gently until the clementines are soft, stirring occasionally.
2 Remove the pan from the heat and set aside to cool slightly, then purée the mixture in a blender or food processor until smooth. Return the puréed clementines to the rinsed-out pan, add the sugar and mix well, then heat gently, stirring continuously, until the sugar has dissolved.
3 In a small bowl, blend the arrowroot with 2 tbsp cold water until smooth. Gradually stir the arrowroot mixture into the clementine purée, then reheat gently, stirring continuously, until the sauce comes to a boil and thickens. Stir in the liqueur to taste. Serve hot.

SERVING SUGGESTIONS *Serve with ice cream or creamy desserts, or with vanilla or lemon cheesecake.*
COOK'S TIP *Once the fruit has been puréed, press the purée through a non-reactive sieve, if preferred, before adding the sugar, and continuing as above.*

350 GLAZED KUMQUAT SAUCE

PREPARATION TIME *15 minutes* **COOKING TIME** *15 minutes* **SERVES 6**

10 oz kumquats
½ cup granulated sugar

⅔ cup water

1 tbsp orange-flavored
liqueur, or to taste

1 Slice the kumquats and place them in a heatproof bowl or large jug. Set aside.
2 Place the sugar in a saucepan with the water. Heat gently, stirring continuously, until the sugar has dissolved, then bring the mixture to a boil and boil rapidly, without stirring, until the syrup is a golden brown caramel color.
3 Remove the pan from the heat, carefully stir in 4 tbsp boiling water and return to a low heat to dissolve the caramel. Stir in the liqueur to taste.
4 Remove the pan from the heat and let cool for 5 minutes, then pour the caramel over the kumquats, and stir to mix. Serve hot or cold. If serving cold, set aside to cool completely, then serve, or cover and chill in the refrigerator before serving.

SERVING SUGGESTIONS *Serve with individual chocolate sponge puddings, chocolate mousse, chocolate tartlets, or scoops of chocolate or vanilla ice cream.*
VARIATION *Use small oranges, peeled, sliced, and cut into quarters, in place of kumquats.*

351 KIWI AND LIME SAUCE

PREPARATION TIME *40 minutes* **COOKING TIME** *N/A* **SERVES 8–10** *Makes about 3 cups*

8 ripe kiwi fruit peeled & quartered

Finely grated zest & juice of 1 lime

½ cup medium-fat or full-fat cream cheese

⅔ cup light cream

¼ cup confectioners' sugar, sifted, or to taste

1 Place the kiwi fruit and lime zest and juice in a blender or food processor and mix until smooth.

2 Add the cream cheese and cream and blend until thoroughly mixed.

3 Pour the sauce into a bowl. Stir the confectioners' sugar into the sauce until well combined.

4 Cover and leave the sauce to stand in a cool place for about 30 minutes before serving, so the flavors develop. Stir well before serving. Serve cold.

SERVING SUGGESTIONS *Serve with fresh fruit kebabs, fresh fruit salad, or fruit compote.*

VARIATIONS *Use 1 small lemon in place of lime. Use crème fraîche, plain fromage frais, or natural Greek yogurt in place of light cream.*

COOK'S TIPS *Kiwi fruit, also known as Chinese gooseberry, has a dark-green flesh with edible black seeds. It has a distinctive taste, and adds delicious color and flavor to this sweet sauce.*

Use ripe kiwi fruit for this sauce, to achieve the best flavor. Kiwi fruit are ripe and ready to eat if they yield slightly when lightly pressed.

352 CARIBBEAN COCONUT SAUCE

PREPARATION TIME *10 minutes* **COOKING TIME** *N/A* **SERVES 6** *Makes about 2 cups*

1 large ripe mango, peeled, pitted, & chopped

2 tbsp unsweetened orange juice

scant 1 cup coconut milk

2 tbsp clear honey, or to taste

1 Place the prepared mango flesh in a blender or food processor with the orange juice and blend to form a smooth purée.

2 Add the coconut milk and blend until smooth and well mixed. Add the honey to taste, and blend to mix.

3 Serve immediately, or cover and chill for 1–2 hours before serving.

SERVING SUGGESTIONS *Serve with a mixed tropical fruit compote or salad, or with broiled mixed tropical fruit such as pineapple, papaya, and star fruit.*

353 VANILLA YOGURT SAUCE

PREPARATION TIME *5 minutes* **COOKING TIME** *N/A* **SERVES 4**

½ cup natural Greek yogurt

⅓ cup natural bio yogurt

1–2 tbsp clear honey, or to taste

A few drops of vanilla extract

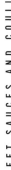

1 Place the Greek and bio yogurts in a bowl and fold gently together to mix.

2 Add the honey to taste and fold in gently, then fold in the vanilla extract. Serve immediately, or cover and chill before serving.

SERVING SUGGESTIONS *Serve with prepared fresh fruit such as passion fruit, nectarines or peaches.*

VARIATIONS *Use almond extract in place of vanilla extract. Use maple syrup in place of honey.*

COOK'S TIP *Serve the yogurt sauce, then sprinkle each portion with a little finely grated semisweet chocolate, if desired.*

354 FRUITY YOGURT SAUCE

PREPARATION TIME *10 minutes* **COOKING TIME** *N/A* **SERVES 6** *Makes about 1¼ cups*

2 cups fresh ripe mixed berries, such as strawberries, raspberries & blackberries, or blueberries

2 tbsp clear honey, or to taste

½ cup natural Greek yogurt

2 tbsp crème fraîche

1 Place the mixed berries in a blender or food processor and blend until smooth. Press the fruit purée through a non-reactive sieve into a bowl and discard the contents of the sieve.

2 Mix the honey with the fruit purée, then stir in the yogurt and crème fraîche until thoroughly mixed. Serve immediately, or cover and chill for about 1 hour before serving.

SERVING SUGGESTIONS *Serve with fresh fruit salad or compote, or with scoops of vanilla yogurt ice.*

VARIATIONS *Use peeled, pitted mango flesh in place of mixed berries. Use a mixture of frozen berries (defrosted) if fresh ones are not available.*

355 BRANDY BUTTER

PREPARATION TIME *10 minutes, plus chilling* **COOKING TIME** *N/A* **SERVES 8**

½ cup unsalted butter, softened

⅔ cup light soft brown sugar (muscovado sugar is ideal)

4–6 tbsp brandy

1 Place the butter in a bowl and beat with a wooden spoon until very soft and creamy.
2 Gradually beat in the sugar until the mixture is light and fluffy. Gradually beat in the brandy, 1 tbsp at a time, until well combined.
3 Transfer the mixture to a serving bowl, cover, and chill for at least 2–3 hours before serving. Store, tightly covered, in the refrigerator for up to 1 week, or freeze for up to 1 month.

SERVING SUGGESTIONS *Serve with Christmas pudding, mince pies, or other festive fruit puddings or pies, or with hot pancakes or baked apples.*

356 RUM BUTTER

PREPARATION TIME *10 minutes, plus chilling* **COOKING TIME** *N/A* **SERVES 8**

½ cup unsalted butter, softened

⅔ cup light soft brown sugar (muscovado sugar is ideal)

4–6 tbsp rum

1 Place the butter in a bowl and beat with a wooden spoon until very soft and creamy.
2 Gradually beat in the sugar until the mixture is light and fluffy. Gradually beat in the rum, 1 tbsp at a time, until well combined.
3 Transfer the mixture to a serving bowl, cover and chill for at least 2–3 hours before serving. Store, tightly covered, in the refrigerator for up to 1 week, or freeze for up to 1 month.

SERVING SUGGESTIONS *Serve with Christmas pudding, mince pies, or mincemeat tart, hot pancakes, crêpes or waffles, or with broiled fruit such as peaches or pineapple.*

357 FRESH RASPBERRY COULIS

PREPARATION TIME *10 minutes* **COOKING TIME** *N/A* **SERVES 4** *Makes about ¾ cup*

2 cups fresh raspberries
1 tbsp confectioners' sugar, sifted, or to taste

2 tsp framboise (raspberry) liqueur or kirsch, or to taste (optional)

1 Place the raspberries in a small blender or food processor and blend to form a purée. Press the raspberry purée through a non-reactive sieve into a bowl to remove the seeds. Discard the contents of the sieve.
2 Add the confectioners' sugar to the raspberry purée to taste, stirring or whisking to mix well. Stir in the liqueur to taste, if using. Serve cold.

SERVING SUGGESTIONS *Serve with fresh mixed berries, sliced peaches, or nectarines.*

358 CRIMSON FRUIT COULIS

PREPARATION TIME *10 minutes* **COOKING TIME** *N/A* **SERVES 6–8** *Makes about 1½ cups*

1 lb prepared fresh ripe red
   summer fruits, such as
   raspberries, strawberries,
   redcurrants, & tayberries
2 tbsp confectioners' sugar,
   sifted, or to taste

1 tbsp framboise (raspberry)
   liqueur or crème de cassis
   (blackcurrant liqueur), or
   to taste

1 Place the prepared red fruits in a small blender or food processor and blend to form a purée. Press the fruit purée through a non-reactive sieve into a bowl to remove the seeds. Discard the contents of the sieve.

2 Gradually add the confectioners' sugar to the fruit purée to taste, whisking to mix well. Stir in the liqueur to taste. Serve cold.

SERVING SUGGESTIONS *Serve with chocolate cheesecake or chocolate mousse, scoops of ice cream or sorbet, or with cold fruit tarts such as cherry tart or apricot tart.*
VARIATION *Use fresh blackberries or blueberries in place of redcurrants or tayberries.*

359 SPICED PEACH COULIS

PREPARATION TIME *10 minutes* **COOKING TIME** *N/A* **SERVES 6** *Makes about 1¼ cups*

14-oz can peach halves or
   peach slices in fruit juice
1 tsp ground mixed spice, or
   to taste

2 tbsp confectioners' sugar,
   sifted, or to taste

2 tsp amaretto (almond
   liqueur), or to taste
   (optional)

1 Place the peaches and their juice in a small blender or food processor and mix until smooth. Add the mixed spice and blend until well mixed.

2 Press the peach purée through a non-reactive sieve into a bowl, then discard the contents of the sieve.

3 Whisk or fold the confectioners' sugar into the peach purée until well mixed. Stir in the amaretto to taste, if using. Serve cold.

SERVING SUGGESTIONS *Serve with cold creamy desserts such as chilled lemon cheesecake, or with creamy fruit desserts, ice cream, or yogurt ice.*
VARIATIONS *Use canned apricots in place of peaches. Use ground cinnamon in place of mixed spice.*

360 SWEET STRAWBERRY COULIS

PREPARATION TIME *10 minutes* **COOKING TIME** *N/A* **SERVES 4** *Makes about ¾ cup*

2 cups fresh ripe trawberries
1 tbsp clear honey, or to taste

1–2 tsp cherry brandy or
   apple brandy (Calvados),
   or to taste

1 Place the strawberries in a blender or food processor and blend until smooth. Press the purée through a non-reactive sieve into a bowl, then discard the contents of the sieve.

2 Add the honey and cherry or apple brandy to the strawberry purée to taste, and stir to mix well. Serve cold.

SERVING SUGGESTIONS *Serve with a platter of prepared mixed fresh fruit, or with panna cotta.*

GOLDEN NECTARINE COULIS

PREPARATION TIME *20 minutes* **COOKING TIME** *15–20 minutes* **SERVES 6** *Makes about 1¼ cups*

4 ripe nectarines, peeled,
   halved, & pitted
2 tbsp freshly squeezed
   orange juice

2 tbsp superfine sugar, or
   to taste
2–3 tsp orange-flavored
   liqueur, or brandy, or to
   taste (optional)

1 Roughly chop the nectarine flesh, then place it in a saucepan with the orange juice
   and sugar. Heat gently, stirring continuously, until the sugar has dissolved. Bring slowly
   to a boil, then cover and simmer for 10–15 minutes, or until the fruit is soft, stirring
   occasionally.
2 Remove the pan from the heat and cool slightly. Mash the fruit mixture, or purée it in a
   blender or food processor, then press the mixture through a non-reactive sieve into a
   bowl. Discard the contents of the sieve.
3 Stir the liqueur or brandy, if using, into the nectarine purée, then taste for sweetness
   and add a little extra sugar, if necessary. Serve hot or cold.

SERVING SUGGESTIONS *Serve with scoops of mixed fruit sorbets, ice cream, or yogurt ice.*

362 ICED BLACKCURRANT COULIS

PREPARATION TIME *15 minutes, plus chilling* **COOKING TIME** *15 minutes* **SERVES 6** *Makes about 1 cup*

3 cups fresh blackcurrants, topped & tailed

½ cup light soft brown sugar, or to taste

1–2 tbsp crème de cassis (blackcurrant liqueur), or to taste

1 Place the blackcurrants in a saucepan with the sugar and 2 tbsp cold water and heat gently, stirring continuously, until the sugar has dissolved. Bring slowly to a boil, then cover and cook gently for about 10 minutes, or until the blackcurrants are soft and pulpy, stirring occasionally.
2 Remove the pan from the heat, cool slightly, then press the blackcurrant pulp and juices through a non-reactive sieve into a bowl. Discard the contents of the sieve.
3 Stir the crème de cassis into the blackcurrant purée, then taste for sweetness and stir in a little extra sugar and liqueur, if necessary.
4 Set aside to cool, then cover, and chill before serving. Serve cold. The coulis may also be served hot, if preferred.

SERVING SUGGESTIONS *Serve with French apple tart, hot pancakes or crêpes, meringues, scoops of ice cream, yogurt ice, or sorbet, or with prepared fresh fruit such as figs or peaches.*

363 BLUSHING BERRY COULIS

PREPARATION TIME *10 minutes* **COOKING TIME** *15–20 minutes* **SERVES 6** *Makes about 1¼ cups*

3 cups prepared fresh
   mixed berries, such as
   raspberries, strawberries,
   blackberries, blueberries,
   & redcurrants

¼ cup superfine sugar, or
   to taste
1–2 tbsp crème de cassis
   (blackcurrant liqueur) or
   framboise (raspberry)
   liqueur, or to taste

1 Place the mixed berries in a saucepan with the sugar and 2 tbsp cold water and heat
gently, stirring continuously, until the sugar has dissolved. Bring slowly to a boil, then
cover and cook gently for 10–15 minutes, or until the fruit is soft and pulpy, stirring
occasionally.

2 Remove the pan from the heat, cool slightly, then press the fruit pulp and juices through
a non-reactive sieve into a bowl. Discard the contents of the sieve.

3 Stir the liqueur into the fruit purée, then taste for sweetness and stir in a little extra
sugar and liqueur, if necessary. Serve hot or cold.

SERVING SUGGESTIONS *Serve with hot pancakes or crêpes, or with caramelized citrus tart.*

364 RASPBERRY VODKA COULIS

PREPARATION TIME *10 minutes* **COOKING TIME** *N/A* **SERVES 4** *Makes about ¾ cup*

2 cups fresh raspberries
1 tbsp confectioners' sugar,
   sifted, or to taste

A dash or two of iced vodka,
   or to taste

1 Place the raspberries in a small blender or food processor and blend to form a purée.
Press the raspberry purée through a non-reactive sieve into a bowl to remove the seeds.
Discard the contents of the sieve.

2 Add the confectioners' sugar to the raspberry purée to taste, stirring or whisking to mix
well. Stir in the iced vodka to taste. Serve cold.

SERVING SUGGESTIONS *Serve with fresh mixed berries or strawberries, or with summer pudding.*

365 EXOTIC MANGO COULIS

PREPARATION TIME *15 minutes* **COOKING TIME** *N/A* **SERVES 6–8** *Makes about 1½ cups*

2 large ripe mangoes, peeled,
   pitted, & diced
Juice of ½ lime

⅓ cup light soft brown
   sugar, or to taste

1 tbsp orange-flavored
   liqueur, or to taste
   (optional)

1 Place the mango flesh in a blender or food processor with the lime juice, and blend to
form a smooth purée. Add the sugar and blend until well mixed.

2 Press the mango purée through a non-reactive sieve into a bowl, then discard the
contents of the sieve.

3 Stir the liqueur, if using, into the mango purée, mixing well, then taste and add a little
extra sugar (and liqueur), if necessary. Serve cold.

SERVING SUGGESTIONS *Serve with tropical fruit salad or broiled fruit, or with mango sorbet.*

Index

ACKNOWLEDGMENTS

My special thanks, once again, go to my husband, Robbie, for his continued support and encouragement with this book and for his enthusiastic tasting of many of the recipes. My sincere thanks also go to Sarah Bradford and Bev Saunder for all their continued and dedicated hard work testing recipes, and to Gwen Whiting for her help with typing recipes.

I would like to thank Julia Charles at Duncan Baird Publishers for approaching me a second time and asking me to write this book, and for her ongoing support throughout this project. I would also like to thank Manisha Patel for her creative design, Rachel Connolly for her comprehensive and thorough editing, Lucy McKelvie for her dedication and patience preparing and styling the recipes for photography, Sailesh Patel for art direction of the photography, and William Lingwood for his delightful food photographs throughout the book.